The Rise and Fall of the Spanish Empire

Also by William S. Maltby

THE REIGN OF CHARLES V

THE RISE AND FALL OF THE SPANISH EMPIRE

William S. Maltby

First published 2009 by
PALGRAVE MACMILLAN

Palgrave Macmillan in the UK is an imprint of Macmillan Publishers Limited,
registered in England, company number 785998, of Houndmills, Basingstoke,
Hampshire RG21 6XS.

Palgrave Macmillan in the US is a division of St Martin's Press LLC,
175 Fifth Avenue, New York, NY 10010.

Palgrave Macmillan is the global academic imprint of the above companies
and has companies and representatives throughout the world.

Palgrave® and Macmillan® are registered trademarks in the United States,
the United Kingdom, Europe and other countries.

ISBN-13: 978–1–4039–1791–1 hardback

ISBN-13: 978–1–4039–1792–8 paperback

This book is printed on paper suitable for recycling and made from fully
managed and sustained forest sources. Logging, pulping and manufacturing
processes are expected to conform to the environmental regulations of the
country of origin.

A catalogue record for this book is available from the British Library.

A catalog record for this book is available from the Library of Congress.

10   9   8   7   6   5   4   3   2   1
18 17 16 15 14 13 12 11 10 09

Transferred to Digital Printing in 2009

For Nancy

CONTENTS

vii

NOTES ON SPELLING AND CURRENCY

Common English equivalents of place names have been used wherever possible (e.g., Genoa, Seville). Where there are no English equivalents, the correct spelling and accents are used. Common English equivalents are also used for kings and popes (e.g., Charles, Ferdinand and Isabella, Alexander) unless there is a possibility of confusion as in the case of Joaõ of Portugal, Juan II of Aragon, and so on, all of whom could be called John. Other personal names receive the accents and spelling appropriate to their own country unless, as in the case of explorers like Columbus and Magellan, a common English equivalent exists. It would be pedantic to call them Cristoforo Colombo or Fernaõ Magalhães. For the same reason, the English equivalents of foreign titles (Duke, Count, Marquis, etc.) are used wherever possible.

Most of the figures provided in the text are quoted in monies of account. The smallest Spanish money of account was the *maravedí*. For most of the sixteenth century, 375 maravedís equaled one ducat. The *escudo* that appears as a money of account after 1590 was the *escudo de diez reales*. It was based on silver rather than gold and had a value equivalent to 340 maravedís. The florin was the primary money of account in the Netherlands. It was generally equivalent to 0.4 escudos. Ten florins or four escudos equaled £1 sterling.

The Spanish coins to which these monies corresponded were the escudo and the *real*. The *escudo* was a gold coin, 22 carats fine, of 3.38 grams. When introduced in 1535 it was worth 350 maravedís, but inflation increased its nominal value to 400 in 1566 and 440 in 1609. The *real* was a silver coin of the same weight, although some were minted at 3.43 grams. It was valued originally at 34 maravedís. Coins of 1/4, 2, 4, and 8 reales were also minted. The last were the famous *reales de a ocho*, or pieces of eight, a currency accepted throughout the world in the seventeenth and eighteenth century. The *peso*, which became the standard currency of the Spanish Empire after 1772, was minted at the same weight and quality of silver as the *real de a ocho*, but a portrait of the king replaced the Pillars of Hercules that had adorned Spanish coins since the reign of Charles V. The United States silver dollar and the Austrian *thaler* were based on the real de a ocho as well. Spain, to its credit, never devalued its gold and silver coins, most of which were minted in America. The coins issued in peninsular Spain beginning in the reign of Philip III were minted from an alloy called *vellón*. While the value of a silver real rose to 275 maravedis by the 1620s, the reales vellón issued to Spaniards were valued at only 34 maravedís.

GENEALOGICAL CHARTS

THE INHERITANCE OF CHARLES V

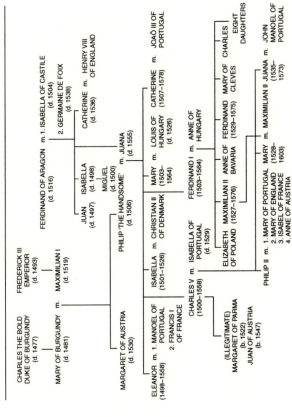

THE PORTUGUESE SUCCESSION

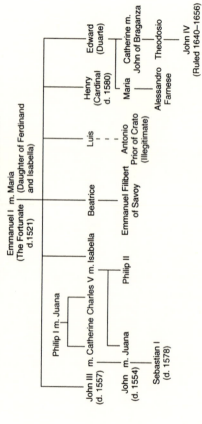

Emmanuel I m. Maria
(The Fortunate (Daughter of Ferdinand
d.1521) and Isabella)

Philip I m. Juana

John III m. Catherine Charles V m. Isabella   Beatrice   Luis   Henry   Edward
(d. 1557)   (Cardinal   (Duarte)
                                                                       d. 1580)

John m. Juana   Philip II   Emmanuel Filibert   Antonio   Maria   Catherine m.
(d. 1554)   of Savoy   Prior of Crato   John of Braganza
                                                                      (Illegitimate)

Sebastian I   Alessandro   Theodosio
(d. 1578)   Farnese

                                                                                              John IV
                                                                                      (Ruled 1640–1656)

THE SPANISH SUCCESSION, 1700

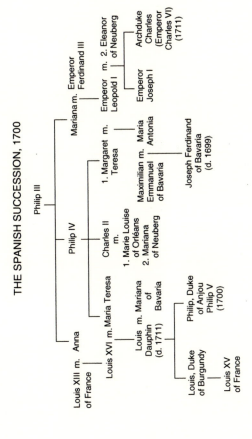

MAPS

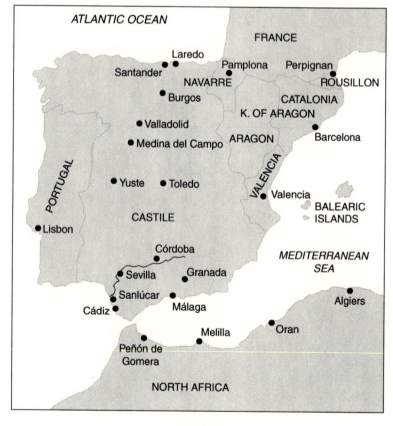

Spain

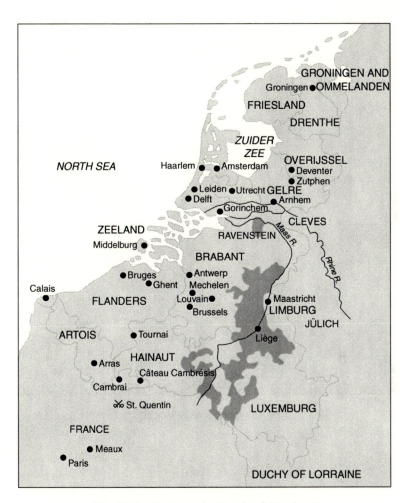

The Netherlands at the Death of Charles V

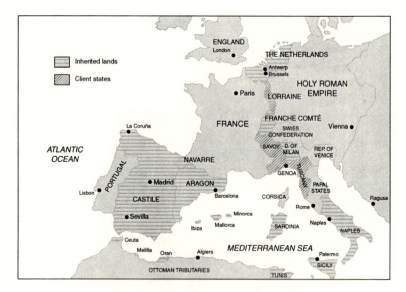

The European Empire of Philip II

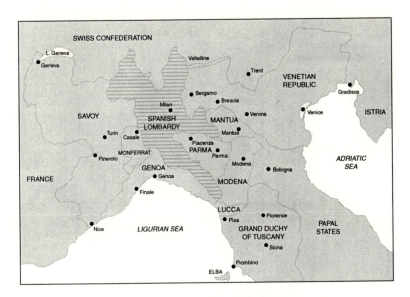

Northern Italy in the 17th Century

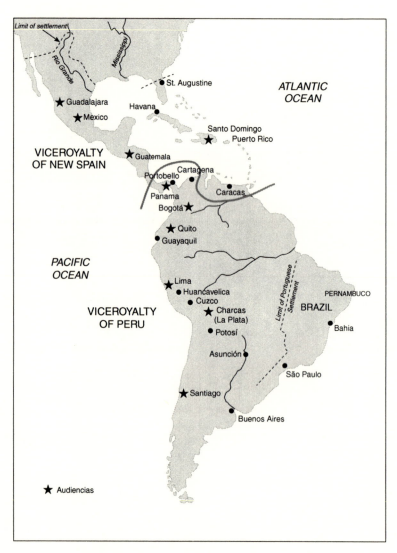

Spanish America under the Habsburgs c.1650

Spanish America under the Bourbons c.1790

Spanish America in 1828

INTRODUCTION

European colonialism, the centuries-long rule of European nations over societies thousands of miles from their shores, has few if any parallels in the history of humankind. No other civilization with the possible exception of Han Dynasty China attempted such a thing, and the Chinese experiment had few long lasting consequences. In contrast, European colonialism shaped the contours of the modern world by helping to foster global integration or globalization, a movement which until the mid-twentieth century proceeded largely on Europe's terms.

The roots of European imperialism lay in the competition for resources among its dynastic states. All of the monarchies in late medieval and early modern Europe faced an unprecedented increase in the monetary costs of war. The transition from feudal levies to paid soldiers, the growing size and complexity of armies, and the development of artillery forced states to increase their revenues if they hoped to survive and prosper. In agricultural economies with a relatively slow rate of growth, this was extremely difficult. Increased taxation could never be more than a partial and highly unpopular solution. More efficient exploitation of the royal domain (the crown's lands and such income-producing privileges as tariffs) helped, but it, too, brought the crown into conflict with its subjects and produced limited returns. Expanding the domain within the borders of a kingdom could be done only by escheat (the reversion of land to the crown in default of heirs), legal confiscations, or other equally unpopular and uncertain means. The best remaining alternative was to acquire new lands by marriage or conquest. When the Dutch broke with Spain in the sixteenth century and became an independent republic, they faced the same problems without the option of expanding by marriage. Their very survival depended upon overseas trade and conquest.

Conquests were always more popular than tax increases or the rack-renting of royal tenants, and offered the hope of new wealth to

1

conquerors and mercantile interests alike. When a conquest could be justified by the Christian missionary impulse it was considered laudable. Almost without exception, the European empire builders shared a common sense of racial and religious superiority. They achieved their conquests by using the superior military organization and technology that had created the demand for new revenue in the first place, and by pitting native peoples against each other to the advantage of the Europeans. Regardless of nationality, the story of the conquerors is one of heroism and crime in almost equal measure, but the empires they created ended badly. Most of them cost the "mother countries" more than they earned, and all too often their dissolution left political and economic havoc in its wake.

Spain was not the first European nation to establish a worldwide empire. That honor, if honor it may be called, belongs to the Portuguese. It was also not the last. The French, British, and Dutch empires developed later but survived into the mid-twentieth century together with a handful of Portuguese colonies. At various times, Danes, Russians, and Germans tried to create their own empires with limited success, but the Spanish Empire was unique in several respects. It was the first to exert direct sovereignty over great land masses and advanced civilizations that contained millions of non-European inhabitants. Moreover it succeeded to an unusual degree in imposing its language, faith, and culture on its new subjects. More than 300 million people speak Spanish today, and it is the primary language of 21 countries. Roman Catholicism became the dominant faith of Central and South America, while Spanish architecture, town planning, art, music, and literature merged with indigenous elements to form a vibrant new culture that has become very much a part of the Western cultural tradition. Part of this achievement was due to simple longevity. Spanish rule in the Americas and the Philippines lasted more than 300 years. Few parts of the French, British, or Dutch empires lasted as long. Spain was also unusual in that for nearly 200 years its empire contained both overseas colonies and European nations with which it shared neither languages, culture, nor even a common border. This combination of European and non-European possessions made Spain the greatest power of the sixteenth and early seventeenth century, but doomed it to unending conflict.

The Spanish Empire was not the work of a single conqueror or even of a single generation, although its greatest and most dramatic expansion occurred in the space of a longer-than-average lifetime. The European empire was created by the improbable success of Ferdinand and Isabella's dynastic strategy. Against all odds, their diplomacy placed Spain, the Netherlands, and much of Italy under the personal rule of one man, the

Habsburg Emperor Charles V. Spain's overseas possessions were acquired by an extension of the process that had created Spain itself. So great was the diversity of this accumulation of territories, its people, and institutions that some modern historians prefer to call it the "monarchy" rather than the empire, but if by empire we mean a group of countries ruled by a single authority, the traditional usage remains justified.

In re-conquering Iberia from the Muslims, the Castilians in particular had developed values, techniques, and institutions that would be transferred to new lands overseas. The acquisition of an Italian empire by Aragon in the fifteenth century and the agreement that unified Aragon and Castile under the rule of Ferdinand and Isabella suggested the imperial system by which separate kingdoms with their own institutions could and would be ruled by a single king. The Spanish may therefore have been better prepared by history and institutional memory for the task of governing an empire than any other European nation. In the face of appalling obstacles of time and distance they created the most complex and sophisticated administrative systems of the age. Despite the Black Legend promoted against it by its enemies and the very real horrors perpetrated in its name, it can also be argued that the Spanish Empire took its ethical and humanitarian responsibilities more seriously than its rivals. That is faint praise, but European colonialism as a whole was based on moral attitudes that have long been unacceptable to the modern world.

Spaniards, of course, did not achieve all this without help. Genoese and German bankers provided capital. Ships and crews from many countries augmented the Spanish fleet, and Spain's European armies were multinational in every sense of the word. Castilians played a dominant role in many aspects of war and administration, but they were too few and their country was too poor to create such a worldwide enterprise without assistance.

The discovery of massive silver deposits in Mexico and Peru—no other colonizing nation enjoyed similar good fortune—determined the empire's history and its economic character. The seemingly endless flow of bullion held the empire together, for without it, the kings of Spain could not have protected their European possessions; but in the end it was not enough. By the middle of the seventeenth century, the empire was in serious decline. The Netherlands Revolt, originally a reaction to the policies of Philip II, had evolved into a generalized European conflict that merged into the Thirty Years' War. Meanwhile, the French, English, and Dutch, having failed to find precious metals on their own, challenged Spain's monopoly in the Americas. For more than a century and a half, Spain fought repeated campaigns on land in Italy, the Netherlands, Germany, and France, and at sea against England and, in the sixteenth century, the Ottoman Turks. The liquidity produced by infusions of New World silver helped make these campaigns possible, but most of the cost fell upon the shoulders of Castilian taxpayers. In the end they could not bear it, for Castile remained, as it had always been, a relatively poor country. American wealth passed directly to foreign creditors or was paid to soldiers stationed on foreign soil where it helped to fuel the accumulation of capital that ultimately produced the Industrial Revolution. In Spain, however, high taxes and a weakening agricultural economy produced an economic crisis. By 1665, Spain had ceased to be Europe's greatest military power. Most of its economy—including the bulk of American trade—was by this time in the hands of foreigners.

The Habsburg dynasty ended in 1700, and with it the European empire assembled by Charles V. Spain, however, remained intact, together with its American colonies. The Bourbon dynasty that replaced the Habsburgs introduced reforms based on French institutions and the ideas of the Enlightenment. In so doing they compromised the ideological foundations of the monarchy, but Spain's wealth and population nevertheless increased throughout the eighteenth century as did its share of the American trade. Unfortunately for the Spanish, France and England grew faster and found ways to mobilize military resources that Spain could not match. Even if the last Bourbons had been competent or popular, the Spanish Empire might not have survived the conflicts of the Napoleonic Age. The collapse of the monarchy in 1808 forced most of the American colonies to govern themselves, and by 1838 Spain's overseas empire had been reduced to Cuba, Puerto Rico, the Philippines. These, too, were lost in the Spanish–American War of 1898.

The rise and fall of the Spanish Empire is obviously a topic of major importance in the world's history; for sheer drama, it is unsurpassed. It has therefore been the subject of an enormous historical literature, much of it of the highest quality. The complexity of the subject, however, has ensured that the best introductory works tend to be long and filled with rich detail that needs to be savored at leisure. This volume does not seek to replace them. It is based instead on the belief that students and the general reader may profit from a concise summary that concentrates on how the empire developed, how it functioned, and why it ultimately failed. The focus throughout is on politics, economics, and institutions in the context of the cultural values and intellectual movements that influenced them. The discussion of such important topics as social and religious history is limited to those issues that affect the political and economic narrative. This in part reflects the purpose of the book, but the Spanish Empire was in fact and theory a cluster of separate European and American realms united only by a common ruler and by economic and military ties of varying strength. The social and religious histories of its components varied too widely to permit facile generalization. Such questions are best examined by studies whose focus is local, or at least regional, and by the careful analysis of documents generated at the local level. Fortunately, there are a host of works on social and religious history available (many of them listed in the bibliography), and students at universities and secondary schools have long been offered course units that deal with race, gender, and other social issues. For them, a brief survey of the kind provided here may prove useful by describing the political, economic, and institutional framework within which the diverse societies of the empire evolved.

When a survey adopts brevity as its goal, it takes on some of the characteristics of an historical essay. This one, at least, is not intended to be revisionist but to base itself firmly on current scholarship. Because the book is intended for non-specialists, there are few discussions of historical controversies and no footnotes. A selected bibliography is provided for those interested in delving more deeply into the literature.

1
IMPERIAL BEGINNINGS

No conqueror created the Spanish empire, nor was its development the result of policy decisions taken by a king or his ministers. It evolved from the process that created Spain itself. Until late in the Middle Ages, Spain had been little more than a geographic expression. The Romans, after conquering its many tribes, divided the Iberian Peninsula into two provinces. In the fifth century the Visigoths established a kingdom centered at Toledo. They collected tribute and introduced elements of Germanic law, but did little to interfere with local or regional centers of power. Then, at the beginning of the eighth century, the armies of *al-Islam* swept over the Iberian Peninsula leaving a handful of Christian communities clinging to its mountainous northern fringe. Almost immediately the inhabitants of those tiny kingdoms began to re-encroach upon the lands that had been conquered by the Muslims. It was the beginning of what has been called the Reconquest, a struggle of nearly 800 years that ended only with the extinction of Muslim Granada in 1492. The experience of those centuries forged Spain, itself an uneasy alliance of many cultures, but relentlessly devoted to expansion.

The Reconquest was the first and most successful of the Crusades, but it was never the simple military action its name implies. The Christian advance remained sporadic until the middle of the thirteenth century. It halted whenever the Muslims achieved political unity, as they did under the Caliphate of Córdoba from 910 to 1031, and advanced whenever Muslim Spain broke up into petty kingdoms, or *taifas*, too weak to defend themselves. Even then, the lack of Christian unity caused temporary reverses as kingdoms, towns, and military entrepreneurs formed alliances with little regard for confessional differences. The turning point came when the

6

Almohads, an Islamic reform movement based originally in North Africa, re-established Muslim unity between 1146 and 1172. Setting aside their differences, the Christian kingdoms of León and Castile, Aragon, and Navarre defeated the Almohads at Las Navas de Tolosa in 1212. The *taifas* re-emerged, only to be swallowed up one by one in the next 40 years. By 1252, only Granada remained as an independent Muslim state on Spanish soil.

By this time, four of the Iberian kingdoms had achieved something like permanence: Portugal, Navarre, Castile, and Aragon. Castile, the largest, was formed in 1230 from León, Galicia, the ancient kingdom of Asturias, and parts of the Basque country. Castile itself had originally been part of the kingdom of León. Portugal broke with León/Castile in 1143 and went on to create a maritime empire that lasted into the twentieth century. The inland kingdom of Aragon merged with the county of Catalonia in 1164, thereby acquiring the wealthy city of Barcelona with its commercial interests in the western Mediterranean and political ties to France. Navarre, although smaller than its neighbors, maintained a precarious independence until the sixteenth century. Castile, Aragon, and Navarre eventually became Spain, but until relatively modern times they remained separate kingdoms that happened to be ruled by the same monarch. The contribution of each kingdom to the growth of a Spanish empire, like the course of its internal development, was therefore very different.

THE IBERIAN KINGDOMS IN THE MIDDLE AGES

Castile evolved from a group of Christian communities which, though different in some respects, shared a common social structure. Neither the Romans nor the Visigoths had been able to exert much influence in the remote valleys of the Cantabrian Mountains or the Pyrenees. Feudalism never penetrated there, and most of the population remained freeholders who lived by subsistence farming supplemented by hunting, fishing, and gathering. In this, northern Spain resembled other highland areas of Europe, and like them, it tended to produce a population surplus. Its inhabitants enjoyed a varied, protein-rich diet, while their scattered farmsteads and isolated settlements limited their exposure to infectious disease. But the productivity of their small fields, like the availability of fish and game, was limited by an unforgiving ecology. There was no way to accommodate population growth by putting new lands into production, and the resources of the forest were by definition inelastic as well. The Spanish north, like the

Alps or the Italian Abruzzi, produced sturdy children, many of whom had to leave as soon as they reached maturity if the community as a whole was to survive.

The Christians who, in the ninth and tenth centuries, began pressing southward into the valley of the Duero River were therefore tough, independent, and highly motivated. Under the sometimes nominal leadership of their kings, they established their settlements in a way that became a pattern for later colonization in the New World. After killing, capturing, or driving off the Muslim inhabitants, they would plant a banner, sound the trumpet, and formally claim the surrounding land in the name of their king. They then established a fortified "town," often little more than a small village, and conducted a *repartimiento*, which allocated land to each settler as freehold property after setting aside a portion for the king. The final stage was to secure formal recognition of their municipality from the crown. This pattern of settlement produced the characteristic social structure of Old Castile: a world of small freeholders living together in fortified villages or towns for protection.

Protection was needed because the new communities continued for many years to occupy a contested frontier. The Meseta of Old Castile is a high plateau with hot summers, cold winters, and rainfall that rarely exceeds 20 inches per annum. The economy of the towns established there was therefore based largely upon herding and ranching, although the fertile bottom land in the river valleys was always used to grow vines and row crops. Raiding and stock rustling provided important supplementary income. To protect themselves, and to launch raids of their own against Muslims and Christians alike, the towns established militias whose chief component was the *caballeros villanos*, or peasant cavalry. Poorer citizens fought as infantry, but every able-bodied male under the age of 70 was obliged by law to be armed and ready to fight on a few hours' notice. The weapons themselves might be provided by a king or lord, purchased, or acquired as booty in earlier raids. Horses, like a family's weapons, were prized, and elaborate regulations governed their maintenance. Part of a militia always remained at home to defend the town walls and gates, but the remainder was free to raid or to accompany the king's armies on campaign. The level of training and discipline in these town militias was remarkably high. They were an important part of Christian armies in all stages of the Reconquest, and the booty they acquired formed a useful supplement to the urban economy.

A portion of that booty was, of course, allocated to the king, as was a share of all new lands conquered by his subjects. Until the fourteenth century, the crown of Castile therefore enjoyed substantial wealth. The kings used it to support their own retinue of knights that served as an elite corps at the heart of their armies. From the eleventh century, the kings also appointed fighting men from these retinues as *tenens* or *alcaldes* to protect their new domains. These lords received landed benefices from the king, but in Castile and León such grants were not inheritable. The *alcaldes* used the proceeds of their benefice to maintain a troop of cavalry based upon a castle or fortified strongpoint. They acted as a mobile defense in case of attack and joined the royal host when the king embarked upon a campaign.

Like the king, these lords maintained a retinue composed largely of professional knights, but in time, free peasants found it necessary to "commend" themselves to one of them in return for his protection. The peasant might then owe him fees or a percentage of their harvest, military service, and the exclusive use of the lord's mill or other facilities. These early *encomiendas*, a term that would have a long and varied history, differed from feudal contracts in that the peasant who commended himself remained armed and legally free. He could, and all too often did, retain his right of private vengeance as well as the right to plead in court. He could choose his own lord or take a new one at any time, and retained full rights over his property as a freeholder. Though later modified to the peasants' disadvantage, this system prevailed in Old Castile until relatively modern times. It may help to account for that lack of servility in the Castilian character that foreigners sometimes chose to regard as arrogance.

After the battle of Las Navas de Tolosa, the acquisition of vast tracts of land in New Castile and Andalusia forced Castile to adopt new measures. Although willing enough to fight for booty or reward, urban or peasant proprietors now showed little interest in abandoning their existing properties for new ones. Faced with a shortage of potential colonists, the crown began to rely more heavily on great lords and on the recently founded military Orders to settle newly conquered lands. The Orders of Alcántara, Calatrava, and Santiago formed late in the twelfth century. Basing their constitutions on those of the Templars and Hospitallers, military orders founded in the Holy Land but also active in Castile, they attracted landless knights who hoped to support themselves by pursuing a military career in Holy Orders. In return for their help in organizing the Reconquest, the military Orders—and the lords—received large grants of land. Muslims who did not flee to Granada or Morocco were sometimes placed in encomienda to these new lordships, but many of the lands, especially in Extremadura and in the vast spaces of La Mancha, had not been heavily populated to begin with. There, the new proprietors expanded the tradition of grazing and ranching that had developed in the trans-Duero region generations before. Their methods and equipment (roundups, branding, the use of corrals, lariats, chaps, etc.) would later take root in the New World.

Towns, however, remained central to the colonizing effort. There were by this time scores of them. Where newly founded, usually by the crown or by one of the military Orders, the Castilians built them on a pattern inspired by that of the Roman camp. Like towns later constructed in America, streets radiated from a central plaza on which the church and municipal buildings, if any, could be found. When the Christians conquered a large Muslim city such as Seville or Córdoba, they converted the mosques to churches, and replaced the existing city government with one organized on the Castilian model of an elected city council and magistrates. By the reign of Alfonso XI (1312–1350), these town governments had become so corrupt and faction-ridden that the king began to appoint royal officials known as *corregidores* to maintain order.

Many Muslims, often the richest and most influential, emigrated to Morocco or Granada rather than accept Christian domination. Those who remained presented a problem for the Castilians, who together with their Aragonese and Portuguese neighbors, became the first Europeans to rule over a large non-Christian population. The Christian model for dealing with these new subjects differed little from that adopted years before by the Spanish Muslims. Tolerance, the *convivencia* lauded by some medievalists, was never an ideal. Canon Law, like the Koran, forbade conversion by force, but special taxes and other forms of legal and social discrimination encouraged many Muslims to convert. The Jews, who suffered similar disabilities, neither emigrated nor converted in significant numbers until forced to do so after a series of anti-Jewish pogroms that began in 1391. The Reconquest was a crusade in law, in fact, and in popular understanding. Those who achieved it hoped to convert their new subjects. Their efforts were not always successful and the conversions achieved were often no more than skin deep, but like Europeans elsewhere, the Spanish and Portuguese had no use for infidels. They justified the Reconquest itself in purely religious terms while reveling in the booty it provided. Their kings, from earliest times, claimed power and privilege because they were God's champions on earth. Duty for king and subject alike lay in the conquest and conversion of non-Christian populations.

By 1300, then, Castile had become not only "a society organized for war," as James F. Powers has called it, but one permeated by a warrior mentality. Men saw conquest and raiding as a normal part of everyday life. Military skill and the ownership of weapons were common at virtually every level of society. The experience of occupying, distributing, and administering new lands, and of governing alien populations had been institutionalized to a degree unknown in the rest of Europe. When a medieval Castilian saw himself as a Christian warrior who might some day acquire unimaginable wealth by fighting on behalf of his faith, he was not, in his own mind at least, engaging in Quixotic fantasies. But because medieval Castile was organized for conquest, it functioned poorly in time of peace. The end of the Reconquest meant the contraction of the frontier. Enterprising men of all social classes no longer had an outlet for their ambitions. Not only lords, but peasants, townsmen, and even priests found no one to fight but each other, and Castile sank into a state of near-anarchy that lasted more than a century.

Much of the sad history of fifteenth-century Castile, like that of contemporary France and England, must be attributed, however, to the personal incompetence of its rulers rather than to any institutional weakness. During the years of Reconquest, the Castilian monarchy had evolved into a highly effective instrument for anyone with the political skill to manipulate it. In theory, the king enjoyed absolute power, delegated to him by God and sanctioned by the Church. That power, however, was not arbitrary. Since the *Fuero Juzgo* of Visigothic times, the monarch's stated function had been to maintain order and justice by means of judicial procedures. The *Siete Partidas* of 1265 described the primary objectives of the law (in order of importance) as: to inspire confidence, to regulate, to command, to unify, to reward, to forbid, and to punish. Jurists and theologians alike understood that legislation—and the conduct of the king—had to be based ultimately on natural law, a concept found in Aristotle and the Scholastics, refined by Roman Law, and accepted by the Church as part of its own legal system. Only the king could promulgate laws, but although new laws could modify and even supercede existing legislation, the old laws could not be discarded. Medieval Castile was therefore, above all, a nation of laws; some would have said a nation of lawyers. The tensions and complexities inherent in its constitutional tradition would, in the conquest of the New World, give birth to a legalism that has seemed strained if not bizarre to non-Spanish observers.

Within the framework of the law, however, the king possessed great power. All officials and judges served entirely at his pleasure. In the course of the Reconquest he had also acquired real property rights over all lands conquered by his subjects. Because he could grant such lands to those who served his interests, this was an invaluable source of patronage. In theory, and for the most part in fact, the monarch was therefore not only the guarantor of a just and stable society, but the greatest *patrón* in a society still based to an extraordinary degree on loyalty and mutual obligation. His subjects expected that he would use these powers benevolently and in their best interests even if they did not fully understand every decision made at court. In the meantime, it was not only their right, but their obligation, to inform the king of injustice and to petition him personally for redress. At no time in the history of the Spanish Empire was this right neglected. Over the centuries, tens of thousands of letters and petitions found their way to the kings. Most were answered, although the response might take years. The role of the king, then, was not to demand unquestioning obedience, but to mediate between his own political and dynastic interest and the demands of his subjects within a framework of civil and natural law. The failure of such kings as John II of Aragon (1458–1479) and Enrique IV of Castile (1454–1474) to manage this difficult task effectively was largely responsible for the disorder of their reigns.

Aragon, too, became a society organized for conquest, but its historical and institutional development bore little resemblance to that of Castile. The king of Castile claimed absolute power limited only by divine will and natural law. He was, however, expected to hear "in generous faith" the advice of his subjects. In Aragon, the oaths of the king's subjects remained conditional on his upholding their *fueros*, or liberties. Its rulers were therefore more limited in their freedom of action, at least in domestic affairs.

Aragon proper was a sparsely populated region similar in culture and language to Castile. In 1164 it merged with the County of Catalonia, the coastal region centered on the city of Barcelona. Alone among the principalities of northern Spain, Catalonia had maintained close ties with the Frankish kingdom to the north and had adopted feudal institutions at approximately the same time. Barcelona had commercial interests throughout the Western Mediterranean. French knights had assisted in the first phases of the Reconquest, but otherwise, the pattern of royal, knightly, and civic initiative in fighting the Muslims resembled that of the other Iberian kingdoms until the reign of Jaume I, the Conqueror (1213–1276).

Sensitive to the needs of Barcelona, Jaume seized the Balearic Islands, long a haunt of Muslim pirates. Then in 1238, he took Valencia, but by agreement with Castile, Valencia became the last Aragonese acquisition on the Iberian mainland. Thereafter, Aragon directed its energies to the Mediterranean. Between 1282 and 1343, the Aragonese royal family acquired Sardinia and Sicily. After years of campaigning and diplomatic maneuver, Alfonso V the Magnanimous became King of Naples in 1442, and made the city his capital. These achievements set the stage for Spain's later dominance in Italy and created, in rough outline, a pattern for imperial governance. The components of the Aragonese/Catalan Empire remained separate kingdoms with their own institutions, united by a common sovereign. When the king was not in residence a viceroy ruled as his personal representative. Moreover, like other monarchs of the age, the kings of Aragon regarded their realms as private property that could be divided at will. When Alfonso V died, he left Sardinia, Sicily, and Aragon itself to his son John II. Naples went to John's illegitimate half-brother Ferrante. A cadet branch of the royal family therefore ruled the kingdom until 1503. During much of this period the two halves of the family remained united for diplomatic purposes.

By the middle of the fifteenth century, both Aragon and Castile had developed experience, values, and institutions uniquely suited to the work of colonization. For good or ill, both had also been forced to confront a problem rare in Christian Europe: how to govern, and if possible to convert, large numbers of non-Christian subjects. Their experience would soon be put to use in unexpected ways.

FERDINAND AND ISABELLA

The marriage of Isabella of Castile and Ferdinand of Aragon on October 18, 1469, began the unification of the Spanish kingdoms and created the nucleus of a much larger empire. Both countries had by this time suffered from decades of intermittent civil war. Isabella, supported by most of the Castilian nobility, succeeded her half-brother Enrique IV in 1474. In an effort to prevent her accession, a faction associated with the late king allied themselves with Portugal, and launched a bloody but unsuccessful war that ended only in 1479. In that year the death of Ferdinand's father made him King of Aragon. Aragon and Castile were now linked by marriage, but the union of the two crowns was—and would remain—personal. By the terms of their marriage agreement, Ferdinand ruled Aragon but had only limited rights in Castile; Isabella as ruler of Castile would have even fewer in Aragon and its dependencies. After each died, their common heir would become ruler of Spain, but he or she would inherit the two kingdoms separately (plus Sicily), and each kingdom would retain its own government, institutions, and privileges.

The arrangement could have been a recipe for disaster. The young rulers differed in interests and personality, and their marriage, in private at least, was not entirely tranquil. Ferdinand, a model for Machiavelli's *Prince*, was cynical and devious but a capable soldier and a master of diplomacy. The deeply religious Isabella was more interested in domestic policy and had the surer grasp of what would today be called public relations. Both, however, were pragmatists at heart. While Isabella lived, the royal couple pursued a common policy.

By necessity, that policy was expansionist. Ferdinand and Isabella are correctly regarded as the founders of modern Spain, but they knew nothing of the modern concept of nationhood and did not consciously set out to create either a nation or an empire. Instead, like other rulers of the day, they based their policies on dynastic interest modified at times by religious considerations. Their first priority was to strengthen royal authority in Castile, now badly eroded by decades of strife and misrule. The situation in Aragon was equally bad, but Ferdinand believed that the kingdom's long-established *fueros* precluded serious reform. Castilian institutions seemed more amenable to change. Even there, however, Isabella lacked the resources or the inclination to impose her authority by force. She needed the cooperation of nobles and town governments, and knew that this required incentives. At the Cortes of Toledo in 1480 Isabella confirmed the nobles in their possession of lands taken illegally before 1466 on condition that they return those taken thereafter. Throughout her reign, she granted *mayorazgos* that allowed them to entail portions of their estates, thereby avoiding the trap of partible inheritance which diluted the wealth of their families. Mayorazgos were an important favor, as were *mercedes*, grants of land and money in return for services rendered, but they were not enough. In the long run, only war and the hope of acquiring new domains could satisfy the ambitions of nobles and towns alike.

If domestic issues encouraged an expansionist policy, the international situation demanded it. Like the other rulers of fifteenth-century Europe, Ferdinand and Isabella believed that to survive they would have to increase their own power and reduce that of their enemies. Their two chief rivals remained Portugal, against which Ferdinand and Isabella had just fought a bitter five years' war, and France. France threatened Spanish interests through its occupation of Cerdanya and Rosselló (Cerdagne and Roussillon), two Catalan territories claimed by Aragon, and by menacing the still-independent kingdom of Navarre. In 1498 it would invade the Italian kingdoms ruled by Ferdinand's cousins.

Ferdinand and Isabella tried to deal with these dynastic rivalries in several ways. As their children grew toward maturity, the monarchs pursued a complex marriage strategy aimed at neutralizing Portugal and isolating France. Like most such strategies in an age of low life expectancy, theirs was partially successful but produced unforeseen results. Alliances alone could not preserve or strengthen their dynasty. They knew that they had to counter the expansion of Portugal at sea by developing overseas interests of their own, and that they would one day face war with France. In either case, expansion of their domains was the price of survival.

It would be wrong, however, to think that royal policy was based solely on *realpolitik*. The religious culture of the later fifteenth century was steeped in prophecies and millennial fantasies. The writings of Christopher Columbus and the preaching of his Florentine contemporary, Savanarola, are two examples of this impulse at work. Like these visionaries, the Queen and the clerics with whom she associated believed that infidels and pagans must be converted to prepare for an imminent Second Coming of Christ, even if the conversions had to be forced. The growing intolerance for Jews and *conversos* (Jewish converts to Christianity) that led to the founding of the Spanish Inquisition was closely related to growing demands for a crusade against Muslims and heathen alike. Ferdinand's apologists saw him as the "last world emperor" who would bring these visions to pass.

The king may not have shared these fantasies with the same degree of enthusiasm, but he knew that they reflected the popular will and had no intellectual basis for rejecting them. Political theory in Spain and elsewhere held that the legitimacy of the monarchy depended on its relationship to God. Kings ruled as God's representatives on earth. Their power might be in theory absolute, but in practice they were to seek the advice of their subjects and rule in accordance with Divine Will and natural law. Much of the chaos in the preceding reign had arisen from the perceived failure of Enrique IV to do either. Ferdinand sometimes tried to moderate the crusading impulses of Isabella and her court, but he never openly rejected their vision of both divine and popular will.

THE CONQUEST OF GRANADA

Granada, the last Muslim foothold on the Iberian Peninsula, therefore provided Ferdinand and Isabella with a unique opportunity. Its fall would complete the Reconquest and bring enormous prestige to the conquerors without threatening the other Christian dynasties of Europe. The Pope, in fact, was pressing them to launch a crusade and had granted them the right to levy a *cruzada*, or crusade tax for its support. Internally, war against the Muslims would divert the martial energies of the nobility and provide them with the hope of new wealth. The Castilian towns would be happy to use their militias in a cause that promised Muslim booty to supplement their otherwise stagnant economies, and a victory could, in time, add to the crown's own revenues. The war for Granada would in fact prove extremely popular, not only in the Spanish kingdoms, but through-out Europe. Volunteers and mercenaries came from as far away as England and Germany to join the king's men, the retinues of the great nobles, and the militias of the Spanish towns in driving the infidel from Europe.

At first, the war for Granada resembled earlier episodes in the Recon-quest. The Granadan border had long been chaotic. Raids and counter-raids caused extensive damage and loss of life, and forced the great lords of Castilian Andalusia to maintain private armies to protect their patrimonies. Royal authority in the region was almost non-existent. In 1482 the Marquis of Cádiz seized the Muslim town of Alhama in what appeared to be a nor-mal raid. This time, however, the royal army moved to support him. In the same year, the growing weakness of Granada's ruler, Muley Hassan, pro-voked a dynastic quarrel between two of his sons who are usually known by their nicknames, El Zigal and Boabdil. Both assumed that, in the tradi-tion of Iberian warfare, each could use Ferdinand and his army against the other. Ferdinand was, of course, happy to encourage their civil war for his own purposes.

Despite Muslim disunity, the war proved long, bloody, and expensive. Ferdinand's basic strategy was to isolate the city of Granada by capturing the surrounding towns and, in particular, the port of Málaga through which the kingdom communicated with North Africa. The Granadan War, like the wars of the Reconquest, was therefore one of sieges interspersed with raids and guerrilla forays on both sides. When Málaga fell in 1487, Boabdil agreed to surrender the city of Granada in return for Ferdinand's help in seizing several towns held by El Zigal. By December, 1489 the Christians had secured the last of them, and El Zigal surrendered to the Christians rather than accept the rule of his half-brother. Boabdil then reneged on his agreement with Ferdinand and barricaded himself in the capital. In spring, 1490, Ferdinand began the construction of a permanent siege camp out-side Granada that became the city of Santa Fe. As the siege progressed, Boabdil began to realize that his cause was hopeless and asked for terms. On January 2, 1492, he surrendered both the city and his kingdom to Ferdinand, and like his half-brother, settled down to the life of a nobleman on one of his estates.

At first, the Spanish settlement of Granada, like the conduct of the war itself, appeared to draw upon the older traditions of the Recon-quest. The Muslims retained their property, their religion, and even their legal and governmental institutions. Soon, however, the generous terms of this settlement broke down. For security reasons, the crown began to encourage the more prominent Muslims, including Boabdil, to emigrate to

North Africa. Six thousand of them left for Morocco in 1493, depriving the Muslim community of its natural leaders. In spite of a royal edict limiting the size of properties held by Christians, Spanish nobles took advantage of their departure, carving out great estates whose inhabitants were placed in encomienda to their new lords.

In 1499, the religious settlement, too, collapsed. The first Archbishop of Granada was the queen's confessor, Hernando de Talavera. An admirer of Muslim culture, he hoped to convert his new charges through preaching and instruction. When the monarchs returned to the kingdom in 1499, they brought with them the Archbishop of Toledo, Francisco Jiménez de Cisneros, who repudiated Talavera's methods and instituted a regime of forced baptisms. Talavera's views had become anachronistic. Forced conversions reflected the triumphalist policies of Isabella, who had established the Spanish Inquisition between 1478 and 1483 and expelled the Jews from Castile only three months after the fall of Granada.

In November, 1499 the Muslims of the Alpujarras, the region to the south of Granada on the slopes of the Sierra Nevada, rebelled. By March, Ferdinand had crushed their revolt, and in 1502, the monarchs ordered the expulsion of all Moors who had not been converted. Most, of course, had nowhere to go. Their conversions were demonstrably false, but the new diocese of Granada had neither the means nor the will to instruct them and the crown had no desire to provoke further rebellions. For the next 50 years, the Muslims of Granada remained nominally Christian while preserving their Islamic faith and its practices. A policy of religious exclusivity inadequately supported by missionary efforts would remain characteristic of later Spanish conquests.

The Moors of Granada remained sullen and discontented. The monarchs could not ignore the possibility that their new subjects might make common cause with their co-religionists in North Africa, or that the 6000 Granadans who emigrated might one day plot to return. To prevent this and also to establish a position in the lucrative African gold trade, the monarchs extended their policy of conquest to the seaports of North Africa. In 1497 the Duke of Medina Sidonia seized Melilla, which remains in Spanish hands to this day. The revolt of 1499 in the Alpujarras increased Spanish fears and inspired the Queen and Cisneros to call for a new crusade in Africa, but nothing was done until after Isabella's death in 1504. In the following year, an expedition took Mers-el-Kebeir. Peñón de la Gómera, Oran, Bugia, and Tripoli fell between 1508 and 1511. These towns became *presidios* or fortified garrisons governed under contract by the great nobles of Andalusia until Philip II placed them under royal control in the mid-sixteenth century.

The North African expeditions took place during a time of troubles in Castile. When Isabella died she was succeeded by her daughter Juana, who was to be assisted by her husband, Philip "the Handsome" of Habsburg, son of the Holy Roman Emperor. Philip, however, died in 1506, and the new Queen suffered a complete mental breakdown that made her unfit to rule. Throughout this period, Cisneros dominated Castilian affairs, but in 1510 Juana's father, Ferdinand, was asked to return to Castile as administrator of the kingdom. It soon became evident that these strong-willed personalities disagreed on North Africa. Cisneros dreamed of a crusade that would conquer all of North Africa for Christ. Ferdinand, ever the realist, wanted only to maintain control of its major ports without imposing Spanish rule on the hinterlands. Ferdinand's view prevailed. The *presidios* of North Africa would remain beleaguered garrisons on the fringes of a hostile Muslim world, neglected by the Spanish government and shunned by its more ambitious subjects because they offered little in the way of plunder or promotion. By the 1560s, they had become a place of exile for those who had annoyed the king.

SPAIN'S FIRST OVERSEAS COLONIES: THE CANARY ISLANDS

In Granada, the Spanish faced a traditional enemy whose social, political, and military organization was comparable to their own, and whose people consciously rejected Christianity in favor of Islam, another great world religion. Spain's first encounter with isolated societies that had no concept of Christianity or of European technology came in the Canary Islands. The Canaries are a group of seven volcanic islands located in the Atlantic off the coast of North Africa. They had been inhabited since prehistoric times by tribes of people who were racially Caucasian, but who knew nothing of Christianity or Islam and who often lived in caves. Although their weapons were simple, centuries of tribal and inter-island warfare had made the Canarians accomplished fighters, and the invaders soon found that European military technology offered no great advantage against guerrillas operating in their own rugged terrain.

In the 1340s both the Portuguese and Aragon had sent expeditions to conquer the islands without success. In 1402, Enrique III of Castile granted the lordship of the Canaries to some French adventurers who seized the islands of Lanzarote, Fuerteventura, and part of Hierro. In 1420, Juan II made a similar gift to his Castilian subject, Alfonso de Las Casas, if he could conquer the rest of Hiero and the island of Gomera. Las Casas did so, and in the next 30 years acquired Lanzarote and Fuerteventura from their French grantees by marriage and purchase. When he died in 1452, he left all four islands to his daughter, Inés de Las Casas, who then married Diego de Herrera. Their descendents retained ownership until early in the eighteenth century.

The three larger islands, Gran Canaria, Tenerife, and La Palma remained unconquered when Isabella reclaimed jurisdiction over them in 1477. For nearly a century, Portuguese mariners had been making their way down the coast of Africa, opening new markets in gold, ivory, and slaves and searching for a route to India that would give them a virtual monopoly of the spice trade. The Portuguese Crown, which fiercely opposed the accession of Isabella, had also annexed the Madeiras and the Azores in the Atlantic. While the Spanish monarchs were still at war with Portugal, and long before the attack on Granada, Isabella determined to contest the growing Portuguese dominance at sea. She also, of course, hoped to convert the Canarians to Christianity. In the treaty that ended the war over Isabella's succession in 1479, the Portuguese abandoned all claims to the Canaries. In return, Castile and Aragon agreed not to sail south of Cape Bojador, a point on the African coast some leagues south of the Canaries

The first expedition sanctioned directly by the Spanish crown departed for Gran Canaria in 1478, a year before the treaty was signed. It was made up of mercenaries commanded by one Juan Rejón, and financed largely from ecclesiastical sources. It soon became obvious that Rejón and his men were uncontrollable and inept. After two years of growing chaos, Isabella sent a much larger force under the royal official Pedro de Vera to depose Rejón and complete the conquest of Gran Canaria. He accomplished this with great difficulty in 1483, largely by exploiting tribal rivalries among the Canarians. The War of Granada delayed further efforts until 1492, when the queen sent another expedition under Alonso Fernández de Lugo to take Palma and Tenerife. Like Columbus, who began his voyage to America in the same year, Lugo negotiated an agreement with the crown that guaranteed him the governorship in perpetuity of any lands he conquered, and, like Columbus, he was financed in part by the Genoese merchant community of Seville. Palma fell almost immediately, but Tenerife resisted until 1496.

By this time, most of the indigenous Canarians had been killed. In an effort to recoup their initial investment, the conquerors tried to sell the survivors as slaves. Isabella, who had justified the conquest as part of her efforts at conversion, promptly forbade this, but her orders were ignored. When the Queen died in 1504, more than 90 percent of the native population had perished or been sold to buyers on the mainland. The developers then recruited Portuguese immigrants to work the land, but even this failed to compensate for the demographic catastrophe of the conquest. When it was discovered that conditions in the islands were perfect for growing sugar cane, an immensely valuable but labor-intensive crop first grown in the Middle East, the conquerors introduced African slavery.

The Canary Islands eventually became a profitable colony and are today part of metropolitan Spain. Their acquisition did nothing to hinder Portuguese activities, but before the last island fell to the conquerors it became obvious that they would be a useful staging area for transatlantic expeditions. Their conquest, however, offered a lesson that came too late to influence the conquest of America. The medieval practice of granting virtually unlimited lordships over new lands made it difficult to establish royal authority thereafter, and the failure to establish royal authority could result in the speedy extermination of the crown's new subjects. Because Ferdinand and Isabella did not see the results of their policies until about 1500, the patterns established in the Canaries would be replicated with disastrous effect in the early settlement of America.

COLUMBUS AND THE BEGINNINGS OF AN AMERICAN EMPIRE

In 1492, when Granada had fallen and the final stage of the campaign in the Canaries had begun, Ferdinand and Isabella authorized Christopher Columbus to sail westward in the hope of discovering new "islands and mainlands" in the Ocean Sea. His voyage marked the beginning of the Spanish Empire in the Americas, a world whose existence had hitherto been unsuspected by most Europeans. The well-known story of how Columbus claimed the New World for Spain demonstrates both the opportunistic character of Ferdinand and Isabella's policy and the inadequate planning that accompanied it.

Columbus was a Genoese merchant and sea captain who had lived for a number of years in Lisbon and acquired much experience in Atlantic navigation. In his travels he had sailed south to Mina, the Portuguese base in West Africa, and north to England, Ireland, and possibly Iceland. In 1478 or 1479 he married a Portuguese woman whose family, although relatively poor, were clients of the duke of Braganza, a leading figure at the Portuguese court. This connection, although weak and ultimately harmful to his cause, gave him limited access at court.

In 1484 or 1485 Columbus appeared before Joaõ II of Portugal with a plan to reach Asia by sailing westward across the Atlantic. The king rejected it for reasons that remain unclear. His experts believed, correctly, that the circumference of the earth was almost one-third greater than Columbus's estimate, and thought that he and his crew would run out of food and water long before they reached Japan. On the other hand, much of the Atlantic seafaring community believed that there was land to the west. Portuguese and Basque fishermen had found carved objects floating in the water that could not have been made in Europe, and on at least one occasion, had discovered a dead man and woman with strange, non-European features in a derelict canoe. Joaõ thought these reports worth investigating, and, after he dismissed Columbus, sent out two Atlantic expeditions that learned more about Atlantic winds and currents but found no land. He probably refused to employ Columbus, not because the explorer was wrong, but because of his distant association with the duke of Braganza. The duke had tried to assassinate Joaõ in the preceding year, and the king may have seen no reason to give jobs to his enemies. Discouraged, Columbus decided to try his luck in Spain.

Ferdinand and Isabella received him cordially in January, 1486. Isabella in particular seemed to be interested, but the war for Granada was at its height and money remained short. She supported him with small subsidies, but made no decision for five years. Columbus used this time to build a formidable lobby on behalf of his project. It included prominent members of the Franciscan Order, the Genoese trading community in Seville, the Duke of Medinaceli, and several key figures in the court of the infante Don Juan. A royal commission appointed to study his proposals came to the same negative conclusion as their Portuguese counterparts, but the monarchs apparently ignored their report. When, in late 1491, the Muslims at last agreed to surrender Granada, Isabella recalled Columbus to court and granted him 20,000 marevedís for expenses. A second commission again rejected his views, but at this point Ferdinand intervened: Columbus was to set forth as soon as possible.

Ferdinand had apparently become convinced that the investment required in an Atlantic expedition would be small and therefore worth the risk. He knew of the Portuguese voyages, and although he almost certainly doubted that Columbus would reach Asia, wanted to ensure that if anything could be found by sailing west, it would go to Spain rather than to Joaõ II. Luis de Santángel, the *escribano de ración*, or keeper of household accounts for the Kingdom of Aragon, encouraged him in this view and found most of the money for the voyage. The budget for the entire enterprise was estimated at 2 million maravedís, a sum comparable to the annual income of a middling noble.

An *ad hoc* arrangement typical of the age would finance the voyage. Santángel borrowed 1.4 million maravedís from the treasury of the Santa Hermandad, the body that supervised the militias of Castile, with a promise to repay it from other government revenues. Columbus provided another 500,000, presumably advanced by his Genoese and Florentine friends in Seville. In addition, the crown ordered the seaport town of Palos to provide two of the three ships needed for the voyage in return for ignoring offenses committed by its citizens. This was a common practice of the age in every country that possessed maritime communities. Kings needed the cooperation of seafarers, always a marginal group that survived only by stretching if not ignoring the law. In this case, the men of Palos had been fishing for tuna south of Cape Bojador on the African coast in violation of the Castilian/Portuguese treaty of 1479. The Pinzón family provided two caravels, their own *Pinta* and the *Niña*, which they leased from the Niño family from the neighboring village of Moguer. The crews, however, would be paid at standard seaman's wages by the crown. Columbus himself leased the third ship, the *Santa Maria*, from a private owner who sailed as its master. Because Castile, not Aragon, provided the public funds for the enterprise, Castile would lay claim to any lands that Columbus found.

As the legal basis for the expedition, Isabella drew up the *capitulaciones* of Santa Fe, so named because she issued them in the new city constructed for the siege of Granada. The capitulaciones were essentially a contract that legitimized potential conquests by affirming both the authority of the Queen and the religious purposes that justified the expedition. Similar documents had been drawn up in various phases of the Reconquest and for the expeditions to the Canaries. Others like them would accompany every subsequent expedition undertaken by Spain in the New World and beyond. They usually granted the commander of an expedition the governorship of whatever lands he conquered and a percentage of the wealth gained by his discoveries. The crown, however, retained authority over him as a governor, the sole right to organize *repartimientos* or distributions of land among the conquerors, and the all-important power to grant charters and privileges to any towns that might be founded.

The provisions of this document, however, were unusually generous. Columbus was to be named admiral, viceroy, and governor general of all islands and mainlands that he discovered in the Atlantic, and granted noble status in Castile. All of these titles would be passed on to his heirs in perpetuity. He would, moreover, receive a salary of 140,000 maravedís for the voyage plus one-tenth of all gold, silver or merchandise found in any lands he discovered, tax free and presumably forever. The remaining 90 percent would go to the crown, but in future voyages, Columbus would be permitted to invest up to one-eighth of the cost and take one-eighth of the profits over and above the 10 percent he was already guaranteed. Finally, as Admiral he would hear all admiralty cases arising from the regions he had discovered and collect the court fees. There was no mention of Asia, although the monarchs included a letter to the Great Khan and ordered an interpreter who knew Arabic to accompany the fleet just in case.

On October 12, 1492, Columbus landed on one of the out-islands of the Bahamas and claimed it for Castile. He believed, and would believe until the end of his life, that he had reached Asia. In the weeks to come, he found other small islands and explored eastern Cuba, which he thought was part of the Asian mainland. All of these places were inhabited by people who impressed the Europeans as primitive, but generous and good natured. Columbus mistakenly called them Indians. At this point, Martín Alonso Pinzón and the crew of the *Pinta* deserted the expedition to go exploring on their own. Columbus moved on to the large island he named Española (Hispaniola), where his flagship ran aground on Christmas Eve and had to be abandoned. Knowing that his only remaining ship, the *Niña* was too small to hold the entire company, he decided to leave 39 men behind and return to Spain. He named the little colony La Navidad because it was founded on Christmas.

The first voyage of Columbus became the basis of all subsequent Spanish claims in the Americas. When Ferdinand and Isabella heard that Columbus had returned, they applied to pope Alexander VI for a bull confirming Castile's possession of the newly discovered lands. Alexander, a native of Valencia in the Kingdom of Aragon, granted them no fewer than four, effectively dividing the world between Castile and Portugal. Joaõ II found the papal grant too generous to Castile and opened independent negotiations with Ferdinand and Isabella. The result was the Treaty of Tordesillas (1494) that gave everything beyond a line 370 leagues (c.1400 miles) west of the Azores to Spain. Everything to the east of the line and south of Cape Bojador would belong to Portugal. Six years later, the Portuguese navigator, Pedro Alvares Cabral, landed on the coast of what is now Brazil. Because the eastern bulge of South America lay east of the Tordesillas line, he claimed it for Portugal. The rest of North and South America would be claimed by Castile.

The privileges granted to Columbus and the kind of colonial establishment they implied rested on the assumption that he would find either

Asia or a group of islands like the Azores. Had Columbus actually found Asia, he intended to establish colonies like those planted by Portugal on the African coast and later in Asia: Small settlements of licensed merchants who traded with the natives while priests from Europe pursued the work of conversion. A garrison would have to protect these "factories," but Spain would not try to rule directly over the population of the hinterland. The Portuguese experience demonstrated that the kind of governorship envisioned by the capitulaciones of Santa Fe worked well in such circumstances. Had Columbus found uninhabited islands, it would have worked just as well, but it was not suited to the complex and unprecedented task of ruling large numbers of people whose culture was wholly unlike that of Europe.

The islands he discovered were not, of course, part of Asia, although he denied this until his death. The people of the Bahamas, Hispaniola, and eastern Cuba fished and practiced subsistence agriculture. They possessed negligible amounts of gold, which they used as personal adornment, and had little or no access to the broader trading networks of the Americas. Ethnically and linguistically, they were of the Taino culture. Their political organization seems to have been limited to village chieftainships unaffiliated with any larger federation. The major difference between the Taino and the Canarians, at least from the Spanish point of view, was that the Taino were not skilled fighters.

Columbus therefore found himself in a difficult, if not impossible, situation. Ferdinand and Isabella regarded the voyage as a royal initiative and had every intention of establishing sovereignty in the discovered lands. New subjects must be protected and, above all, converted to Christianity. The generous powers granted to Columbus placed the burden of this complex mission on a single man whose own motives were mixed and whose leadership skills proved adequate only to the management of a ship. Moreover, the crown's acceptance of a partnership with private investors set the stage for endless conflict between conquerors and the crown. Columbus, though committed to the work of conversion, felt intense pressure to produce a return for his investors, public and private. His men, who had risked their lives on a dangerous and improbable scheme, wanted only to get rich. The tragedy then unfolding in the Canaries would be duplicated on a far grander scale in the Caribbean.

When cultures with radically different values and levels of technology come into contact, the richer, more organized society will almost always exploit its poorer neighbor. Columbus and his men were immediately impressed by the hospitality and gentleness of the Taino, and astonished by the fact that they wore no clothes. Some of the Europeans took their nakedness as a sign of prelapsarian innocence; others saw in it only barbarism and immorality. Columbus himself was of two minds on the question, but it seems to have occurred to him almost from his first contacts that the docile Indians would make excellent slaves. On the first voyage, he was deterred from enslaving them by his own concern for the conversion of the Indians and by the crown's policy forbidding the enslavement of subjects unless they rebelled against royal authority. The second voyage changed his mind.

Columbus returned to Hispaniola in November, 1493 with 17 ships and more than 1200 men. This time he took a more southern route and made his first landfall in the Leeward Islands. There he encountered the Caribs, a fierce and warlike people who were enemies of the Taino, and who greeted the Europeans with a shower of arrows. Clearly, the Caribs would reject both conversion and Castilian sovereignty. They were also cannibals. This charge, made by both Tainos and Spaniards, was at one time questioned by modern scholars, but it now appears to have been correct. From the first, Columbus regarded the Caribs as potential slaves.

When he at last reached Hispaniola, he found that his little colony had vanished. The marooned sailors had extorted food and gold from the Indians and either raped the women or taken them as concubines. The natives, driven to desperation, had finally killed them. To Columbus, this meant that the Indians had rebelled, and were therefore at least technically subject to enslavement. He still hoped to convert them and make them loyal subjects of the crown, but as it became obvious that no Asian trade goods would immediately be forthcoming, Columbus began to look for gold, spices, and other commodities to send back to Spain. Finding only negligible amounts of gold and nothing else of value, he began to fear that the crown and his Genoese backers would withdraw their support before he could locate the Asian mainland. When he sent a portion of his fleet back to Spain for additional supplies, it carried the small amount of gold he had found and the first consignment of Indian slaves.

By this time, the Europeans had grown restive. Most of the men on Columbus's first voyage were impoverished sailors from Palos and Moguer. The second voyage brought more sailors, a smattering of Portuguese, Catalans, and Italians, and a cadre of tough peasants from the hardscrabble world of Extremadura and western Andalusia. There were no women. A contingent of soldiers from the Castilian *Hermandades* who had fought in the Granadan War and now lacked employment accompanied them. Before sailing, the soldiers traded the horses and weapons provided by the crown for substitutes of poorer quality and pocketed the difference. Isabella later blamed Columbus for not bothering to check on them in advance, but the whole episode says something about the early colonists. They were, almost by definition, desperate folk to whom stepping off the edge of the world was better than starving at home.

Whatever the policies of the crown or the rationalizations of Columbus, such men would have no compunctions about taking what they could. Some went off to hunt for gold on their own. One such group under Alonso de Hojeda and another under Vicente Yañez Pinzón actually founded colonies that were later confirmed by the Queen. Still others followed the example of the murdered colonists at Navidad and settled down to oppress the Indians in the immediate neighborhood. Clearly, the great captain who led fleets across the trackless ocean could not control his men on land. Columbus responded to these troubles by leaving the colony in the hands of his brother, Bartolomé, and going off in search of the Asian mainland. While he was gone, a faction of colonists rebelled under the leadership of Francisco Roldán. They controlled part of the colony until Columbus returned on his third voyage in 1498.

Columbus finally ended Roldán's rebellion by making two important concessions. First he allowed some of the men to form independent colonies of their own, thereby assuming the privilege of repartimiento reserved to the crown by the capitulaciones of Santa Fe. He then formally granted some of them the right to exploit Indian labor through what he called encomiendas. These encomiendas, like their Old World counterparts, did not involve grants of land or other property. Instead, the encomendero gained the right to demand labor services from Indian chiefs who assigned groups of tribesmen to him, often as virtual slaves. In some cases the labor service could be commuted for tribute in kind. Columbus, however, broke with tradition in one important respect. The New World encomendero assumed no responsibility for the welfare of his charges, religious or otherwise. Having granted these privileges to the rebels, Columbus had to extend them to his supporters as well. Isabella regarded the repartimientos as the usurpations they were, and disliked the Columbian interpretation of encomienda, not only because it oppressed her new subjects, but because she feared that, together with the repartimientos, it created the potential for a new quasi-feudal class whose privileges could one day threaten royal authority.

Meanwhile, the Indians had begun to die in large numbers. Some were killed in conflicts with the settlers; others perished from privation and overwork. European diseases, to which they had no immunity, exacted a terrible toll. The settlers, too, began to sicken and die from diseases that remain hard to identify from contemporary descriptions. Fleets sent back to Spain for supplies carried increasingly dire reports of conditions in the colony, and, in violation of the Queen's direct orders, more Indian slaves. Exasperated, Isabella decided to send Francisco de Bobadilla with full powers to investigate the situation and deal with it as he saw fit. When he arrived on August 23, 1500, new rebellions had broken out. Columbus and his brother were off hunting rebels in the interior, and the bodies of seven Europeans now decorated a line of gallows erected at the water's edge. Appalled, Bobadilla felt that he had no choice but to assume control of the colony. In October, 1500 he sent the Columbus brothers home in chains. Isabella released them when they arrived and restored most of the Admiral's privileges, but his career as a colonial administrator was over.

The chaos uncovered by Bobadilla, and the realization that the discoveries of Columbus involved far more than a handful of islands, forced Ferdinand and Isabella to develop a more systematic approach to their Atlantic enterprise. Their first priority was to determine the limits of their new possessions. Between 1500 and 1502 they authorized 12 new voyages of discovery, including a fourth and final expedition by Columbus. The monarchs remained confident of his navigational skills, but would never again trust him as a governor.

They also had to bring order to the colony on Hispaniola. In September, 1501, they appointed Nicolás de Ovando governor of "the islands and mainland" in the Indies. By "mainland" they meant Cuba, whose outlines had not yet been discovered. Ovando arrived at Santo Domingo in February, 1502, with 2500 men including farmers and artisans. Ferdinand and Isabella still hoped that large amounts of gold would be found in the islands, but realized that they needed to create a permanent infrastructure to support mining and prospecting. For this reason Ovando carried with him a royal auditor (*veedor*), a factor, an assayer of precious metals (*fundador y mercado de oro*), and an *alcalde mayor*, or Chief Justice of the Indies. By 1520 enough gold had been extracted by placer mining to cover the cost of the first expeditions, but by 1525 the deposits were exhausted.

Ovando restored order to Hispaniola, not by abandoning the methods of Columbus, but by extending them. He executed large numbers of Indians and Europeans alike and expanded the encomienda and repartimiento systems. Ovando seems to have adhered more closely to the medieval ideal of the encomendero as a protector and Christianizer of the Indians than did Columbus, but his influence on the behavior of the colonists remained limited. By this time, Indian mortality had created a chronic labor shortage like that of the Canaries. The conquests of Puerto Rico (1508), Jamaica (1509), Cuba (1511), and the establishment of a colony at Darién on the Isthmus of Panama (1509) were primarily attempts to find new supplies of labor, although the leader of the Darién colony, Vasco Nuñez de Balboa, found the time in 1513 to discover the Pacific Ocean and claim it for Spain.

Meanwhile, little had been done to Christianize those Indians who had survived the first conquests. This distressed the pious Isabella until her death in 1504, but the Church found it difficult to recruit suitable priests willing to brave conditions in the New World. Finally, in 1510, four Dominicans came to Santo Domingo, and were outraged by what they found. One of them, Antonio de Montesinos, preached a memorable sermon against the greed and cruelty of the encomenderos. In 1512, Ferdinand responded to his complaints with the Laws of Burgos, which established a wage rate for encomienda workers and placed the system as a whole under the supervision of royal officials. It was too late. The colonists largely ignored this legislation, and Indian mortality continued to mount. Modern estimates of Indian deaths in the islands have ranged from 50,000 to 8 million. The first figure is almost certainly too low, but given the limitations of Indian technology and the island environment, both of which would tend to limit the size of the original population, the true figure was probably closer to the former than the latter. Whatever it may have been, the conquest had resulted in genocide, although this had never been the colonist's intent. The Spanish did not want the Indians to die; they wanted to profit from their labor. They also found Indian women attractive. Decades would pass before significant numbers of Spanish women could be induced to emigrate. Many, perhaps most, of the colonists formed liaisons with Indian women and had many children by them. As a result, the DNA of Tainos and Caribs survives in the modern population of the islands, but within three decades the Indian cultures themselves had vanished.

Despite their efforts and intentions, Ferdinand and Isabella had failed to protect or Christianize their new subjects in the islands. Their attempt to provide an economic and administrative framework for the new colonies was not much more successful. Their first priority, after restoring a measure of order on Española, was to regulate trade and communications with the Indies. In 1503, the crown established the *Casa de Contratación* at Seville. Based on the Consolats de la Mar established in the kingdom of Aragon during the fourteenth and fifteenth centuries, it was intended to preserve the Indies trade as a Spanish monopoly conducted through one authorized port. Its staff of royal appointees licensed ships, organized convoys, inspected cargoes, and collected duties, including a fifth of all bullion shipments for the crown. In time it developed advisory and judicial functions as well, and became an important element of imperial administration.

A second and equally pressing issue involved the structure of colonial government. The arbitrary behavior of Columbus and Ovando in the islands and Fernández de Lugo in the Canaries proved that the crown could not depend entirely on the discretion of its governors. The powers granted to them had been too broad. The capitulations of Santa Fe had made the powers granted to Columbus hereditary. The crown honored that obligation by appointing Columbus's son, Diego Colón, to replace Ovando as governor in 1509, but modified the original agreement in significant ways. The finances of the colony were placed under the supervision of royal officials, and Diego was instructed to consult regularly with an informal junta within the Royal Council headed by Bishop Juan Rodríguez de Fonseca, the crown's chief adviser on American affairs since 1493. The government also rejected Diego's claim to rule over islands and mainland alike by appointing new governors in Panama, Puerto Rico, and elsewhere. In 1511 Ferdinand, acting as regent of Castile, established the first American *audiencia* at Santo Domingo. Originally a three-man court that heard appeals from lower courts as well as cases involving the crown, it placed judicial authority firmly in the hands of royal officials other than the governor. The Laws of Burgos further restricted the governor's powers to grant encomiendas and repartimientos. To protect his rights, Diego Colón filed suit against the crown. The issue was not resolved until 1536, long after Diego himself had died. In a negotiated compromise, the Columbus family relinquished its governmental privileges in return for a tenth of the crown receipts from Española, the island of Jamaica, and a huge estate in Panama. No such powers would ever again be granted to a colonial governor, but when Ferdinand died in 1516, the status of the colonial governors remained unclear, and no constitutional entity was as yet charged with the management of American affairs. The situation in the Indies remained fluid, if not chaotic, but the foundations of an American administration were becoming visible.

2

THE CREATION OF AN EMPIRE IN EUROPE

Important as the discovery of America proved to be, the founding of its first colonies was never a major preoccupation of Ferdinand and Isabella. Their highest priorities remained the ordering of Castile and the protection of their realms from European challengers. With the settlement of their disputes with Portugal, the greatest threat to Spanish interests remained France. The French held the Catalan counties of Cerdanya and Rosellón (Cerdagne and Roussillon), while a French family, the Albret, ruled Navarre, the tiny kingdom that straddled the western passes of the Pyrenees. Both regions offered the French easy military access to the Iberian peninsula. The kings of France also claimed the Aragonese kingdom of Naples, based on their descent from the Angevin dynasty that had ruled there until it was supplanted by Alfonso the Magnanimous of Aragon in 1443. A cadet branch of the Aragonese dynasty had ruled there ever since, and although Naples was not part of Ferdinand's patrimony, he was obligated by kinship and treaty to protect it. From 1492 until his death Ferdinand therefore devoted most of his attention to Europe. Although he could not have foreseen it, his military, diplomatic, and dynastic policies became the foundations of a vast Spanish empire in Europe.

From the beginning of their reign, Ferdinand and Isabella had worked to construct an anti-French alliance that included England, the Duchy of Brittany, and the Emperor Maximilian I. In the process they created a first-rate diplomatic corps based on resident ambassadors, an Italian innovation that had not yet been copied by the states of northern Europe. When, in 1492, the new King Charles VIII of France decided to invade Italy in an effort to make good the Angevin claim to Naples, the Spanish therefore had several assets in place: Good relations with much of Europe, excellent intelligence (their resident ambassadors also served as spies), and a cadre of fighting men hardened in the campaigns for Granada. It was not quite enough. France had more than twice the population of the Spanish kingdoms and far greater wealth. Spanish artillery was no match for that of the French, and the Spanish infantry, tough as it was, had not yet found a way to defeat the Swiss pikemen who fought as mercenaries for France. Ferdinand, if he hoped to protect the Aragonese possessions in Italy, would have to rely on diplomacy as well as force. Informed of Charles's intentions by the Spanish ambassador, Ferdinand raised the issue of Cerdanya and Rosellón. As Charles did not want a war in the foothills of the Pyrenees while he was engaged in Italy, he ceded both territories to Aragon in the Treaty of Barcelona (1493). It was the first of several diplomatic triumphs and could not have been more gratifying to Ferdinand and his Catalan subjects.

The French invasion of Italy, when it came in January, 1494, began a series of wars that lasted ten years and ultimately brought Ferdinand the Kingdom of Naples. Already king of Sicily and Sardinia, he may have hoped from the beginning to displace the cadet branch of his family that had ruled there since 1443. He succeeded in part because of good luck and the weakness of the Neapolitan dynasty, but his cunning diplomacy and military success won him the grudging admiration of Europe and greatly expanded the foundations of Spanish power in Italy.

His great diplomatic achievement was to create and maintain the Holy League, an alliance of all the Italian states including the Aragonese Pope, Alexander VI. The army with which Ferdinand twice expelled the French from Italy was therefore predominantly Italian, although strengthened by Spanish veterans of Granada and by German *Landsknechte* whose skill and discipline as pikemen approached that of the Swiss. Gonzalo de Córdoba, a Castilian who had played a major role in the War of Granada, commanded this force in most of its engagements. Gonzalo was known as "the Great Captain," in part because he eventually developed the combination of pikemen supported by arquebusiers that ended Swiss domination of the battlefield and paved the way for a century and a half of Spanish military predominance.

The combination of Gonzalo's army and Ferdinand's diplomacy proved unbeatable. The armies of the League drove the French from Italy for the first time in 1497. Meanwhile, Ferdinand and Isabella concluded treaties with England and with the Emperor Maximilian I. To seal the agreements, their daughter Catherine of Aragon married Arthur, Prince of Wales. Then, in a double marriage, their only son Juan married Maximilian's daughter Margaret of Burgundy and their second daughter Juana married Margaret's brother Philip "the Handsome" of Habsburg. Neither England nor the Habsburgs provided major assistance to Ferdinand in Italy, but the marriages would have important, if unforeseen, consequences.

Charles VIII, the object of these schemes, died unexpectedly in 1498. Ferdinand now feared that, in the absence of a French threat, the Holy League might turn against Spain in attempt to rid Italy of foreigners once and for all. In a piece of chicanery remarkable even for him, he concluded the secret Treaty of Granada (1500) with Charles's successor, Louis XII. The agreement actually brought the French back into Italy by promising to divide Naples between Louis and Ferdinand. Once again, the French invaded Naples, and in 1501 captured King Federico, the last surviving member of the Aragonese dynasty. Gonzalo de Córdoba and the armies of the League drove the French out again by 1503 after using the new tactics to defeat them at Cerignola. At this point, luck intervened on Ferdinand's behalf. In 1504, Federico died in France, and Ferdinand became King of Naples by hereditary right. Louis XII recognized him as king in 1505, but the issue never really died. In the next half-century, the French would fight seven wars on Italian soil without dislodging Ferdinand or his successors. The Kingdom of Naples remained under Spanish rule until 1707.

Ferdinand's last territorial acquisition came in 1512. The tiny Kingdom of Navarre dominated the most important pass between France and Spain. Its population, most of whom were either Basques or Spaniards who spoke a dialect of Castilian had few affiliations with France, but since 1484 it had been ruled by a French family, the Albret. Ferdinand had always coveted Navarre for its strategic value and because it had once been ruled by his father, John II. In 1512, his army launched a successful invasion on the pretext that France and Navarre were conspiring to invade Castile. His ally the pope quickly deposed John II of Albret and proclaimed Ferdinand King of Navarre. Like Naples, it was incorporated into the Kingdom of Aragon, but retained its royal title, its coinage, and its own political institutions. Three years later, for reasons that remain unclear, Ferdinand placed the kingdom under the Crown of Castile. Its privileges and governmental institutions, however, did not change.

THE INHERITANCE OF CHARLES V

Important as they were, Ferdinand's acquisitions in Europe pale before the consequences of his dynastic policies. To guarantee the peace with Portugal, Ferdinand and Isabella had married their eldest daughter, Isabella, to Emmanuel I. As part of their diplomatic efforts to isolate France in the 1490s, they had, as we have seen, given their second daughter, Juana to the Habsburg Archduke, Philip "the Handsome." At the time, Ferdinand and Isabella assumed that their only son, Juan, would inherit the Spanish kingdoms, but Juan died an unmarried teenager in 1497. Isabella of Portugal died in 1498, leaving a young son who then became the Spanish heir until he too died in 1500, the year in which Juana gave birth to her first son, Charles of Habsburg. As Juana was now the oldest surviving heir, the infant Charles was now in line for the Spanish inheritance, but his parents were still very young. Had it not been for further domestic tragedies, he might have waited decades for his throne.

The years after the death of Isabella of Castile in 1504 tested whatever unity Spain and its nascent empire possessed. In her will, the Queen followed the letter of her pre-nuptial agreement and left Castile and its possessions to her eldest surviving daughter, Juana. She excluded King Ferdinand from the succession, but made him "governor of the kingdom" until Juana could rule in person. If Juana could not rule—she had already begun to exhibit symptoms of a mental disorder—Ferdinand would govern until little Charles reached his twentieth birthday. In the meantime, Juana's husband Philip could style himself Philip I of Castile, but was to be excluded from power. These arrangements foundered on Philip's determination to rule in his own right. Soon after the royal couple arrived in Spain, he and a faction of nobles hostile to Ferdinand drove "the Old Catalan," as they called him, out of Castile. Furious, Ferdinand tried to prevent Juana and Philip from inheriting Aragon as well by marrying Germaine de Foix, a niece of Louis XII of France. Had these two produced a child, Aragon and Castile would again have been separated, but their efforts proved unsuccessful.

Then, in September, 1506, Philip I died unexpectedly at the age of 28. Juana's mental condition now deteriorated to the point that she could not, and indeed would not, govern. The Royal Council appointed Cardinal Cisneros to administer Castile on her behalf, but by 1510 the cardinal's irascible personality and autocratic methods had alienated powerful elements in the kingdom and Ferdinand was asked to return under his old title of "governor." He ruled Castile as regent for his daughter until he died in

1516. Ferdinand resented the Habsburgs to the end, but failure to produce a child in his old age forced him to recognize Charles, son of Juana and Philip I, as heir to Castile, Aragon, and its Italian possessions.

By this time, Charles was 16 and had already inherited most of what is now Belgium and the Netherlands from his father. In the course of the fourteenth and fifteenth centuries the Dukes of Burgundy had built a vast estate that stretched from the foothills of the Alps to the shores of the North Sea. They held some of these lands from the King of France, but most were Imperial fiefs. When Charles the Bold, the last Valois Duke of Burgundy, died in 1477, Lorraine, Burgundy, Picardy, and parts of Artois reverted to the French crown. His daughter Mary inherited the rest of his estate, and preserved most of it by marrying Emperor Maximilian I. When Mary died, their son Philip the Handsome inherited her fiefs and passed the Burgundian inheritance to his eldest son when he died. At six, Charles therefore became Duke of Brabant, Limburg, and Luxemburg. He was also Count of Holland, Zeeland, Hainaut, Namur, and the Franche-Comté. He held all of these states as vassal of his grandfather, the Emperor Maximilian, whose authority in the Netherlands had never been more than nominal. As Count of Flanders and Artois, Charles remained a vassal of the king of France, but French rights in these counties had long been unenforceable as well.

Although not a kingdom, the Burgundian lands were an independent principality, perhaps the richest in Europe. Charles's aunt, Margaret of Austria, ruled them as regent during his minority until 1515 when Charles deposed her with the help of an aristocratic faction headed by the Grand Chancellor of Burgundy, Guillaume de Croye, lord of Chièvres. The young archduke governed thereafter in his own name, though for some years he remained under the influence of Chièvres. Long before he set foot in Spain, Charles was therefore among the greatest potentates in Europe. He was soon to become greater yet.

The 17-year-old youth who arrived at Laredo in 1517 to claim his Spanish inheritance was of medium height with a prominent chin, a reticent manner, and no knowledge of Spanish. His new subjects were unimpressed, and thoroughly disliked his "Flemish" courtiers. Led by Chièvres, the new king's entourage used the first months of the reign to gorge themselves on the more lucrative offices in Castile. The Castilians grumbled, while Valencia and Catalonia refused to acknowledge Charles as king until he appeared there in person. Then, in January 1519, Charles's grandfather, Emperor Maximilian I died, leaving him the hereditary lands of the Habsburgs: Austria, Styria, Carinthia, and the Tyrol, together with the County of Alsace, and several counties in Swabia and the Breisgau. Charles now became the leading candidate to succeed Maximilian as Holy Roman Emperor.

Emperors had to be chosen by the seven imperial electors: the archbishops of Mainz, Cologne, and Trier, and the four secular rulers of Brandenburg, the Palatinate, Electoral Saxony, and Bohemia. The election of Charles as Emperor Charles V on June 28, 1519 required massive bribes and an army of mercenaries to protect the electors from the other leading candidate, Francis I of France, whose own armies threatened to intervene. The campaign cost the enormous sum of 835,000 florins. Using projected revenues from Castile and the Tyrol as collateral, Charles borrowed the money from Italian and German bankers, with 65 percent of the total coming from the Fugger bank of Augsburg. Similar arrangements would be made throughout the reign whenever Charles embarked on a new and expensive project.

The election brought Castilian discontent to the boiling point. Already unhappy with a foreign king and his rapacious counselors, the Castilians now realized that Charles would almost certainly be an absentee ruler and that he would use their resources to support causes in which they had no interest. Several Castilian towns rebelled before Charles left for Germany in May, 1520. Unrest spread, and within a few months developed into the generalized urban uprising known as the *comunero* revolt. Fortunately for Charles, the high nobility grew alarmed at the increasingly radical tone of the revolt and suppressed it before Charles returned to Spain in 1522. By this time Chièvres had died. Charles then showed that, left to his own devices, he could be a masterful politician. His settlement of the revolt balanced conciliation with judicial force, and from that time forward Castile became the most loyal of his kingdoms. The concerns of the rebels, however, had been justified. The inheritance of Charles V, as he is now called out of deference to the imperial title, drew the Spanish kingdoms into a host of entanglements on the continent of Europe.

THE EUROPEAN EMPIRE OF CHARLES V

Charles now ruled the Netherlands, Spain, the Aragonese kingdoms in Italy, and the German Empire. The union of these polities was, and would remain, entirely personal until his death. Their individual constitutions, and Charles's place within them, varied enormously, as did their ability to generate revenues for projects beyond their own immediate needs. The European empire of Charles V was not, in other words, a Spanish empire in the constitutional sense, but by the end of his reign Spain would become the dominant power within it. A brief description of the empire's major components suggests the reasons for this development.

The Holy Roman Empire, from which Charles derived his imperial title, was not a kingdom, but a federation of more than 200 princely states and free cities, most of whom pursued their own policies with little regard for the emperor. The larger principalities resembled the monarchies of Western Europe with their own chanceries and representative institutions. Some of the lesser princes survived by acting as military contractors, selling their service to the highest bidders. More than 80 imperial cities had achieved virtual self-government in the period of imperial disintegration after 1250, and many possessed their own militias. In theory, the emperor was supposed to determine foreign policy and serve as the empire's military leader. In practice he could act only with the consent of the Imperial Diet, a body so large and diverse that it rarely agreed on anything. Towns and princes alike formed their own alliances within the empire and sometimes conducted diplomatic relations with France and the elective monarchies of Eastern Europe.

Imperial administration was rudimentary at best. Maximilian I had created an imperial court (*Reichskammergericht*) to adjudicate disputes between states, but its members were appointed by the Diet. The Common Penny, an imperial tax created in 1498, was collected by the Diet, not the emperor, and completely ignored by many of the states. An emperor could secure military and financial support from the Diet, but only after pursuing delicate and complex negotiations with individual princes and the towns. Earlier emperors, including Maximilian, had survived largely on revenues from their hereditary lands. Charles would do the same, but the Habsburg properties in Austria and Germany could do little to assist him. Early in the reign, Charles ceded them and their revenues to his younger brother Ferdinand whose help he needed in dealing, not only with the German princes, but with Turkish pressure on the Empire's eastern borders. The German Empire, in other words, added little to Charles's resources but greatly increased his responsibilities.

The wealthiest, most urbanized region in Europe, the Netherlands, was another patchwork of city and provincial governments divided by intense localism. Each town had its own government, militia, and charter of privileges, and each province had its provincial estate, a representative body that included members from the towns and from the land-holding nobility. Charles, however, was the hereditary ruler of each province. He appointed the *stadholder*, who governed it as his personal representative, and many of the lesser officials in the provincial administration. Moreover, the provincial estates acknowledged their obligation to support him with taxes in the form of grants known as *aides*, or, in Flemish, *beden*. These grants, however, were not perpetual. "Ordinary" grants to cover the basic cost of government were usually renewable for several years at a time, but the larger "extraordinary" grants needed for a war or other emergency were not. If he needed additional funds, Charles requested them from each provincial estate, whose members responded with a list of demands and grievances. If Charles and the representatives could reach an *accord* on these matters, the *aide* would be forthcoming, usually as a one-time payment for a specific purpose. Redress of grievances, in other words, preceded the supply of funds.

The Dukes of Burgundy had also developed a rudimentary central government to deal with matters involving all of their provinces. Each province elected representatives to the States-General, a central parliament with authority over tolls, taxation, currency, and the declaration of war. Here, too, redress preceded supply, and individual provinces sometimes refused to honor grants voted by the Estates-General if the emergency in question did not threaten their immediate interests. Other central institutions included a Privy Council that advised the prince on policy, a Council of Finance, and the High Court of Mechelen. The latter was an appellate court that dealt with cases arising between provinces. Typically, several provinces including the Duchy of Brabant did not recognize its jurisdiction.

Although fractious and decentralized, the government of the Netherlands functioned reasonably well under Charles V. His regents, Margaret of Austria (restored in 1517) and his sister, Mary of Hungary, who governed from 1530 to 1555, were capable politicians. The Burgundian nobility, unlike their counterparts in some countries, provided a unifying element in the life of the region. Bound to the prince through their common membership in the prestigious Order of the Golden Fleece, they served as provincial stadholders, voted in the estates, and commanded the armies of the Netherlands in the frequent wars that convulsed the region. Important, too, was the sophisticated system of bonded debt developed by the towns and provinces to fund their tax obligations. The Netherlands raised enormous sums of money in the course of the reign. They also proved capable of defending themselves militarily, but the terrible crises through which they passed left neither men nor money for Charles's projects in other parts of Europe.

His Spanish inheritance brought Charles Castile, Navarre, and the Aragonese Empire consolidated by his grandfather Ferdinand during the Italian wars. The kingdom of Aragon contained three rather disparate principalities. Aragon itself remained a dry, isolated land with a few great estates and a larger number of properties held by minor nobles. The city of Valencia with its rich, irrigated hinterland, had a large Morisco population and suffered from grave social tensions in the early years of the new reign. The suppression of the *Germanías*, a series of rebellions contemporaneous with the Comunero revolts in Castile, brought the region a certain measure of calm after 1519. Historically, Catalonia, with its great city of Barcelona, had been the heart of the kingdom and the driving force behind its acquisition of a Mediterranean empire. From the fourteenth century onward, however, terrible visitations of the plague reduced its population by half while bank failures, political unrest, and growing economic competition from Genoa nearly destroyed its trade. By the mid-fifteenth century, the glories of medieval Barcelona had become little more than a memory.

Each of the three component states had its own Cortes (Corts in Catalan), but these bodies met together as a Cortes General to deal with matters involving the entire kingdom. Unlike the Cortes of neighboring Castile, the Aragonese assemblies possessed real legislative authority, and in financial matters redress of grievances preceded supply. Each body elected a subcommittee of its Cortes known as the Generalitat or Disputació that contained a deputy and an *oidor* or auditor from each of the three estates (four in the case of Aragon, where the lesser nobility constituted a fourth estate). These men paid the crown subsidies, controlled their collections, and served as spokesmen for the Cortes in all dealings with the king. The strength of these constitutional arrangements protected the kingdom's cherished *fueros*, or rights, until the last years of Philip II, and—together with the country's undeniable relative poverty—ensured that Aragon's contributions to the imperial treasury would be modest.

To Charles, Naples and Sicily were the most valuable parts of his Aragonese inheritance. He and his successors regarded the two kingdoms as a first line of defense in the struggle against the Turks, and Naples provided him with a strategic base on the Italian peninsula. They were also wealthy enough to provide large revenues for the crown, but despite certain cultural similarities, the problems of governing the two states were different. Sicily had been part of the Aragonese Empire since 1282, when the islanders had expelled the Angevins in a bloody revolt. There was no nostalgia for French rule and, whatever their internal differences, the Sicilians remained loyal to Spain. Sicily's *parlamento* was stronger and more representative than that of Naples. Its three *bracci* or estates represented the church, the titled nobility, and a variety of corporations including the towns and the university. As in the Netherlands, redress of grievances preceded supply, but every three years the Sicilians voted an "ordinary" grant that ranged from 100,000 florins to 175,000 at the end of the reign. From 1532 to 1556, they provided no fewer than ten "extraordinary" grants in varying amounts in addition to maintaining a fleet of galleys. Sicily's cooperation in fiscal matters arose almost entirely from fear of the Turks, and most of the money was spent locally.

Otherwise, Sicilian politics remained a hornet's nest of factional rivalries and open vendettas that tried the patience of the Spanish viceroys. Most of these men were Castilian grandees, and few sought to remain in their posts for more than two or three years. In the long run, however, the endless vendettas guaranteed the permanence of Spanish rule, not only because they prevented the development of a real opposition, but because the Sicilians readily accepted the government as a referee in their disputes. Under Charles V, the Sicilians preferred to appeal the decisions of their own courts to those of Spain in the hope of receiving more objective justice. Philip II chose instead to reform the Great Court of Sicily, on which several Sicilian barons held seats by right of inheritance. By threatening to appoint Spaniards to Sicilian courts, he maneuvered the *parlamento* into accepting a compromise. The court would be packed with qualified Sicilian jurists appointed by the crown; the barons could retain their seats, but their opinions would no longer carry judicial weight. The basic principles of Roman and Spanish law were thereby extended to Sicily, which, like Naples, had been founded as a feudal state on the Norman model.

Naples, although larger and wealthier than Sicily, had weaker institutions and was at first less securely attached to the crown. Many Neapolitans carried resentments against the Aragonese regime that dated to the time of Alfonso the Magnanimous. They rebelled unsuccessfully on the death of Ferdinand of Aragon in 1516, and, when the French launched an invasion of the kingdom in 1528, an important faction of Neapolitan barons supported their efforts. Most of these people lost their estates after the invasion failed, and were replaced by Genoese and other north Italian investors who had supported Charles V. The nobility, however, remained factionalized and continued to rule the countryside in alliance with bandit gangs whose power continued to influence Neapolitan and Sicilian life throughout the Spanish period and beyond. Between 1532 and 1553, an able viceroy, the Castilian Don Pedro de Toledo, maintained order by playing the nobles against each other and tried without much success to eliminate the *banditi*. His efforts to introduce the Spanish Inquisition, however, met with total failure.

Despite these problems, the weakness of Neapolitan institutions permitted the viceroys to extract great sums of money from the kingdom. The

Neapolitan barons dominated a weak *parlamento* in which supply preceded redress. The city of Naples, one of the largest in Europe, had its own representative institutions, or *seggi*, with which the viceroy dealt separately. Lack of baronial unity and the fear of Muslim raids favored generous grants that went far beyond the needs of the kingdom and helped to finance the emperor's European campaigns, but the financial demands of the crown grew so onerous that even Viceroy Toledo claimed that they were destroying the economy. By mid-century the economies of both Sicily and Naples were in decline, although climate change and the impact of Genoese control over Neapolitan trade may have done more harm than taxes. Under Philip II, Neapolitan grants as a component of imperial revenues declined as well.

Sardinia, the third of the Italian kingdoms, remained largely peripheral to imperial affairs. A poor and sparsely populated island, its Cortes met but once every ten years to provide modest grants that rarely covered the cost of protecting it against Muslim raiders. When Philip II established the Council of Italy in 1555 to oversee Italian affairs, Sardinia remained under the authority of the Council of Aragon.

With a population that probably numbered between 5 and 6 million people, Castile was the largest of Charles's possessions. By most measures it remained a poor, largely agricultural society, but its system of finance and government had evolved in ways that made it uniquely useful to its ruler. The Cortes, Castile's parliament, was generally cooperative. The nobles, whose partnership with the crown had been cemented by Charles's careful handling of the comunero revolt, rarely attended because they did not pay taxes. Only representatives of the 18 royal towns voted on revenue measures, but since the reign of Isabella, royal officials known as *corregidores* supervised municipal elections and could if necessary disqualify undesirable candidates. For all practical purposes, members of the Cortes were therefore selected with the approval of the crown. Moreover, in Castile, supply preceded redress. The Cortes presented the grievances of its constituents and negotiated money matters with considerable skill, but Charles usually obtained the subsidies he needed.

Taxes that had long since been voted in perpetuity further strengthened his position. The *alcabala*, which dated in its earliest form from 1296, was in theory a levy of 10 percent on all transactions. It had long since become a capitation tax, administered by the towns, and produced about 1.25 million ducats per annum during most of the reign. Other perpetual sources of revenue included customs duties, a transit tax on the movement of sheep, and the *cruzada*, originally levied on the clergy during the war of Granada and funded from the sale of indulgences. Together, these taxes covered more than the ordinary costs of government and provided Charles with a predictable source of revenue. More than any other ruler of the day, the king of Castile could borrow against future returns and budget for contingencies.

He could also count upon what was probably the most effective administration in Europe. In theory, the power of the crown was absolute. The Royal Council, reformed by Isabella in 1480 and staffed mostly by lawyers who served at the ruler's pleasure, advised the crown on legislation and appointed its officials. The most important of these served on the *contaduría mayor de la hacienda*, which collected money, and the *contaduría mayor de cuentas*, which disbursed it. A powerful set of administrative controls limited corruption. All royal officials were subject at the end of their term to a *residencia*, a formal inquiry that examined their actions in detail. Should suspicions arise in the middle of an official's term, the Royal Council could appoint a *visita* to investigate them. Moreover, Castile, unlike the Netherlands, possessed a uniform legal code in which all subjects were in theory equal under the crown. The *audiencia* of Valladolid served as an appellate court for the north; the *audiencia* of Granada for the south. Their officials were subject to both *residencias* and *visitas*, and the Royal Council could if necessary serve as a final court of appeal. Church courts became subordinate to the royal courts after 1504.

The subordination of ecclesiastical courts reflected the position of the Spanish church in general. Ferdinand and Isabella had been able to wrest control of episcopal appointments from the papacy in both Castile and Aragon. This enabled them to initiate a wide-ranging reform of the church under the guidance of Cardinal Cisneros, who corrected at least some of the abuses that would produce the Protestant Reformation in northern Europe. The Inquisition, founded by Ferdinand and Isabella, dealt with matters of doctrine and morals. It, too, was controlled by the Crown.

In Castile, Charles therefore possessed a realm whose financial, ecclesiastical, and legal systems were as firmly under his control as anything could be at a time when poor communications, inadequate information, and established privilege limited the effectiveness of all governments. It also had the best army in Europe. Officers and men trained in the Italian wars under the guidance of Gonzalo de Córdoba and his disciples made up the fighting core of Charles's multinational armies. Like Castile's administration, the army, improved and reorganized in the course of the reign, became a major bulwark of the Emperor's power. In terms of usable finance, manpower, and organization, Castile was therefore the most valuable of Charles's possessions. After 1519, its acquisition of a vast new empire in America would further increase its importance.

THE EMPEROR'S WARS

The sheer extent of Charles's European domains, together with his own ideological and personal commitments, involved him in almost nonstop warfare. His adversaries accused him of seeking universal empire, but most of these struggles were, from his point of view, defensive. Some of his non-Spanish advisors, including the Chancellor of the Holy Roman Empire, Mercurino de Gattinara, sought to restore what they saw as the universal monarchy of antiquity, but Charles offered them little encouragement. He distrusted theories in general, especially those that unnecessarily frightened his neighbors, and based his policies on two basic principles: the preservation of his inheritance and the protection of the Catholic faith.

The most important threat to his inheritance came from Francis I of France, the only European potentate whose wealth and power approximated his own. Rivalry between Charles and Francis was perhaps inevitable. Francis does not seem to have thought, as Richelieu later did, of France as a strategic island surrounded by Habsburg territories, but he resented his loss of the imperial election to Charles and wanted to revive French claims to Naples, Milan, Flanders, and Artois. He and his son, Henry II, fought campaigns against Charles and his successor in no fewer than 16 years. The conflict ended only with the Treaty of Câteau-Cambrèsis in 1559.

France possessed enormous wealth. Moreover, its position as a compact mass of territories surrounded by Habsburg lands was actually a strategic advantage because the French could force Charles to fight on as many as three fronts without overly extending their own lines of supply and communication. France could strike at any time in the Netherlands, Italy, and the Pyrenees from its own territory, while the emperor's communications—and often his armies—had to move by long and often dangerous routes around the French periphery. In each war, the emperor raised multinational armies to fight in Italy and the Netherlands while relying on Spanish troops to guard against French attacks on Navarre and Catalonia. Despite these disadvantages and the enormous cost of the French wars, Charles ultimately prevailed. The Habsburg–Valois conflict, as it is often called, increased the Emperor's holdings in the Netherlands and made him the virtual master of Italy.

In the Netherlands, the French army normally confined itself to attacks on the southern provinces. In the north and east they used surrogates, the most dangerous of whom were the Duke of Gelre (Gelderland) and his successor, William "the Rich," Duke of Cleves, who inherited Gelre in 1538. Gelre was both wealthy and strategically important, for it controlled the passage of the Rhine between Germany and the Netherlands. Under its brutal and gifted marshal, Martin van Rossem, Gelre invaded Friesland, Groningen, and Overijssel in 1521–1522, Utrecht in 1527, and the heartland of Brabant in 1542. The Netherlanders repelled each of these attacks at great cost in blood and money, and by 1544 Charles added Tournai, Utrecht, and all of the northeastern Netherlands (Friesland, Groningen, Overijssel, Drente, and Gelre) to his realms.

The French failed in Italy as well. They continued to fight until 1544 even though the Emperor had established military superiority in the Peninsula by 1528. In that year he induced the Genoese fleet under Andrea Doria to abandon the siege of Naples. The Spanish general Antonio de Leyva then crushed the French army at Landriano, giving the Duchy of Milan to Charles. Milan was the strategic key to the Po valley and historically a fief of the Empire. Charles restored it to Francesco Maria Sforza in 1530, but when Sforza died five years later, the Emperor used his imperial authority to name himself Duke. With the French collapse in Italy, Milan became the hub of imperial and, later, Spanish power in Europe. The duchy's arsenals and its usefulness as a center for military recruiting made it valuable; its control of the lines of communication between Italy and the north made it vital. Under Charles and his successors, traditional Milanese institutions continued to function under the eye of an imperial lieutenant-general whose chief responsibility was to defend Lombardy. He was assisted by the Senate, an appellate court whose approval was needed for all ducal edicts and appointments. Its 12 members, nine of whom had to be Milanese, were appointed by the ruler for life, but there was no representative assembly. Taxes were very high, but nearly all of the revenues were spent on the defense of Lombardy.

With Milan and Naples secure, the Emperor began to spin a web of patronage that made the other North Italian states his clients, and ultimately the clients of Spain. He secured Parma and Piacenza, when their pro-French ruler, Pier Luigi Farnese, was assassinated, perhaps with imperial connivance. Although Pier Luigi's successor, Ottavio Farnese, was married to Charles's illegitimate daughter, the Emperor seized Piacenza to secure his good behavior. The emperor's only son and heir, Philip II of Spain (born 1527), would understand the dynamics of threat and reward as well as his father. When he ascended the Spanish throne in 1556, he returned Piacenza to the Farnese, thereby securing their support for years to come. In the lower valley of the Po, Charles ensured the loyalty of Ferrara by reconciling its ruling family with the pope. At Mantua, he elevated Ferrante Gonzaga to Duke, confirmed him in his disputed succession to Montferrat, and granted him a number of important military commands. These cities and their networks of fortification neutralized the influence of the emperor's greatest Italian rival, the Republic of Venice, by blocking its military access to the Italian mainland.

In Tuscany, the loyalty of Florence was assured until 1589 when Charles acceded to the request of pope Clement VII and restored the Medici in 1530. In 1554, he supported Cosimo de' Medici's attack on the neighboring republic of Siena, and brokered an arrangement by which his son Philip became Vicar of Siena only to subinfeudate it to Cosimo. Philip, however, retained the strategically important fortresses along the Tuscan coast—Porto Ercole, Orbetello, Porto San Stefano, l'Ansedonia, and Talamone—and placed them under the control of Naples.

Of all these arrangements, the Emperor's relationship with Genoa was perhaps the most important. Genoa's fleet of war galleys dominated the Western Mediterranean and its bankers remained essential to the Emperor's finances. Having bribed Andrea Doria to abandon the French cause in 1528, Charles found it easy to preserve his loyalty and that of his fellow oligarchs by granting them estates and commercial concessions in the Kingdom of Naples. Long-term contracts ensured that the Genoese fleet would patrol the Western Mediterranean and support Spanish/Neapolitan ventures in the region, while the placement of ever-larger loans with Genoese bankers tied the Republic's economy to Spain for the remainder of the century and beyond.

By 1544, Savoy, alone among the Italian states, remained under French control. With an eye to the future, Charles gave its young Duke, Emmanuele Filiberto, refuge at his court. In 1553 he appointed him commander-in-chief of his forces in the Netherlands. When Charles abdicated as ruler of the Netherlands, Savoy became regent for his heir Philip II, and in 1559 defeated the French at St. Quentin, the last battle of the Habsburg–Valois wars. A grateful Philip secured the restoration of his duchy by the Treaty of Câteau-Cambrèsis. For all practical purposes Italy was now, and would long remain, a component of the Spanish empire.

From the emperor's point of view, the French wars were a great success, but they distracted him from dealing with two other issues that were in some ways closer to his heart. The rise of the Ottoman Empire during the fourteenth and fifteenth centuries brought a new focus to the age-old conflict between Islam and Christendom. Fully equal to the West in wealth and military sophistication, the Ottoman state was also relentlessly expansionist, and directly threatened not only the Emperor's patrimony but his faith. The Turks conquered most of Hungary in 1526. In 1529 and 1532 they forced the emperor to take the field against them when they besieged Vienna, capitol of the Habsburg hereditary lands. Logistical problems and the onset of winter forced the Turks to retreat on both occasions, but the continued Turkish presence in Hungary posed a threat to the Austrian heartland until Charles's brother Ferdinand negotiated a truce with the sultan in 1547.

Meanwhile, the Muslim pirates of North Africa, undeterred by the garrisons established under Ferdinand and Isabella, intensified their raids on the Spanish and Italian coasts. Their leader, Kheir-ed-din Barbarossa, had placed himself under the sultan's protection, making Tunis and Algiers part of a semi-autonomous province of the Ottoman Empire with a permanent Turkish garrison. Protests over Barbarossa's depredations forced Charles to mount costly expeditions against Tunis in 1535 and Algiers in 1541. He captured Tunis with little difficulty, but the attack on Algiers failed because an October storm destroyed the Spanish/Italian invasion fleet. Charles went to his grave regretting that he had not done more to defeat the great enemy of Christendom.

The emperor's failure to resolve the problems of Germany on his own terms proved equally distressing. The drift toward princely autonomy within the Empire became a powerful current with the advent of the Protestant Reformation. Two years before Charles's election, the Saxon monk Martin Luther launched an attack on the sale of indulgences by the church. By the time Charles convened the first Diet of his reign at Worms in 1521, Luther had become the center of a movement that threatened to destroy both the Empire and the unity of western Christendom. Politically, the heart of Luther's message had become an assault on papal authority. It appealed to many Germans, whose anticlericalism was already well-developed, and to princes and city governments who saw in the Reformation an opportunity to gain control of church resources and patronage in their own states. At a deeper level, it threatened to sweep away centuries of religious thought and practice with its doctrine of salvation by faith alone.

Charles was determined to resist the Reformation on several grounds. Personally, he remained a devout adherent of the Old Church for whom Luther's teaching held no attractions. He believed, moreover, in the medieval theory that political authority, and the authority of the emperor in particular, derived from the God's Grace as mediated by the Church. The office of Holy Roman Emperor was in fact sacred and quasi-priestly in its own right, a symbol of Christian unity derived ultimately from the age of Constantine. Practically, he saw that the towns and princes who favored the Reformation wanted to use the church's resources to increase their autonomy at the expense of the Empire. Charles nevertheless tried to achieve a religious settlement through negotiation at Augsburg in 1530, but efforts foundered on the intransigence of the Catholic princes, including his brother Ferdinand. A group of Protestant princes and towns formed the Schmalkaldic League in the following year. When a second attempt at reconciliation failed at Regensburg in 1541, Charles became convinced that only military action could save the empire. War, however, did not come to Germany until 1546 when Charles's army outmaneuvered the Schmalkaldic League on the Danube and then routed the army of John George of Saxony at Mühlberg in March, 1547. Five years later, the Protestants, reorganized and with new leadership, surprised the Emperor and drove him across the Alps into Italy. An army raised by the Castilian duke of Alba came to his rescue, but the reign ended with an uneasy religious compromise, the Peace of Augsburg (1555).

The French assisted the Protestants in these latter wars, and tried to cooperate from time to time with the Turks. The papacy, fearing Charles's growing power in Italy, sometimes allied itself with France. Such combinations, although worrisome, tended to founder on differences of culture and purpose. A more serious problem was that the Emperor could not approach any one of these conflicts without worrying about the others. Their simultaneity prolonged his struggles and made them far more costly than they might otherwise have been. He therefore failed to achieve decisive results against either the Turks or the Protestants. The French wars, however, strengthened and expanded his authority in the Netherlands and gave him effective control over the Italian Peninsula. By 1561, France itself had fallen into a civil war that effectively neutralized it until the 1590s.

IMPERIAL FINANCE

The cost of the emperor's many wars was, of course, enormous. In most years it exceeded the revenues of all his states combined. Like the other princes of his day, he therefore lived largely on credit. From the 1540s, wars in the Netherlands had been financed almost entirely with bonds issued by the various towns and provinces and pledged against specific sources of public revenue. These instruments, like the municipal bonds of today, provided guaranteed payments at fixed intervals, and could be bought and sold at market rates on European bourses. Because the credit of Netherlandish towns and provinces was better than the emperor's, interest rates on this funded debt remained at a manageable 4–10 percent. The system was financially sound, but caused taxes to rise more rapidly than the rate of inflation. In 1520 the Netherlands contributed about 500,000 ducats to the emperor. By 1555 the annual receipts had reached 3.25 million. It was a heavy burden, but Netherlanders could console themselves with the thought that all of this money was consumed locally by the Regent's government in the wars with France and Gelre.

For expenses outside the Netherlands, Charles relied upon an older and far more costly system of finance. His officials borrowed money by *asiento* or agreement from private bankers. At the beginning of the reign, most of these loans were made by the Fuggers, the Welsers, and a handful of smaller German banks. Italian firms, the most important of which were the Genoese Dorias, eventually acquired about half of this business. The German share dropped to about a quarter, with Spanish and Netherlandish banks covering the remainder.

Asientos differed from bonded debt in that payment of both interest and principal was to be made at a specified future date (normally at one of the quarterly fairs of Antwerp or Genoa). As unforeseen emergencies arose and the size of armies increased, payment was often delayed, sometimes for decades. Bankers expected this, and charged interest rates of 12–20 percent on these loans, plus handling charges and service fees that continued to mount as long as the balance remained unpaid. Of this "floating" debt, 29 million ducats with a repayment obligation of no less than 38 million was secured against Castilian revenues alone. By 1557, much had been paid off, but 12 million in principle remained, exclusive of fees and penalties. In that year, Charles's son Philip, now Philip II of Spain, stopped payment on these loans and eventually restructured them by offering his creditors *juros* (bonds) at rates of between 6 and 7 percent.

Wars, however, continued—as did borrowing at usurious rates. The Spanish state bankruptcy of 1557 was followed by similar restructurings in 1575, 1596, 1607, 1627, and 1647, yet bankers continued to make loans whose terms they knew to be largely fictional. The reasons for this apparent folly were complex. In an agrarian economy with low or even negative rates of growth, few other investments returned 6 or 7 percent. Bankers reasoned that even loans converted to bonds would at least be paid over time, and with the build up of fees, penalties, and service charges on the original *asientos*, they could provide income over many years. In the meantime, if a banker could somehow secure payment before the next bankruptcy, his returns would be very much larger. The royal secretaries who arranged asientos encouraged such thinking by telling bankers that payment of existing loans would be delayed if no new loans were forthcoming. Other incentives to lenders included trading rights, monopolies in crown territories, and even the right to collect some of the taxes on which their loan was based. The Doria family, for example, enjoyed an immensely lucrative contract by which they provided galleys for the imperial fleet. They acquired estates in Naples that had been confiscated from the rebels of 1528, and were given monopolies that enabled them to gain control of much of that kingdom's export trade. Concessions on a smaller scale were granted to other lenders. Over time, the government's chronic insolvency created vast networks of mutual dependency that were often of more benefit to others than to itself.

The system devised by Charles and his ministers provided emergency funding as needed, and tied Europe's financiers to the fortunes of the empire. It could not, however, be sustained without far higher levels of economic growth than his states could provide.

Germany, which had probably contributed no more than 3.23 million ducats between 1520 and 1555, contributed nothing after the emperor's abdication. Naples, which had contributed 8 million ducats in the same period, and the Netherlands, which contributed vastly more, had both reached the practical limits of taxation. Aragon, Sardinia, and Sicily contributed only enough to sustain themselves. Castile became the borrower of choice because, of all Charles's kingdoms, it alone produced more tax revenues than it required for its own protection.

Taxes in Castile rose throughout the reign, but the Emperor's advisors believed that the overall burden of taxation had far to go before it seriously damaged the economy. Modern studies have generally agreed. Castile prospered under Charles V, while taxes rose at no more than the approximate level of inflation. Philip II, however, continued the fiscal policies of his father. The debt mounted and taxes continued to rise until by the 1590s they began to create real economic distress at a time when agricultural yields declined, probably as a result of climate change. The financial system contributed by Charles V to his Spanish successors proved to be the most damaging part of his legacy.

THE SPANISH ASCENDANCY

The importance of Castile as a source of revenues and credit was the most important reason for Spain's emergence as the dominant power among the emperor's European possessions, but there were others. Spain provided the cadre of professional soldiers at the core of his armies. They rarely numbered more than a fifth of his troops in the field, but their training, loyalty, and discipline made them indispensable. Spanish commanders such as Antonio de Leyva, the Marquis del Vasto, and the Duke of Alba became more prominent as the reign progressed. Castile's government was also more amenable to the Emperor's will than those of his other kingdoms. Traditional privilege, the bane of other monarchies, was far weaker than in the Netherlands or the German Empire and the administration, controlled largely by secretaries like the great Francisco de Los Cobos, was extremely efficient by the standards of the day.

On a personal level, Charles came to appreciate Spanish culture and its values. Spanish policy had long been anti-French. Even in Catalonia there was at this time no pro-French faction of the kind that had long existed in the Netherlands or in the Italian states. Moreover, hatred of the Turks and of Islam in general had deep roots in Spanish history and culture. The annual depredations of the North African pirates reinforced it, and the Cortes usually demanded that Charles expend more effort on the Muslim threat rather than less. Heresy, too, found little acceptance in Spain. The best efforts of the Inquisition uncovered no more than a few dozen Spanish heretics, only a handful of whom may actually have been Protestants. Spain remained firmly Catholic while the number of Protestants in Germany and the Netherlands grew throughout the reign.

German Protestantism was a powerful movement that enjoyed substantial political and military support. Charles acknowledged that he could do little or nothing to defeat it by accepting the Peace of Augsburg at the end of his reign. In the Netherlands, Protestants remained a small minority, but many Catholics, including some provincial and municipal authorities, tolerated beliefs that most Spaniards found abhorrent. The emperor issued ferocious *placards* or edicts against heresy which, although not always enforced, served to limit its growth in his lifetime, but Germany and to a lesser extent England remained sources of reinfection. When he died, heresy was under a measure of control, and his lifelong alliance with the great nobles remained intact. The 17 provinces were loyal, but Charles no longer shared the values of many Netherlanders. The Spanish may not have wanted their money spent in faraway Germany, but they could not in conscience object to the Emperor's religious policies. It is little wonder that, as the reign progressed, the Emperor grew more attached to his Spanish kingdoms. He had long since learned Castilian, and now used it as a matter of preference. Even his confessors were Spanish. When, sick and exhausted, he decided to abdicate his offices, he chose a monastery in the remote Castilian province of Extremadura as his place of retirement.

As Charles approached the end of his reign, certain conclusions seemed inescapable. The first was that the French, the Turks, and the Protestants would remain a threat. He could not foresee that the accidental death of Henry II would plunge France into nearly 40 years of civil war or that the Turks and Protestants would abide by the treaties they made with his brother Ferdinand. He could see no end to war, and no new source of monies to support it other than Castile. Charles had always intended that his son Philip would inherit the Spanish and Italian kingdoms. Charles's brother Ferdinand, elected King of the Romans in 1531, would be the next Holy Roman Emperor. It was assumed that Ferdinand, following imperial tradition, would then arrange for the election of his own son Maximilian as King of the Romans, and that Maximilian would become emperor after Ferdinand's death. The Netherlands were historically part of the Empire and would therefore have gone to Ferdinand and Maximilian, but in 1548 Charles declared them independent and named Philip as their future ruler. Three decades of warfare with France had convinced him that the provinces could not survive without the financial and military might of Spain. He may also have feared that membership in the Empire would expose the Netherlands to even greater inroads by the Protestants.

Two years later, to his brother's horror, he therefore reopened the issue of the imperial succession. Charles now believed that the German Empire could not survive without Spanish help and wanted Philip elected King of the Romans rather than Maximilian. This initiative failed because the electors feared Spanish power and would never have accepted it, but the Duchy of Milan was now added to Philip's responsibilities as a kind of compromise. To further secure the safety of the Netherlands, Charles arranged a marriage between Philip and Queen Mary of England in 1554. The union was unpopular with the English and ended with the death of the childless Queen in 1558. Philip tried to maintain an alliance with her successor, the Protestant Elizabeth I, but it soon became obvious that the emperor's vision of England as a political counterweight to France was doomed. When Charles died at the monastery of Yuste on September 21, 1558, Philip (now Philip II of Spain) ruled all of his father's realms outside Germany and Austria. He also inherited his father's problems and his debts, including full responsibility for the Netherlands. Meanwhile, the enormous and largely unanticipated growth of Castile's empire in the New World was beginning to suggest the means by which these responsibilities might be fulfilled.

3

THE CONQUEST OF AMERICA

When Charles of Habsburg ascended the throne of Castile in 1517, the kingdom's empire in the New World had grown little since the days of Columbus. The original colony on Hispaniola had been reorganized and Cuba conquered. In 1509, the unofficial expedition under Balboa established a colony on the Isthmus of Panama and discovered the Pacific Ocean. Four years later Balboa was superceded and then executed by a legally sanctioned force under Pedro Arias (Pedrarias) de Avila. No great wealth was found in any of these places. Then within two decades a new wave of conquests toppled the great stone-age empires of Mexico and Peru and added them, together with their enormous wealth, to the patrimony of Castile. The forces that achieved these conquests were tiny by any standard, European or American, and were first launched by military entrepreneurs with little or no royal participation. Years elapsed before the Crown established its authority in the new territories. By this time millions had died and ancient cultures had perished, some of them virtually without a trace, while a flood of gold and silver wrung from the mountains of the New World enriched the Spanish treasury. Few episodes in history have been the subject of more vivid historical narratives, but the reasons for European success remain the subject of controversy.

THE CONQUEST OF MEXICO

In 1519, Diego de Velázquez, the governor of Cuba, asked for the king's permission to send an expedition to the American mainland where reports indicated the existence of a civilization far richer than any that had yet been found. He appointed Hernán Cortés to lead it. Cortés was 33, son of a respectable family from Extremadura who had gone to Cuba at the age of 19 and distinguished himself in a variety of lesser positions. Without waiting for the royal authorization to arrive, Cortés immediately and illegally set forth with 600 men, 16 horses, and 14 artillery pieces to subdue the empire of the Aztecs.

For 1500 years, a succession of advanced cultures had occupied the Valley of Mexico: Olmec, Teotihuacán, and Toltec. The term Aztec refers to the group of eight Nahuatl speaking tribes that inhabited the valley at the time of the conquest. The most powerful were the Mexica, originally a semi-nomadic tribe from the north that, after many vicissitudes, adopted the culture of the Toltecs and established themselves on an island in the middle of Lake Tezcoco. In the early fifteenth century they formed a confederation with two of the neighboring tribes and conquered the remainder of the valley. When Cortés arrived the Aztecs, who in aggregate numbered perhaps 1.5 million people, ruled or extorted tribute from a population of at least 5 million (some estimates are far higher). Their island capital, Tenochtitlán, had more than 200,000 inhabitants, making it larger than any city in contemporary Europe. The Spanish thought it the most beautiful city in the world and likened it to a larger, more magnificent Venice.

The conquest of such an empire required cunning, ruthlessness, courage, and luck. The Aztecs were warriors who had terrorized their neighbors for more than a century. At the beginning of the campaign, their army was large enough to have overwhelmed the Spanish force in spite of European superiority in technology and organization. Cortés therefore allied himself with the Totonacs and Tlaxcalans, neighboring peoples who paid tribute to the Aztecs and hated their rule, but had retained armies of their own. The Aztecs might still have been able to defeat this combined force, but their Emperor Montezuma allowed Cortés to penetrate the heart of his empire without serious opposition. Perhaps he believed, as some Aztec sources have suggested, that the Spanish leader was the god Quetzalcoatl. It is more likely that he thought that the Spaniards, with their ridiculously small army, were freebooters who could be bought off with gifts and diplomacy, or with luck, isolated in the capital and killed. If so, his confusion is understandable. He had heard of the Spanish fondness for gold and, like many modern historians, mistook its significance. Cortés and his followers wanted gold, but they wanted it primarily to secure favor from the crown and to pay off their investors. They would take a share if they could, but their larger goal was different: they wanted to live the life of Spanish lords in the New World with vast estates and thousands of Indian subjects to work them. Their primary mission was territorial conquest. Unable to believe such temerity, Montezuma received the Spanish force, now reduced to about 400 men, as honored guests in his capital.

Cortés knew that his situation was now extremely perilous. Separated from his Indian allies, surrounded by an increasingly hostile population, and confined to a complex of buildings in the city, he decided to take the Emperor hostage. No sooner had he done this than Cortés learned that an expeditionary force sent by Governor Velázquez had arrived at Vera Cruz, not as reinforcements, but to punish him for disobeying orders. Leaving a skeleton force under Pedro de Alvarado to hold Montezuma, he met the invaders and convinced most of them to abandon their mission and follow him. When the combined force returned to the capital, he found Alvarado and his men besieged by a population that had been enraged by Spanish conduct. Shortly thereafter, Montezuma died, probably from being stoned by his subjects when he tried to calm them. Without the Emperor as a hostage, Cortés and his men fled the city with heavy losses in June, 1520, and retreated to Tlaxcala where they began to organize a new and far more massive assault.

Unlike its beginnings, the final stage of the campaign was adequately manned and took full advantage of European technology and military organization. It also benefitted from one of the most effective, if unintended, applications of biological warfare in history. Over the winter of 1520–1521 Cortes assembled a much larger army of Spanish troops from the islands supplemented by a far larger host of Indian auxillaries, some of them recruited from Aztec tribes that resented the dominance of the Mexica. He had ships built on the coast and carried in sections over the mountains to be reassembled on the shores of Lake Tezcoco where they were used to blockade food shipments from the mainland. The siege of Tenochtitlán began in April, 1521. Cortés soon realized that fighting in the city's narrow streets neutralized the European advantage in technology and tactics, and set out to destroy the city stone by stone. On August 13, the Spanish captured Cuahtemoc, Montezuma's heroic successor, and forced him to surrender. By this time, only a quarter of the city's buildings were left standing, its inhabitants were starving, and thousands had perished from smallpox, a European disease against which the Indians had no immunity.

The fall of Tenochtitlán gave Spain control over the entire Valley of Mexico and much of the surrounding territory as well. There was little or no continued resistance in the countryside because most of its inhabitants either hated the Mexica or saw no great difference between them and the Spanish. The Aztecs had been a military and priestly aristocracy that extorted tribute and labor services from a population whose primary loyalty had always been to their *calpulli* or commune. The new Spanish lords were different only in that they did not demand victims for human sacrifice as well. They insisted that the Indians convert to their religion, but the old gods, if not wholly discredited, were now seen as weaker than the god of the White Men.

The Aztec empire fell, then, not because its leaders were paralyzed by religious fantasies, or because, as one recent theory has it, because the Indians thought of warfare as a ritual of dominance whose purpose was to ensure a supply of prisoners for sacrifice. The history of their conquests demonstrates that the Aztecs knew well how to slaughter enemies and seize their property. Their empire fell because it commanded the loyalty of neither its subjects nor it allies, nor could its military organization and stone-age weapons stand in the long run against the Europeans. Even if Montezuma had destroyed Cortés and his first expeditionary force, it would not have prevented other Europeans from following in his footsteps. By this time, the empire would further have been reduced by European diseases. The sense of inevitable doom that pervades Aztec accounts of this first contact between two great warrior civilizations was in retrospect fully justified.

In the decade after the conquest of Mexico, expeditions led by Cortés's captains Pedro de Alvarado and Cristóbal de Olid claimed most of Central America for Spain. Another force launched from Panama by Pedrarias de Avila met Alvarado as he moved southward into Nicaragua. None of these efforts uncovered great wealth or centers of population comparable to the Valley of Mexico, but they added new lands and thousands of Indian subjects to the growing empire. Otherwise, the conquest of the Mexican periphery proved in some respects more difficult than that of the Aztec empire. The Mayan civilization of the Yucatan and adjacent Guatemala had declined by the beginning of the sixteenth century, but it put up a formidable struggle against the Spanish that lasted from 1527 until 1542. The Chichimec peoples to the west and northwest of the Valley of Mexico proved equally valiant. Nuño de Guzmán required 12 years to conquer what became the province of New Galicia (now the states of Michoacán, Nayarit, Jalisco, and Sinaloa). The Mixtón revolt of 1541 nearly overturned his efforts, but five years later the discovery of silver in this area brought an influx of colonists that consolidated the conquest. These campaigns were conducted with extraordinary savagery, as were those of Francisco de Ibarra, who established Spanish claims to northern Mexico between 1562 and 1575.

This sparsely settled region, which the Spanish called Nuevo Vizcaya, would remain a violent frontier for many years. Here the crown encouraged Franciscans and Jesuits to establish missions that would then be protected by a small *presidio* or military garrison. The missions were basically agricultural villages operated by Indians under the sometimes heavy-handed guidance of the friars. The Spanish knew that the work of conversion could succeed only with settled populations. Nomadic Indians would simply drift away from areas of Spanish control and nullify their conversions through contact with pagans. The mission system became the basis of frontier settlement for the next two centuries and enjoyed a modest success despite runaways, occasional revolts, and frequent attacks by neighboring tribes. By the 1590s missions extended into the pueblo country in the upper Rio Grande valley and were struggling to succeed in northern Florida, but long before this, the Spanish had concluded that some places were simply not worth conquering. Great empires with settled populations were easier to subdue than semi-nomadic peoples whose territories lacked a strategic center—and far more profitable. For this reason, the heroic explorations of North America by Coronado, De Soto, and Cabeza de Vaca did little more than strengthen Spanish claims to regions that no one at this point intended to colonize.

THE CONQUEST OF PERU

The empire of the Incas stretched from what is now Ecuador to the northern parts of modern Chile and Argentina. Like that of the Aztecs, the Incan social system was based on tribes made up of kinship groups, but the Andean *ayllu* differed from the Mexican *calpilli* in that its members were geographically dispersed. Peru is characterized by distinct ecological zones determined by altitude and rainfall. A coastal desert cut by narrow river valleys could, with irrigation, support a modest agriculture based on vegetables, squash, cotton, peanuts, and cassava. On the Andean slopes, maize and beans give way to grains and potatoes at about 11,000 feet. Between 13,000 feet and the snow line is the *puna*, a frigid grassland that provides pasturage for llamas, alpacas, and other American relatives of the camel. Because erratic rainfall can cause crop failures in any of these regions, and because no single region can supply all of life's necessities, the *ayllu* long ago developed a strategy of agricultural diversification. They established settlements in each of the ecological zones—often many miles apart—collected their produce, and distributed it more or less equally to all of their members. Each *ayllu* had an ancestral village which it regarded as its spiritual home, but neither it nor the tribe of which it was part had a true territorial base. Politically and economically, the Andean region was therefore better integrated than its Mexican counterpart.

The supreme Inca, who ruled over the entire region, was regarded as a descendant of the Sun God, and therefore sacred. In reality he descended from the chiefs of the Inca tribe which, like the Aztecs, had established an imperial polity on the wreckage of earlier empires during the fifteenth century. He ruled with the assistance of a large army and an even larger bureaucracy whose primary function was to ensure the continued distribution of goods. The Inca collected tribute from his subjects, but always reserved a part of it in huge government warehouses to be redistributed in times of famine. This was an important source of imperial patronage, and seems to have been accepted as an extension of the distributions practiced by the *ayllus*. A system of compulsory labor known as the *mita* seems to have been accepted in the same spirit. Communal survival had long depended not only upon diversification and redistribution but on cooperative efforts to provide irrigation in the lowlands, terracing on the slopes, and the maintenance of an elaborate system of roads to unite the various regions. The Inca and his administrators had long provided direction for many of these projects. In theory, the Empire of the Sun should therefore have been harder to conquer than Mexico. More distant from the American centers of Spanish power, it was geographically larger, more centralized, and probably more populous. There were no armed tributary nations like the Tlascalans with whom an invader could ally, yet the Spanish force that destroyed it was not only smaller than the one commanded by Cortés but deeply divided against itself.

The conquerors of Peru, Francisco Pizarro and Diego de Almagro, had been followers of Pedrarias de Avila in Panama. Unlike Cortés, they came from the very bottom of Spanish society. Pizarro had herded swine in his native Extremadura and was probably illiterate. Almagro was an orphan from Castile who fled to America to avoid criminal prosecution. Drawn by reports of a wealthy empire to the south, the two launched an unsuccessful exploratory expedition in 1524. In 1527 they penetrated as far as Tumbes, where they found a respectable quantity of gold. Pizarro then went to Spain in 1528 and secured a license for conquest from the crown that named him Governor of Peru. Almagro remained behind to seek financial backing in Panama. When they launched their attack on Peru in December, 1530, both men were grizzled veterans in their fifties.

Pizarro went first with 180 men, including his four half-brothers. Almagro, already angry at Pizarro's elevation to the governorship, remained behind to raise more troops. When Pizarro arrived at the northern city of Tumbes, he found the Inca's empire in crisis. Smallpox, possibly introduced by one of Pizarro's earlier expeditions, had killed many natives including the Inca himself. The ruler's death set off a bitter civil war over the succession between two of his sons, Huascar and Atahualpa. Pizarro soon learned that Huascar had recently been captured by forces loyal to Atahualpa, and that Atahualpa was at that moment marching south to Cuzco to assume the title of Inca. Pizarro moved to intercept him, and the two forces, one huge, the other tiny, met at the nearly abandoned town of Cajamarca. In a replay of Cortés's strategy, Pizarro invited Atahualpa to meet with him. When the Emperor arrived in the town center with an enormous entourage, the Spanish took him hostage in a sudden ambush that left several thousand Indian soldiers dead.

Once again, an American ruler had failed to take the Spanish seriously. Atahualpa admitted before his death that he allowed Pizarro to reach Cajamarca with the intention of surrounding and destroying the Spanish, but the Spanish struck first. Even then, the Emperor did not believe that the white men had really come to conquer. Tales of Spanish greed led Atahualpa, like Montezuma, to believe that he could buy them off with a golden ransom in return for his release. For eight incredible months, tens of thousands of warriors commanded by the Inca's best generals did nothing while treasure was gathered from Cuzco and other places. Then, in April, 1533, Almagro arrived with another 150 men. By this time the treasure had been received and melted down for shipment to Charles V and Atahualpa's followers in Cuzco had murdered Huascar. Atahualpa was now useless to the Spanish. At Almagro's insistence, Pizarro had the Emperor garroted, and the two commanders embarked on a campaign against Cuzco itself. Assisted by chieftains loyal to Huascar's side of the royal family, the Spanish fought a series of successful battles against heavy odds before entering the capital on November 15.

In contrast to the situation in Mexico, resistance did not end with the death of the emperor and the loss of his capitol. Sebastián Benalcázar, eventually assisted by Almagro and a third invasion force from Guatemala under Pedro de Alvarado, required two years of hard fighting to gain control of the northern province of Quito. To preserve order in the heartland, Pizarro installed Huascar's younger brother, Manco, as a sort of puppet Inca, and went off to build a new capital at Lima near the coast. He left his incompetent half-brothers, Juan and Gonzalo Pizarro, with a small garrison at Cuzco while Almagro and his followers set forth to subdue Bolivia and Chile. The misbehavior of the Cuzco garrison and the prodding of tribal leaders provoked Manco into repudiating his policy of cooperation. He raised an army and besieged Cuzco while another Indian force surrounded Lima.

Massive Spanish reinforcements soon relieved the new capital, but the siege of Cuzco lasted until April, 1537, when Almagro and his "Men of Chile" returned. Embittered by their failure to find anything of value in the south and by what they saw as the usurpations of the Pizarros, they relieved the city but arrested the Pizarro brothers. It was the beginning of a civil war among the Spanish that outlasted the execution of Almagro by Francisco Pizarro in 1538 and the murder of Francisco by Almagro's followers in 1541. The first viceroy sent by the Crown to restore order died fighting against the forces of Gonzalo Pizarro, and it was not until 1548 that Pedro de la Gasca, a priest skilled in both war and diplomacy, established royal authority in Peru. Indian resistance, however, continued. Strife among the Spaniards encouraged Manco Inca to launch further rebellions, and eventually to establish an independent Incan state in the Vilacabamba valley between Cuzco and Lima. The enclave survived in one form or another until 1572 when the Viceroy Francisco de Toledo destroyed it and executed the last Inca, Tupac Amaru.

As in Mexico, the conquest of Peru inspired others to embark on conquests of their own. No fewer than three expeditions, two from the Caribbean and one from Peru, descended upon the Chibcha kingdoms of what is now Colombia. The Caribbean forces were headed by Gonzalo Jiménez de Quesado, who had conquered the Chibcha kingdom of Tunja, and a German conquistador, Nikolaus Federmann. At Bogotá they encountered the Peruvians under Sebastián de Benalcázar who had led the successful campaign against Quito. To avoid civil war, the three conquerors agreed to accept the arbitration of the king. Benalcázar was eventually named governor, and Santa Fe de Bogotá became the capital of the region called New Granada. The Indians to the south proved more resistant. Undeterred by the earlier difficulties of Almagro and his men, Pedro de Valdivia invaded Chile and became mired in a long and bloody struggle with the Araucanian Indians. He founded Santiago (1541) and several other cities, but could not go beyond the Bío-bío River. South of that line, the Araucanians, whose military virtues inspired the conquistador Alonso de Ercilla's epic poem *La Araucana*, maintained their independence for years to come.

Like North America, the vast tracts east of the Andes were claimed by Spain but largely neglected. A foraging expedition under Francisco de Orellana lost its way in 1541 and floated downstream the length of the Amazon. Most of the Amazon basin fell within the limits assigned to Spain by the Treaty of Tordesillas, but no attempt was made to exploit the region until the Brazilian settlements of the twentieth century. Although the basin of the Río de la Plata presented fewer geographic and climatological obstacles than the Amazon, it too remained largely unsettled. Pedro de Mendoza founded Buenos Aires in 1535. When the Indians destroyed it in 1541, he and his men moved up the Rio de la Plata to Asunción in what is now Paraguay. They found no great Indian civilizations and no mineral wealth, and for many years the Spanish settlements in the region remained small and largely dependent on smuggling goods between the Atlantic and the mining that developed around Potosí in Upper Peru. Europeans made little effort to settle Patagonia and the great pampas of Argentina until the nineteenth century.

THE PHILIPPINES

Spain's most remote colony joined the empire in 1565. In 1519 Charles V dispatched an expedition under the Portuguese navigator Ferdinand Magellan. Its purpose was to reach the Spice Islands by sailing west. Magellan hoped to prove that the longitude of the islands lay within Spanish territory as determined by the papal bull of 1493. In an extraordinary feat of seamanship and endurance, Magellan and his multinational crew discovered the strait that bears his name and crossed into the Pacific, making landfall at Guam in March, 1521. From there he went to the Marianas, and then on to the archipelago that would eventually be named the Philippines. He died there on the island of Mactán in a skirmish with the natives, but the remnants of his expedition proceeded to the Moluccas. One leaking ship full of spices and 21 survivors eventually returned to Spain under the command of the Spanish navigator Sebastián del Cano. It was the first circumnavigation of the globe.

When two subsequent expeditions, including one launched from Mexico by Cortés, failed to reach the Moluccas, Charles ceded them to Portugal in 1527 for 350,000 ducats. The islands that became the Philippines remained theoretically within the Spanish line of demarcation. In 1542 an expedition from Mexico, financed in part by Pedro de Alvarado, landed there and named the archipelago for crown prince Philip, but more than 20 years passed before Philip, now Philip II of Spain, authorized an expedition of settlement under Miguel López de Legazpi. The king's purpose was not conquest, but the establishment of a trading colony on the Portuguese model. Legazpi and his men left New Spain in November, 1564, and landed on Cebu in April, 1565. After six years of misery they established themselves at Manila in 1572. Administratively, the new colony was part of New Spain, but received an audiencia of its own in 1583.

In the beginning, the Chinese and Portuguese tried without success to dislodge the Spaniards. Manila, however, soon evolved into an entrepot where Japanese and Chinese merchants traded silks and porcelains for Spanish silver. Each year in June or July the Manila Galleon made the six months' journey to Acapulco with a cargo of eastern luxuries. In March, it returned laden with silver. In the early years, three or four ships occasionally made the trip. In 1593, the crown limited their number to two, but in most years, only one actually sailed. On at least 30 occasions a ship was lost at sea, often disappearing without a trace. On one occasion, when the galleon arrived at Acapulco after a voyage of 12 months, the entire crew was dead. Only the immense value of this trade, which reached a peak of 12 million pesos in 1597, made the journey worth the risk.

The Philippines, then, were an important acquisition, but the Spanish colonists never became numerous enough to seize control of the entire archipelago. When Legazpi and his men arrived, Islam was already well-established on the southern islands of Mindanao and Palawan, and had begun to make inroads on Luzon. The northern peoples, most of whom spoke Tagalog and practiced their own native religions, seem to have accepted Spanish rule as a desirable alternative to the Muslims. Five Augustinian friars who accompanied Legazpi were soon joined by missionaries from the other orders, and the inhabitants of Luzon's coastal lowlands quickly adopted Christianity and a measure of European ways. Because few Spanish women made the arduous journey across the Pacific, intermarriage was common. The settlers, however, made little or no effort to extend their authority to the mountainous hinterland. Expeditions against the Moros, as the Spanish called them, failed to break the hold of Islam in the south, and Moro raids and acts of piracy troubled the Spanish settlements until 1850.

THE PROBLEM OF GOVERNANCE

Unlike the French and British settlers of North America, the conquerors of Central and South America imposed their rule on vast, settled populations with elaborate, long-established political and social institutions. Ethnic Spaniards would never become more than a small minority in a vast land. Although most of them came from modest if not squalid backgrounds, they sought to emulate the social values of the Castilian aristocracy. Few if any hoped to cultivate the new lands as their peasant ancestors had cultivated the old. Their goal was to find precious metals and to establish landed estates for themselves that would, they hoped, make them the equal of lords. They therefore put down roots where they found mineral deposits, a settled population of Indians capable of providing labor, or both. They built some of the more important centers, like Mexico and Bogotá, upon the ruins of Indian capitals; others, like Lima, were new foundations. The distance between the centers of Spanish settlement was often immense. Communications between them and with the mother country involved arduous, time-consuming journeys by land and sea, but few of the ports that served these routes developed into major centers. On the mainland at least, the Spanish tended to avoid coastal regions. They found them unhealthy and, in later years, vulnerable to pirate raids. Vera Cruz in Mexico, Lima's port of Callao, and the Panamanian ports long remained transient communities with little permanent infrastructure.

Most of the emperor's European possessions had long histories as independent kingdoms whose established institutions continued to form the basis of their government under Habsburg rule. Native polities in America were no less sophisticated, but the Spanish either could not or would not integrate their institutions with European and Christian norms. As we shall see, they would for a time tolerate a measure of Indian self-government at the local level. Otherwise, they sought to impose new institutions based selectively on those of Castile, but with few of that kingdom's traditions of representative government.

In America as in Castile, the chartered municipality would be the basis of political and social life. Physically, the new towns were constructed according to a universal plan or *traza*. A grid of streets surrounded a central plaza around which were the church, the governor's house, the *cabildo* or city hall, the jail, and the houses of the most prominent citizens. This scheme, a self-conscious imitation of the ancient Roman camp, had been used in the founding of cities in New Castile during the Reconquest. Although many *vecinos* or citizens held agricultural land and the highest ambition was to create a *hacienda* or landed estate, few Spaniards wanted to live in the countryside. Spanish society in both Europe and America was, and remains to this day, essentially urban.

People measured their status by the proximity of their residence to the town center. Away from the plaza homes grew more modest and the formal pattern of streets gave way to winding, unpaved lanes. The *barrios* or *colaciónes* that grew up on the outskirts of every city were largely inhabited by urbanized Indians who worked in domestic service or construction and by a growing class of *mestizos* or persons of mixed race. A majority of mestizos descended from Spanish settlers and their Indian concubines. Few Spanish women emigrated to America until years after the first settlement. In the interim, some of the conquistadors married Indian women. If they eventually took brides from Spain, they saw no reason to abandon their mistresses but established them, together with their children, in households on the edge of town. The *barrios* soon became microcosms of the Latino world to come: a rich stew of Indians, mestizos, and poor whites with a composite culture of its own.

The founding of Spanish towns in America followed the pattern established by the Reconquest and by the crown's original agreement with Columbus. Military entrepreneurs, most of whose financing came from private sources, received a *capitulación* from the king that set forth the terms of conquest. This document asserted that in the event of conquest, the crown would assume full sovereignty and real property rights over the new lands. The conqueror would, however, become the colony's governor, often for life, with the right to grant lands and encomiendas to his followers as agent of the crown. In some cases the governorship could be passed on to the conqueror's heirs; in others, the governor was also granted the medieval title of *adelantado*.

Before claiming inhabited lands, the commander of the expedition (or more often an attending priest or notary) was commanded to read a document called the Requirement (*requirimiento*) that ordered the natives to acknowledge the authority of the Pope and King of Spain. If the natives rejected this proclamation, or, as was usually the case, did not reply because they were hiding from the Spanish, the would-be conqueror was justified in launching a "just war" against them. When the conquest was complete, the settlers planted the royal standard and drew up a petition to the crown. In it they acknowledged their status as vassals of the king, accepted their commander as royal governor, and requested a formal charter making their conquest a royal town.

In authorizing new expeditions of discovery and conquest, Charles V had at first followed the precedents established by Ferdinand and Isabella. This basically proprietary system worked no better for Charles than it had for his predecessors. The new governors used land and labor grants as patronage to increase their own power over the white settlers. Few if any of the conquerors did much to protect the Indians, whose real property rights were often ignored and who were abused by the encomenderos on the mainland as they had been in the islands. Indians everywhere continued to die in alarming numbers. Peru, the worst case, descended into civil war and anarchy, but even at its best the system threatened royal control. Cortés in Mexico proved as capable at governing as he had been at war. He rebuilt Tenochtitlán as the Spanish city of Mexico and maintained order while making himself popular with colonists and Indians alike. The Emperor rewarded him with lands and titles, but recalled him to Spain in 1527 because he feared his growing independence.

Charles eventually solved the problem of American governance by adopting a system not unlike that used by the Aragonese in Italy. Mexico (officially the Viceroyalty of New Spain) and Peru would be governed by viceroys who served as the king's personal representatives. The viceroys were always from noble Spanish families and were expected to maintain a king's estate. Some, including Antonio de Mendoza in Mexico (1535–1550) and Francisco de Toledo in Peru (1569–1581), were brilliant administrators. Viceregal decisions, however, were at all times subject to royal approval. The mechanism for that approval predated the viceroyalties themselves. In 1524, Charles created the Council of the Indies to advise him on American affairs and to hear appeals from the colonial audiencias. By doing so he gave constitutional form to the junta of advisors that had been meeting for years under the presidency of Bishop Fonseca. The Council of the Indies ranked second only to the Council of Castile in precedence. It met daily except holidays and disposed of an enormous amount of business with the help of a large staff which, in addition to its judicial functions, prepared legislation on American matters for the king's approval and recommended all colonial appointments.

Each of the two kingdoms was divided into several provinces with governors of their own. The first governors had of course been conquerors whose powers dated from their original *capitulación*. Assisted in part by precedents established during 30 years of litigation with the Columbus family, the crown gradually managed to replace most of these men and their descendants with royal bureaucrats. The new governors, like their predecessors, held broad powers, but their decisions were subject to review by the nearest audiencia and ratification by the viceroy. By the end of the reign, the larger provinces had acquired audiencias of their own: Mexico (1529), Panama (1538), Lima (1542), Guatemala (1544), Guadalajara (1549), and Santa Fe de Bogotá (1549). All but Lima and Bogotá fell within the Viceroyalty of New Spain. Philip II added audiencias at Charcas (in Bolivia), Quito, and Santiago de Chile to the viceroyalty of Peru between 1559 and 1565.

The New World audiencias, like those of Castile, served primarily as appellate courts. They differed from the Old World model because their right to review the decisions of governors and viceroys gave them an administrative function as well. In practice, they served not only as courts, but as advisors to the king's appointees. Their members were lawyers appointed by the Council of the Indies which tried to ensure impartiality by choosing only peninsular Spaniards with no connection to the region in which they were to serve. In provinces, the president of the audiencia served as governor and, if the military situation warranted it, captain-general. Captains-general on the more remote frontiers reported only to the crown. There was no rigid organizational chart in the early Spanish empire. The needs of the situation and the perceived skills of the proposed official governed appointments, titles, and even salaries.

This system provided the basic structure of American government until the end of the Habsburg era, but for the first 25 years of the reign, the implementation of policy remained inconsistent and fraught with bewildering reversals. The innate pragmatism that subordinated organizational rigidity to local needs made the crown unwilling to discourage further enterprise by depriving loyal subjects of their rewards. The replacement of *conquistadores* by bureaucrats from Spain was therefore a delicate process. Except in cases of serious misconduct, it proceeded slowly and inconsistently until the wave of conquests subsided in the 1540s.

THE PROBLEM OF THE INDIANS

With few exceptions the conquerors saw the native population as little more than a source of free labor. The crown and its officials saw the Indians as a source of tribute, but also as new subjects to be Christianized and protected. No one thought it desirable to integrate them with the Spanish or make them a part of Spanish municipalities. Most of the Indians therefore continued to be governed by their hereditary chieftains and to live in traditional towns or villages where some, at least, of the old customs were preserved. Ironically, the social organization of the old New World empires combined hierarchical and communitarian elements that seemed in many ways familiar to the conquistadores. The Indians had always been governed by chiefs who lived in towns and were assisted by a hereditary class of tribal elders. This ruling class was supported by levies of labor and tribute at least as onerous as those of medieval Spain. *Ayllus* and *calpullis*, like many Spanish villages, were composed of related families who often cooperated in the raising of crops and in meeting the demands of the lords. Although *ayllus* had multiple locations and the Mexican *calpullis* normally did not, the relationship of both to their urbanized chieftain and his *principales* resembled the situation of Castilian villages subject to a municipality

The Spaniards may not at first have understood the importance of tribal relationships, *ayllus*, or *calpullis*, but the relationship between the larger Indian towns and their tributary villages encouraged them to think that Indian cities could be remodeled along Spanish lines. In the middle years of the sixteenth century viceregal governments designated the larger towns as *cabeceras*, with an elected governor and a cabildo. The governor, almost always the local cacique, was responsible for collecting tribute with the help of an army of lesser officials, all of whom were Indian. The *principales* or elders of the community became the town's electorate. They alone could be elected as the *alcaldes* and *regidores* of the cabildo, unless, as sometimes happened in later years, no Indian candidate of sufficient standing appeared. As in Spanish towns, the *alcaldes* served as magistrates, so that Spaniards played no role in the ordinary administration of justice. The Indians accepted these arrangements while adapting them to their own culture. Spanish efforts to impose term limits, for example, were steadfastly resisted by Indians who had traditionally elected their chieftains for life.

To impose a measure of control, the crown established the office of *corregidor de indios* in 1531. By the 1560s, all of the Indian communities had been placed in *corregimientos* governed by a royal appointee who was always Spanish and often a Spaniard of American origin with close connections to the local landholders. The responsibilities of these officers suffered from an inherent contradiction: they were to ensure the material and spiritual welfare of the Indians and at the same time collect the tributes owed by the Indian communities to the crown. As they were appointed for only two or three years and derived their modest salaries from a percentage of the tribute, the temptation to extort goods and money from the Indians proved irresistible. The government's constant attempts to restrain the *corregidores de Indios* by flurries of legislation proved largely ineffective. At the same time Spanish officialdom did not seek to micromanage Indian affairs. Corregidors might intervene in cases of serious financial or judicial irregularities, but for the most part allowed the Indians to govern themselves as long as tribute was forthcoming. Tribute commonly took two forms. The first, a capitation tax commonly paid in cash or in kind to the crown by an Indian town and its subject jurisdictions, was negotiated by the corregidor and the cacique. The difference between the agreed sum and the much larger amount collected from the peasants supported the cacique, the *principales,* and the cost of municipal government. Indian tribute collectors knew their communities, and commonly took everything beyond what they thought a family could live on until the next harvest.

Until the 1540s most labor tribute was exacted within the institutional framework of the encomienda. The conquerors had granted encomiendas to their men, which meant, as in the islands, that the encomendero assumed responsibility for the protection and spiritual welfare of a group of Indians in return for their labor. The cacique was responsible for supplying the workers. As in the islands, the system proved inherently abusive. Encomenderos rarely fulfilled their end of the bargain. Instead they overworked the Indians and frequently mistreated them, often to the point of death. Caciques, of course, had traditionally imposed labor tribute on their people as well and continued to do so after the conquest under conditions little better than those created by the Spaniards.

Given the conditions under which Indians were forced to live, it is not surprising that the size and importance of their communities declined steadily throughout the sixteenth century. Native populations before and after the conquests cannot be accurately determined, but most authorities would agree that the absolute decline in the number of native Americans on the mainland was almost as dramatic as it had been in the islands. The violence of the conquest and the disordered conditions that followed it cost thousands of Indian lives, although many survivors undoubtedly chose to flee beyond the limits of Spanish settlement. Privation and the brutal conditions imposed by the encomienda system took their toll, but the greatest killer was pandemic disease. Lacking immunity to European ailments, hundreds of thousands succumbed to smallpox and other plagues. Some of the symptoms described correspond to nothing known to modern medicine. In some cases, as in Central America and Peru, European diseases preceded the coming of the conquistadors. By most counts, the native population of Mexico, Central America, and Peru had dropped by about 80 percent in 1570. Further pandemics in the 1570s and thereafter caused further declines until the mid-seventeenth century, after which the native population began a slow recovery.

It should be noted, however, that the documents on which these estimates are based referred to people who were legally and administratively defined as Indians; that is to say, those who lived in Indian communities or who were obliged to provide labor services or tribute because of their legal status as Indians. People of mixed race did not ordinarily fall into this category, nor would Indians who had left their communities or found ways to escape the tribute system through marriage or other means. Racial mixing had become very common by the 1570s, but there is no doubt that pure-blooded Indians—or those who were so defined—experienced one of the worst demographic catastrophes in history.

The worst of the pandemics occurred in the 1540s. Long before this, the government began to take steps to remedy the situation of the Indians. Charles V, like his grandmother Isabella, was both deeply religious and jealous of his reputation. The mistreatment and slaughter of subjects entrusted to him, as he thought, by God, was intolerable, and many Spaniards shared his views. As a result, despite the often unfortunate results of Spanish policies and the charges later made by Spain's detractors, no other European colonial power worked as diligently to provide justice for the indigenous populations it had conquered.

From the first discoveries by Columbus, the best minds in Spain had addressed themselves to two related questions: what was the legal and moral basis of Spain's claim to the Indies, and what position should the Indians occupy within a Christian commonwealth. By the 1520s, their efforts had escalated into a controversy that spread beyond the halls of the university to involve court factions, high officials, and the Emperor himself. The Indians soon found a powerful champion in Bartolomé de Las Casas, who had come to the Indies with Ovando in 1502 and later acquired an encomienda in Cuba. Under the influence of Montesinos, he renounced his holdings and eventually joined the Dominican Order. Eloquent, persistent, and long-lived, Las Casas became a gifted publicist who orchestrated a decades-long campaign against Indian slavery and the abuses of the encomienda system. The Dominican theologians at the University of Salamanca supported Las Casas. Domingo de Soto, Francisco de Vitoria, and Melchor Cano—all men with international reputations as theologians—declared that the Indians met Aristotle's definition of rational beings and therefore could not be enslaved. Vitoria came close to denying that Spain had a legitimate claim to the Indies. A number of prominent Franciscans supported the encomienda as an institution, but even they agreed that Indian slavery was intolerable. To his credit, Charles V favored Las Casas and the Dominicans through-out his career, but for many years their shared determination to help the Indians foundered on the objections of the colonists.

For more than 20 years, the government vacillated, alternately abolishing and then restoring the privileges of the encomenderos. Some of the con-fusion arose from the emperor's conflicting priorities. His commitment to the physical and spiritual welfare of his new subjects cannot be doubted, but experience seemed to show that the Indians, with few exceptions, would not work for Europeans unless compelled to do so. Given the small number of European settlers, the economic survival of the colonies was thought to depend upon compulsory labor on the land and in the mines. The mines were especially important because Charles and his government needed gold and silver. Much has been written about the Spanish obsession with gold as an impetus to colonization, but it was not unique. Long before the formulation of mercantilist theories, Europeans measured a nation's wealth by its store of precious metals. Gold and silver paid for armies, and armies were the source of a ruler's power. The later empires of France, England, and the Netherlands searched avidly for gold, but, unlike the Spanish, would discover little. In Mexico and Peru, the Spanish found wealth sufficient to alter the balance of European power in favor of Charles and his successors. In the 1540s, they discovered large silver deposits near Zacatecas and Guanajuato in Mexico. Cerro Rico, literally a mountain of silver, was discovered at about the same time at Potosí in Upper Peru (now Bolivia). Gold existed only in smaller quantities except in the northwestern provinces of New Granada (modern Colombia), where a large placer-mining operation lasted until the end of the colonial era. Production in all of these areas reached significant levels only in the last years of the Emperor's reign, but Charles, beset with enemies on every side, was determined to exploit each new source of specie to the fullest.

The New Laws of 1542 brought the question of Indian labor to a crisis. In 1530, the king had for the second time abolished both Indian slavery and the encomiendas, only to restore the latter in 1534 when the colonists and their supporters on the Council of the Indies insisted that the Indians could not otherwise be persuaded to work. Las Casas and his allies then took their case to Rome where, in 1537, they secured a Papal Bull that condemned Indian servitude in all its forms. By this time, opinion in the Spanish homeland had already begun to turn against the excesses of the conquerors. The New Laws, drawn up the Council of the Indies and promulgated by the king in 1542, declared that Indians could no longer be enslaved for any reason, and that slaves whose owners could show no clear title to them must be freed. No new encomiendas could be established, and those held by clerics, royal officials, and colonists who had abused their Indians had to be surrendered immediately. While other colonists who had clear title to their encomiendas might retain them, they could no longer pass them on to their heirs, and could receive no tribute from the Indians beyond the share that would otherwise be claimed by the crown. Officials known as Protectors of the Indians were assigned to each district to enforce the rules.

To the colonists this was confiscation of property legally granted to them by the crown in return for service in the conquests. The New Laws provoked the revolt of 1544–1548 in Peru. In Mexico, Viceroy Antonio de Mendoza wisely refused to publish the decrees with the full support of a *visitador* sent from Spain to enforce them. So violent was the reaction that the crown compromised. In 1545–1546, it repealed the laws that abolished existing encomiendas and forbade inheritance, but passed new legislation that limited inheritance only to the encomendero's wife or child. The sections forbidding personal servitude and the enslavement of Indians, however, remained, as did the office of Protector of the Indians. The encomienda, in other words, survived as an institution, but became less important with the passage of time. In 1555, the Viceroy of Mexico received permission to extend the inheritance of encomiendas to the third generation as long as he did so "*por via disimulación*," by which the government apparently meant secretly or under false pretenses. Many years later, in the reign of Philip III, inheritance was extended to the fourth and fifth generations, but in practice, most *encomiendas* had long since reverted to the crown under the old rules or for want of a successor. In Peru, the two-generation rule remained until 1629 when the impoverished government of Philip IV allowed extensions in return for a hefty payment. There were few takers. In the meantime, Viceroys produced reams of legislation restricting the activities of encomenderos, and in, theory, protecting the Indians.

Many of these regulations proved impossible to enforce. Most quickly became irrelevant. By 1560, the massive decline in Indian populations, the growth of a cash economy, and the introduction of European crops had begun to create an economy in which there was little need for encomiendas. Settlers converted their property into vast *haciendas* that combined stock raising, a practice unknown to the Indians, with a diversified mix of European and American crops. Paid seasonal laborers from nearby Indian communities supplemented a cadre of permanent employees who might be Indian, Spanish, or of mixed race. The Indian communes had for the most part retained their property and tribal organization throughout the age of conquest. Those in the vicinity of European settlements combined the intensive agriculture and barter systems of their ancestors with occasional wage labor for the Europeans. That labor, however, was not aways voluntary. When Mexican landowners could not obtain enough workers for their planting or harvests, it became possible after 1570 to apply to the viceroy for a *repartimiento*, which by this time had come to mean a draft of forced, paid laborers. In theory at least, this privilege was tightly controlled and rarely granted. In practice it appears to have been much abused

The mining industry weathered the change as well. Most of the Mexican silver deposits were located in under-populated regions outside the boundaries of the old Aztec empire. Neither encomienda nor repartimiento could function among semi-nomadic and often hostile peoples. Almost from the beginning the owners staffed their mines with *naborías*, Indian workers separated from their communities in Central Mexico by the conquest, and by importing a limited number of African slaves. These people, together with a cadre of professional miners from Spain and Germany, evolved into a mixed-race force of highly skilled wage workers. In Peru, Viceroy Toledo adapted an Inca institution, the *mita*, to provide labor for the mines at Potosí. As part of their tribe's annual tribute to the crown, Indian chiefs from certain districts in different parts of the country were ordered to select a specified number of workers who would then move to the mines for ten months, accompanied by their families and possessions. While there, the workers were paid and fed by the mine owners while the *ayllu* maintained their property for them at home.

Elsewhere, the introduction of African slavery compensated for the decline in Indian populations. At no point in the debate over the Indians did anyone, even Las Casas, object to the enslavement of Africans. Indians could not be enslaved because they met Aristotle's definition of rational beings. Africans, according to learned opinion, were not rational and could be enslaved at will. It was a position shared at that time by all Europeans. In fact, it was the Portuguese that first brought slaves to the Spanish colonies after the middle of the sixteenth century. English, French, Dutch, and Spanish slavers would follow. Modern estimates of the numbers of Africans brought to the Spanish colonies are as unreliable as estimates of Indian mortality during the conquest. They range from 75,000 to 290,000 between 1450 and 1600, and from 455,000 to 1.5 million in the seventeenth century. In any case, by 1600, the placer mines of New Granada, the pearl fisheries, and the growing sugar industry in the Caribbean islands would all be staffed by slaves imported from Africa. Elsewhere, African slaves remained a small minority, although they probably outnumbered Spaniards in many areas.

When Charles V abdicated in 1556, Spain's New World empire had assumed something like its final shape. The Rio de la Plata and much of northern Mexico were still an undeveloped frontier and years would pass before Spain wrested southern Chile from the Araucanians, but in the conquered areas royal authority had been firmly established under an administration whose basic structure would change little until the eighteenth century. The influence of this extraordinary legacy was not felt immediately in Europe. What Alfred W. Crosby has called the biological exchange had scarcely begun. It would require many years before such New World crops as potatoes, tomatoes, and maize found acceptance in Europe. If the

Indians had already been decimated by European diseases, no comparable American plagues (with the possible exception of a new strain of syphilis) afflicted the conquerors. Even the vast deposits of bullion found in Mexico and Peru would have little influence until well into the reign of Charles's successor, Philip II. The potential, however, was immense. In 1535 Charles had funded the successful invasion of Tunis almost entirely from the golden treasure sent to him from Peru by Pizarro. By the 1570s, Philip II's share of American silver would increase his revenues by at least 20 percent.

4

IMPERIAL ORGANIZATION
UNDER THE HABSBURGS

The Habsburgs governed the Spanish empire according to principles that had been universally accepted in Western Europe during the middle ages but are largely foreign to modern political thought. They—and their subjects—believed that all political authority was an extension of God's sovereignty. Kings ruled by divine grace as God's surrogates on earth, subject only to the restrictions imposed by divine and natural law. Any other form of government was by definition illegitimate. In theory the king's power was therefore absolute. He was commander-in-chief in time of war, royal officials served entirely at his pleasure, and his edicts formed the basis of all legislation, but he could not exercise his power arbitrarily. His decrees could not violate moral and natural law as defined by the church, nor could they be inconsistent with the great body of legal rulings that had evolved in Spain since Roman times.

In practice, this meant that kings and queens had to seek the counsel of their subjects to determine if their actions were both moral and legal. They normally did so by creating a royal council composed of notables both lay and clerical, but they were also expected to hear and respond to the petitions of their vassals. To fail in these obligations was to rule as a tyrant. Moreover, as in the other monarchies of Western Europe, the ruler had no authority to levy taxes without the consent of his subjects. He or she was entitled only to the proceeds of the royal domain, which included revenue from crown lands and from a number of precisely defined rights and privileges including customs duties. The crown could confiscate property for cause as determined by a court of law, but could levy taxes only with the

73

consent of its subjects, usually as given by vote of a representative body such as the Cortes of Castile.

The governmental structures created by Ferdinand and Isabella, and by their grandson, Charles V, were therefore absolutist, personal, and based on the model of household governments typical of the middle ages. The size and complexity of Spain's empire, however, forced its rulers to extend and elaborate these institutions to a degree unparalleled in other European countries. The basic structure of government under the Habsburgs survived until the Bourbon reforms of the eighteenth century, not only because Spanish government was honest and efficient by the loose standards of the age, but because the ideological assumptions that supported it remained unchallenged. This was not the case in England, Scotland, and those parts of the Netherlands that eventually broke from Spanish rule. There the success of the Protestant Reformation—and in England the revival of common law—brought changes in government that had no impact on Spain or its Italian and American possessions. To a society that remained overwhelmingly Catholic, the structure of the Spanish state embodied the ideal of legitimacy itself.

That society, however, was dauntingly complex. As we have seen, the kingdoms of Charles V were separate constitutional entities that happened to be ruled by the same prince. With the exception of Mexico and Peru, each kingdom or province was governed by its own laws and possessed its own administration and representative body. Because the American kingdoms had been founded by conquest and lacked European precedents, their laws and government were based on the institutions of Castile. The king's regent in the Netherlands and the viceroys he appointed to govern Aragon, Catalonia, Valencia, Navarre, Naples, Sicily, Sardinia, New Spain (Mexico), and Peru enjoyed broad powers, in part because of their distance from the court. When communications required weeks or months they had to make important decisions on their own, but those decisions were at all times subject to royal approval. No viceroy wished to have his edicts overturned by the king or a royal council. Most of them therefore sought the advice of local notables, and negotiated carefully with representative bodies where such bodies existed. In the Americas, the audiencias served as viceregal councils in addition to their judicial and administrative duties. In the Kingdom of Naples, the Collateral Council, a body composed of five notables called the regents, advised the viceroy on general policy. There was also a Judicial Council and a Council of Finance.

These arrangements mirrored the councils by which the kings of Aragon and Castile had governed since the middle ages. The Royal Councils of the two kingdoms had at first been little more than committees of nobles and clergymen appointed on an ad hoc basis to advise the king. Under Ferdinand and Isabella, the councils of Castile and Aragon not only provided advice, but became the highest appellate courts in their respective kingdoms. They supervised the crown's financial departments, and recommended the appointment of royal officials. Ferdinand and Isabella had also created three new councils to advise them on the Inquisition, the military orders, and the *cruzada*, or crusade tax. In this as in so many other things Charles V elaborated on the policy of his grandparents. One of the first acts of his reign was to create a Council of War. Then, in 1522, he created the Council of State to advise him on the broader issues of imperial and foreign policy. Both were from the beginning imperial in scope. Charles appointed their members from his different realms, largely on the basis of proximity and expertise. Charles never established a permanent capital, and like the kings of the Middle Ages, traveled incessantly, a practice which left him dependent for advice on whoever was available at the moment. Under the sedentary Philip II (1556–1598), appointments in both councils became more permanent—and more Spanish.

The other royal councils acquired broader responsibilities as the empire grew. When Ferdinand became president of the military orders in Castile and Aragon, the Council of the Orders automatically assumed responsibility for the orders' activities in Italy and North Africa, including the governorships of the North African *presidios*. The Council of the Inquisition transcended national borders almost from its inception. When Charles reformed the Castilian government in 1524, he created a Council of Finance by detaching its fiscal operations from the Council of Castile. This body incorporated the functions of the *hacienda*, which collected and administered crown revenues, and the *contaduría mayor de cuentas*, a board of auditors. The latter assumed empire-wide importance as supervisors of the Emperor's credit operations when he became dependent on Castilian revenues in the latter part of his reign. He created two other councils by splitting them off from existing bodies. The Council of the Indies, created in 1524, ended the arrangement by which a subcommittee of the Council of Castile managed American affairs. Italy remained under the supervision of the Council of Aragon until 1555 when Philip II, at his father's suggestion, created the Council of Italy.

The Council of State remained primarily advisory. The others combined functions that would today be considered legislative, executive, and judicial because the modern concept of a separation of powers had no place in an absolutist polity based in theory upon divine will. The king was responsible for both administration and legislation, and, in the Roman imperial tradition, administrative edicts had the force of law. Complaints, protests, and proposals for action might be referred to the appropriate council by the king and his officials, or by petition. Petitions could come from the cortes or *parlamentum*, a municipality, a corporation (e.g., a guild or a university) or a private subject. If the councilors agreed to discuss the matter, the council's secretary summarized their conclusions in a *consulta* which was then submitted to the king. If the king approved their recommendations, he issued a *cédula* or edict that had the force of law. If he did not approve, or—as was more often the case—had suggestions or reservations about the proposal, he returned the consulta for modification.

Once issued, a royal edict had the force of law, but in the Indies, at least, it was not always carried out. An official who believed that conditions had changed or that implementation of an order might be imprudent for other reasons could have recourse to a unique legal formula: *se obedece pero no se cumple* (it is obeyed, but not carried out). A law of the Indies since 1528, it was a logical compromise between theoretical absolutism and the practical problems of time and distance.

Judicial review was built into the process from the beginning and actually preceded legislation because the Council, most of whose members were lawyers, also served as the highest appellate court in the regions it governed. Councils suggested only those measures they believed to be in conformity with existing law and were unlikely to overturn their own decisions. When they did so, it was because a petitioner was able at some later date to demonstrate a conflict between a particular cédula and an established legal principle. The Council then tried to reconcile the difficulty in another consulta which led to another cédula that modified the original decree. Oral argument was rare in the Spanish legal system. Courts and Councils alike relied on written briefs that were, by Anglo-Saxon standards, mercifully brief, but it is fair to say that the Spanish Empire ran on paper.

In some ways the secretaries were therefore the most important officials in the Spanish government. They made up a council's agenda and summarized its deliberations for the king. As such, they were the primary link between the sovereign and his administration. Most of them came from relatively humble backgrounds and lacked university degrees. Senior secretaries trained promising young men—including their sons—as their apprentices, and maneuvered them into new secretarial positions as they became available. These secretarial "schools" became important political factions in their own right, and, as we shall see, formed connections with other centers of power at the court and in the countryside.

The administrative functions of a Council lay primarily in the area of personnel. It vetted candidates for offices in the royal administration and recommended them to the king for approval. At the end of an official's term it appointed a committee known as a *residencia*, which examined every aspect of the appointee's conduct in office and had the power to levy fines for legal or fiscal misconduct. Complaints about the official's actions while in office might cause the council to appoint a *visita*, or committee of inquiry whose recommendations could result in dismissal, financial penalties, and even prison. These provisions applied to viceroys as well as to lesser officials, and served as an impediment to administrative misconduct and the arbitrary use of power. These institutions, like the judicial process, depended in part upon the willingness of ordinary subjects to protest what they saw as injustice. The archives are full of petitions and letters of complaint addressed not only to councils and audiencias but to the person of the king. It is a tribute to the crown's sense of itself as a repository of divine justice that most of these complaints received an answer and at least some measure of consideration.

The Netherlands did not receive a council of its own until 1588. By that time the northern provinces had long since rebelled and established themselves as an independent republic. Under Charles V and in the early years of Philip II, the 17 provinces continued to be governed by a regent who was always a woman of the royal family. She, like the Italian viceroys, was assisted by a Council of State, a Council of Finance, and a Privy Council which dealt with legal matters. Until 1567–1568 the councilors were prominent Netherlanders and the basic mechanisms of government remained as they had been at the accession of Charles V. Both Charles and his son communicated directly and extensively with the regent, the states-general, and the provinces using their own local titles. There was no attempt to integrate the Netherlands with the imperial administration until the ill-fated reforms of the 1560s.

Except in the Americas, the Habsburgs retained the existing structures of local government with little modification. In Spain, Italy, and the Netherlands, local governments fell into two main categories: seigneurial and royal. Seigneurial communities were governed by a bewildering array of agreements made centuries before when tenants placed themselves under the protection of a lord. In the Netherlands, southern Italy, and parts of the Kingdom of Aragon, most of these agreements were feudal and tenants were the legal subjects of their lords. In most of Castile the tenants remained subjects of the crown, while owing various dues and services to their lord. This greatly limited the jurisdiction of seigneurial courts, but in both systems the lord's courts administered justice at the local level, and the lord's appointees dealt with the everyday business of government.

Municipalities chartered by the crown (or in the Netherlands by the ruler in his capacity as Duke or Count), normally possessed a council elected by the tax-paying citizens. The council in turn elected the equivalent of a mayor and appointed the town secretary, a police chief, and other municipal officials. The wealthiest citizens tended to dominate the town councils, and, except in Castile, enjoyed little direct interference from the crown. In Castile, the disorders of the fifteenth century had resulted in a far more restrictive system dominated by a royal official known as the *corregidor*. The corregidor normally served a two-year term. He presided over the city council, which was composed of *regidores* appointed by the crown for life. This body appointed the *alguacil*, or police chief, the *escribano*, or secretary, and the *fieles*, who supervised the lands and departments of the municipality. The *alcalde*, or chief magistrate, had both civil and criminal jurisdiction, and, except in a few towns with special privileges, was appointed directly by the crown as well.

Villages, the basic political and social units of early modern society, were normally subject either to a lord or to a municipality. In Castile, a number of them had petitioned for, and received, municipal status by the sixteenth century—a distinction that seems to have had little to do with either their relative wealth or the size of their populations. As in other parts of Western Europe, the peasants of Spain, Italy, and the Netherlands dealt with many local concerns themselves. The village leaders who resolved minor infractions and disputes, allocated the common lands, and negotiated with outside authorities might be chosen by vote or by some form of negotiated consensus. The political process used in any given village is often unrecoverable owing to the lack of written records.

In establishing a system of local governments for the Americas, the Crown had to consider the values and expectations of two completely different populations. The governments established for Spanish settlers and those Indians who left their own communities to live among them were based loosely on Castilian precedent. As we have seen, viceroyalties might contain several provinces. Each province was in turn divided into *corregimientos*, headed by a corregidor or, in New Spain, an *alcalde mayor* who was appointed by the crown and who reported to both the provincial governor and the regional audiencia. A corregimiento might contain one or more chartered municipalities whose lands could extend for hundreds of square miles. The municipalities were governed by a Cabildo whose members were normally selected by the corregidor. In a few cases, they were elected by the property owners of the town, but in either case, regidores were drawn from the wealthiest and most prominent families and often served for life. The Cabildo imposed local taxes, allocated the municipal lands, supervised the town's market, and maintained order with the assistance of a host of officials: the *alguacil mayor* (chief constable), the *depositario general* (public trustee), the city attorney, and the *escribano* or town secretary. A *fiel ejecutor* regulated prices, weights, and measures, and tried to ensure a steady supply of food for the community while the *mayordomo* was responsible for maintaining the town's property. Lesser alcaldes served as police officers and magistrates in rural districts and in the neighborhoods of the larger cities. The cabildo appointed them all, but the corregidor was supposed to ensure that they acted at all times in the best interests of the crown.

As we have seen, Indian governance evolved into a parallel system, or perhaps a parody, of that established for the colonists. There seems to have been no deliberate attempt to displace the ruling Indian families, but election or appointment, even when it resulted in continuity of personnel, undermined the hereditary principle of traditional Indian society and weakened the authority of the chiefs.

The Spanish imperial system had its weaknesses, but tyrannical behavior by the crown and isolation from its subjects were not among them. Paternalism and an almost naïve faith in the power of regulation reflected a determination to rule justly and according to Christian religious principles. The unquestioned right of subjects to communicate with the crown mediated, but could not erase, the human weakness of its officials. The government's greatest failing lay not in its institutions or intentions, but in the fact that it could do nothing quickly. The process of decision-making by consulta often seemed interminable. The resolution of legal issues took even longer. Part of this was due to the innate conservatism of a system that had always been risk-averse and became more so with the passage of time. Legalism, a feature of Spanish society as a whole, and the need to consider every conceivable aspect of a problem generated tons of paper as well as often unconscionable delays. Charles V, who was not himself fond of paper work, recognized at least part of the problem and ordered the foundation of a central archive at Simancas in 1545. It contains not only correspondence and the deliberations of councils, but copies of documents filed in the archives of kingdoms, provinces, and courts throughout the empire. The Council of the Indies established another great repository of documents at Seville. In a measure designed to reduce legal disputes, the emperor decreed that when a notary retired he had to deposit copies of every document he had ever notarized with the archives of the province in which he lived. This edict applied to the Netherlands as well as to the Spanish and Italian king-doms. The empire's record-keeping was therefore centuries ahead of its time. Its archival collections remain a treasure house for historians; they are at the same time a measure of the problems faced by the administrators who created them.

COMMUNICATION AND TRADE

Sheer distance increased the problem of governance. Communications with Spain's European possessions required weeks or even months. A letter from Peru spent a minimum of eight months in transit, mostly at sea. More months might elapse while the appropriate council debated its contents and drew up a consulta for the king. By the time the king emended the consulta, drafted his cédula, and dispatched it, those who sent the original petition might well have died or left office. Legal cases, with their appeals and endless requests for additional documents, could last decades.

In the absence of modern technology, there was little that the king and his servants could do to provide safe and speedy communications. Until 1568 dispatches between Spain and the Netherlands often went by sea. After that, interference from the Dutch rebels and their English sympathizers made this already dangerous route impossible. Land communications were han-dled under contract by an Italian family named Tassis (the original spelling was Tasso). They operated relays of horse-mounted couriers that could, under ideal conditions, carry dispatches between Madrid and Brussels in about two weeks. Conditions, however, were rarely ideal. The roads of the day were little more than dirt tracks, dusty in summer and muddy the rest of the year. Moreover, the shortest road to Brussels lay through France, a coun-try whose intentions were suspect even when the two kingdoms were not actively at war. The couriers did not advertise their purpose and were nor-mally left unmolested, but there was always a chance that vital papers might fall into enemy hands. To prevent this, Spanish secretaries wrote in elabo-rate substitution ciphers which, unlike code, could not be deciphered unless the reader possessed the key. If a cipher book fell into enemy hands the ciphers were changed, but days or even weeks might elapse before the gov-ernment learned of such a loss. Fortunately for Spain, such events were rare.

Communications between Spain and Italy were more secure than those with northern Europe. Fast war galleys carried dispatches on a regular basis from Spain's eastern ports to Naples and Palermo. Winter storms posed a greater threat to this route than the North African pirates, who rarely challenged heavily armed ships. On land, the Tassis family couriers managed communications within the Italian kingdoms and with Spain's client states in Northern Italy.

Communication with the Americas faced problems of a different magnitude. From the earliest days of empire, the need to control not only communications but trade complicated the inherent difficulty of transatlantic travel. Ferdinand and Isabella had decreed that all commerce with the New World be limited to Castilian subjects and conducted through the Casa de Contratación at Seville. Charles V attempted to liberalize these policies in the 1520s, but later revoked his edicts. Concentrating trade with the American colonies in a single location made it easier to collect royal taxes, prevent smuggling, and control the flow of emigrants. Seville was chosen in part because its large population and rich agricultural hinterland facilitated the manning and victualling of great fleets. It was also a royal town whose municipal government was supervised by a crown-appointed corregidor. Other ports in southwest Spain were small and controlled by great nobles: the marquis of Cádiz or the duke of Medina Sidonia. Unfortunately, Seville lay some 50 miles from the ocean on the banks of the Guadalquivir River, a shallow stream with many sandbars. Large inbound ships had to be at least partially unloaded at Sanlúcar de Barrameda, the Duke of Medina Sidonia's little port at the river's mouth, before undertaking the hazardous, weeklong journey upstream. Outbound ships faced the same problems in reverse. By the end of the Habsburg era, the increased silting of the Guadalquivir made it necessary to transfer virtually all shipping operations to the deepwater ports of San Lucar or Cádiz.

In theory, however, the Casa de Contratación registered all American imports and exports and levied taxes on them. The most important were the *almojarifazgo*, or export duty with a nominal rate of 5 percent, and the crown's share of imported bullion which amounted to 10 percent on bullion from New Spain and 20 percent from Peru. The *almojarifazgo de indias*, also at 5 percent, was levied in the Indies on exports to Spain and constituted an important part of viceregal revenues. The Casa also attempted, with limited success, to interdict the movement of books banned by the Inquisition and the emigration of foreigners and people of Jewish or converso extraction. The trade itself was organized by the *consulado* of Sevilla, a merchant guild whose statutes and functions resembled those of the far older consulado of Burgos which had long regulated the Spanish wool trade with Flanders. Its members not only conducted trade on their own but served as agents for the large number of foreign traders in the city. It leased ships, licensed cargos, and financed voyages.

For protection against hurricanes and pirates and to prevent smuggling, the crown prohibited single ship voyages to and from the New World as early as 1526. Thereafter, merchant ships sailed in convoys accompanied by heavily armed galleons provided by the crown. A fee known as the *avería*, collected by the Casa de Contratación as a percentage of each cargo's value, paid for this protection.

By the 1560s, bullion from the Americas had become vital to Spain's military power. Beginning with the ordinance of October 18, 1564, the crown began to organize the treasure fleets on a formal basis. The selection of routes and timetables presented formidable problems, but the system developed in the 1560s lasted with modifications until the end of the colonial era. Two fleets sailed annually to the New World. Under ideal circumstances, the first departed from Seville in April or May for the 10- or 12-day voyage to the Canaries. After taking on additional water and provisions, the *flota*, as it was called, followed the trade winds westward to the Antilles. After a month or so, it made landfall at Dominica or one of the neighboring islands before re-victualling at Puerto Rico. The voyage to San Juan de Ulúa, the rather exposed anchorage that served the city of Veracruz, usually consumed another month owing to westerly headwinds in the Gulf of Mexico. From Veracruz, goods and messages had to be transported inland to Mexico City, more than 200 miles away. Fairs whose organization reflected those of Europe provided a venue for payment and the consignment of goods at Veracruz, Mexico City, and even Puebla.

Ships destined for South America (the *tierra firma* fleet, sometimes called the *galleones* in the seventeenth century because of its more numerous escorts) left Seville in July or August, and followed the same transatlantic course as the flota to the Antilles. From there they turned south toward Cartagena in what is now Colombia. The same westerly winds that slowed the Mexican flota allowed the *tierra firma* fleet to reach its destination on what sailors call a beam reach in only about two weeks. Cargoes destined for Peru then went on to Nombre de Dios in Panama to be off-loaded for shipment across the Isthmus. The late departure from Spain risked hurricanes to avoid the diseases of the rainy season, but the mortality of Spanish crews on the north coast of Panama was appalling at any time of year. The ships wasted little time at the Nombre de Dios fair before returning to the healthier, more defensible, harbor at Cartagena. From Nombre de Dios, mule trains carried the goods for Peru overland to the city of Panama on the Pacific Coast. The route, part of which followed the valley of the Chagres River, was called the "Road of Crosses" because of the hundreds of graves that marked the roadside. From there, everything was loaded once again on a convoy destined for Callao, the port of Lima. Prevailing winds from the south and a powerful Antarctic current meant that the Callao fleet normally required four or five months to reach its destination.

The return trip from Callao to Panama normally took only three weeks, but this time the ships were laden with tons of bullion. At Panama, everything had to be loaded onto the backs of mules for transshipment across the Isthmus. When word reached the ships anchored at Cartagena that the Callao fleet had arrived, they returned to Nombre de Dios to load their cargoes. The heavily armed escort galleons carried as much of the silver as possible, often ballasting their hulls with silver ingots, but they did not linger. Nombre de Dios was not only unhealthy; it was virtually indefensible. The treasure ships reassembled with the fighting galleons of their escort at Cartagena before departing for Havana to rendezvous in March with the flota from Mexico. From Havana, the combined treasure fleet passed through the Straits of Florida and followed the Gulfstream to about 40 degrees north latitude before turning east to the Azores, a journey that normally consumed about a month. From the Azores to Sanlúcar de Barrameda required another three to four weeks. The last stages of the voyage were the most dangerous because pirates tended to lie in wait near the Azores and off Cape San Vicente. In the Azores the fleet and its escorts were on their own, but closer to home the authorities often dispatched additional warships to the vicinity of the Cape if they learned that the fleet was on its way.

Beginning in the 1560s, increased pirate activity in the Caribbean forced the crown to strengthen security in the colonies. The greatest danger came, not from the individual ships that preyed upon local trade, but from small fleets that sailed with the tacit—and sometimes overt—approval of the French, English, or Dutch governments. These fleets would not normally molest the treasure ships at sea: the hovering presence of six or more escort galleons saw to that. Instead they made amphibious attacks on the places where Spanish ships gathered to load cargo or supplies. Over the next 200 years, the fortifications of Cartagena, Havana, and San Juan de Puerto Rico grew ever more massive and sophisticated as the number of attacks increased. St. Augustine in Florida, where in 1565 a French Huguenot colony had been massacred by Spanish troops, was fortified as well lest it serve as a base for attacking the fleets as they proceeded north along the coast. Little, however, was done at San Juan de Ulúa and Nombre de Dios, in part because both were considered too unhealthy to support permanent garrisons. Instead, officials made every effort to coordinate the transport of goods overland with the arrival of the ships, which were loaded as quickly as possible and sent on their way under the protection of their escorts. Neither town ever developed a large permanent population or a substantial infrastructure. In 1597, operations at Nombre de Dios were transferred to the nearby settlement of Portobello which, although eventually fortified, offered few advantages over its predecessor.

Even the Pacific coast of Spain's empire proved vulnerable. In 1575 the first English ship, commanded by the pirate John Oxenham, appeared on the Pacific coast. Then, in the winter of 1577–1578, Francis Drake rounded Cape Horn and attacked towns and shipping in Chile and Peru before completing his celebrated circumnavigation of the globe. It was by far the most profitable of Drake's expeditions, and eventually forced the Spanish to establish what they called the Armada of the Southern Sea, in reality a modest squadron to protect the treasure ships on their voyages from Callao to Panama.

Viceregal treasuries paid most of the enormous cost of this protection, but the empire had to protect its communications and the shipments of bullion on which much of its credit depended. By the late sixteenth century, American bullion had become vital to the success of Spanish imperial policy. In *American Treasure and the Price Revolution in Spain*, Earl J. Hamilton found that officially registered shipments of gold and silver increased from 979,484 ducats in 1506–1510 to a maximum of 42,221,835 in 1591–1595. Of this amount, about 40 percent went to the crown, including the royal fifth and taxes paid by the colonists. The rest was credited to private accounts. The crown's share declined thereafter, but even at its peak, revenue from the Indies rarely amounted to more than 20 percent of revenues from Castile. The importance of this vast flow of silver lay in the liquidity it provided. Without it, Philip II could not have supported his foreign policy.

Most of the silver registered to private accounts was probably paid to merchants in return for goods imported from Spain. The American mines consumed large quantities of mercury for the amalgamation process that separated silver from its ore. Mercury deposits at Huancavalica in Peru helped to supply the needs of Potosí, but Mexico was wholly dependent on mercury from Almadén in Spain, supplemented on occasion by imports from mines in Croatia. Spanish colonists did not readily adapt to the American diet, and imported large quantities of grain, wine, and oil, together with manufactured goods and European clothing. Before stock raising became established in the New World, they also imported horses, cattle, and hogs. Most of this was paid for in silver, but the colonies also exported sugar, dyestuffs, pearls, and eventually tobacco. The African slaves who produced these commodities had to be imported as well. Spain had no presence in sub-Saharan Africa and the African slave trade operated apart from the officially sanctioned flotas. Portuguese slavers trading under official license (*asiento*) competed with Dutch and English entrepreneurs whose activities, while illegal, were often tolerated by Spanish officials.

The slave trade in a sense symbolized why the flota system could not and did not ensure the maintenance of Spain's desired monopoly on trade with the New World. With limited industry and no direct access to African labor, Spain could not fully supply the needs of its colonists. The relative predictability of the fleets' movements made it possible for foreign traders to slip into American ports whose inhabitants were usually willing to buy not only contraband slaves, but European goods at prices that were generally lower than those brought by the flotas. Although the system remained in effect until the end of the Habsburg era and beyond, its benefits to the crown declined. By the last quarter of the seventeenth century, Spain's control of its colonial trade had become little more than a polite fiction.

WAR AND DEFENSE

War, rather than the promotion of social or economic welfare, was the primary business of the early modern state. During much of the sixteenth and seventeenth centuries it consumed ten times more revenue than all other functions of Spanish government combined and was by itself responsible for the crown's enormous debt. The task of defending the empire and supporting the foreign policy goals of the Habsburg kings was in fact so costly and so complex that the government never developed an administrative structure equal to the task.

In theory, military affairs in the Iberian Peninsula, North Africa, the Atlantic, and the Mediterranean islands fell under the purview of the Council of War, which also served as chief appellate court for cases arising under the code of military justice. The Councils of Flanders, Italy, and the Indies governed the conduct of war in their respective jurisdictions. The *Junta de Galeras*, a subcommittee of the Council of War, dealt with the problems of the Mediterranean galley fleet, while a subcommittee of the Council of the Indies coordinated defense for the Americas. By the 1580s these arrangements had become inadequate. Under Philip II, the revolt of the Netherlands, the annexation of Portugal, and wars with England and the Turks forced the empire to support large armies in distant places and to maintain fleets in both the Atlantic and the Mediterranean. The task of coordinating these varied elements forced Philip to experiment with a series of reforms, none of which proved entirely satisfactory.

Local defense, in Spain and the Indies, posed serious problems. By necessity, thousands of miles of coastline went virtually undefended. A system of watchtowers constructed under Charles V and backed by cavalry stationed in Valencia and Granada tried to protect those kingdoms from Muslim attack by sea. Royal fortresses guarded the French frontier, the North African presidios, Minorca and Ibiza, as well as the major choke points of the Atlantic trade: Havana, San Juan, and Cartagena. In Spain, Italy, and the Indies, municipal—and in some parts of Europe, seigneurial—militias provided a secondary line of defense. The militias were almost always poorly trained and poorly equipped, but the soldiers who manned royal garrisons were often little better than the militiamen. Low pay and months of tedium encouraged many to live in town and pursue a trade with predicable effects on training and discipline. War was as much a skilled profession in the sixteenth century as it is today. Amateurs stood little chance against a well-trained army, but garrisons backed by a municipal militia sometimes gave a surprisingly good account of themselves against pirates and other raiders.

The armies that projected Habsburg authority abroad were international in composition and far better trained than the militias. Their Spanish component rarely amounted to more than 20 percent of the whole. Recruitment in Spain followed the Western European norm. All of the men were volunteers recruited by captains who held commissions from the crown. Some of them signed up for the recruiting bonus and then deserted, but if the captain could hold his troop together they marched to Cartagena on the Mediterranean coast. They then embarked for the Kingdom of Naples where they trained for two or three years before proceeding to the battlefields of the north. In 1536 Charles V organized the Spanish infantry into *tercios* with a nominal complement of about 3000 men divided into 12 companies. Commanded by a *maestro de campo* and a small staff of officers, each tercio theoretically contained more or less equal numbers of pikemen and arquebusiers with a handful of musketeers for special duty. In fact, the number of men and companies varied enormously, as did the ratio of pikes to shot. This was in part because from the end of the French wars in 1559 until the 1630s the tercio was rarely used as a tactical unit. Large set-piece battles like Ceresole (1544) had produced unacceptable casualty rates in an age when good men were hard to train and even more difficult to recruit. Wherever possible, Spanish commanders tried to keep their forces intact by fighting wars of maneuver enlivened by skirmishes fought at the company level. Unlike most armies of the day, the Spanish tercios provided surgeons and field hospitals for the wounded in return for a small deduction from the soldiers' pay.

The tercios developed a formidable reputation as skirmishers and assault troops—an elite force whose superior morale made them the core of the army until their defeat at Rocroi in 1643. But the bulk of Spain's European army consisted of Italians, Germans, and Walloons, most of whom were supplied by military contractors for a single campaigning season. Contemporary opinion regarded the Italians as almost equal to the Spanish as all-round soldiers, the Walloons as superior marksmen, and the Germans as best at holding a defensive position. In the Netherlands, the government of the regent, or (after 1567) the captain-general, administered contracts, pay, and provisioning for the Army of Flanders with little interference from the Council of War. After 1588 the newly created Council of Flanders assumed oversight for these functions. Funding came from taxes levied on the provinces under Spanish control supplemented by large annual subsidies from the royal treasury.

Spain's survival as a worldwide empire depended on sea power as well as armies, but the challenge of maintaining fleets in four oceans (the Mediterranean, the Atlantic, the Pacific, and the Caribbean) stretched Spanish administration to its limits and may have been beyond the capacity of any early modern state. Charles V followed medieval precedent and used naval contractors to provide his warships, their commanders, and their crews. Until 1555, the Mediterranean galley fleet contained ships hired from Genoa and from the Spanish contractor Bernardino de Mendoza. The viceregal governments of Naples and Sicily paid and provisioned their own contingents. When Charles required ships for service in the Atlantic he hired them from his Spanish and Netherlandish subjects, or from foreigners with little regard to their ethnicity. Unlike Henry VIII of England he made no effort to create a specialized naval administration. The needs of a multinational empire with worldwide responsibilities were unlike those of a relatively small, homogeneous kingdom with little need to project naval power outside its home waters.

Philip II, an administrator at heart, would have preferred to control naval affairs directly, but even he found the task daunting. Unhappy with Mendoza's performance, he tried to royalize the management of the Spanish galleys after the contractor's death by placing construction, command, and manning in what was called *administración*. That is to say royal officials built the ships and managed them under the supervision of the *junta de galeras*. The enormous and costly expansion of the galley fleet before and after the Battle of Lepanto (1571), forced the king to re-evaluate this policy. The crown lacked the men and the money to build the ships required and was forced once again to seek help from contractors. No Spanish contractors agreed to meet the king's terms, but he was able to place most of the Sicilian and Neapolitan galleys under contract where they remained until 1590. The results, once again, were unsatisfactory, but by this time, the Turkish threat had diminished and the government's attention turned to the Atlantic. The galley fleet deteriorated, and, after about 1600, North African pirates roamed the Western Mediterranean almost at will.

The need for an Atlantic fleet became evident with the expedition of John Hawkins to the Caribbean (1567) and the outbreak of the Netherlands Revolt (1568). The Consulado of Seville hired escorts from private ship owners for the American convoys until 1577 when Philip II ordered the construction of several galleons under the supervision of royal officials to help protect the Atlantic trade. Most of the hundreds of ships involved in the annexation of Portugal (1580) and in the Armada of 1588 served, however, under contract from private and foreign owners. Both fleets were in fact multinational efforts under Spanish command. The Armada disaster of 1588 forced the king to develop the first truly royal navy. Beginning with 12 1000-ton galleons, the so-called Twelve Apostles, the shipyards of Cantabria produced more than 60 warships for the king between 1589 and his death in 1598, most of them under *administración*. The size of the armadas sent against England in the last years of the reign, however, ensured that contracting would continue on a major scale.

The Indies fleet had a somewhat different history. In 1591, the Council of the Indies found evidence of corruption in the Casa de Contratación. The Council therefore signed an agreement with the Consulado of Seville to collect the *avería* (the fee levied on merchant ships for their protection at sea) and administer the escort galleons assigned to the Atlantic run. The ships themselves—ten 500-ton galleons and four dispatch boats—were built by the crown. The creation of the *junta de armadas* in 1594 recognized at long last that warfare in the North Atlantic could not be divorced from defending the American convoys. It included both the presidents and secretaries of the Council of War and the Council of the Indies, and represented a serious effort at administrative integration. The crown also created a *junta de fábricas* to deal with the complex problems of ship construction and the production of munitions. By this time, the vast sums of money involved in Spain's imperial defense had encouraged corruption on a massive scale. In 1593 supervision of the comptrollers who audited military and naval accounts was taken from the Council of War and returned to the Council of Finance which had appointed them prior to 1573.

None of these changes solved the basic problem of coordinating military action on multiple fronts, nor did they provide impeccably honest military administration. Moreover, the cost of building and manning ships by *administración* proved overly expensive. Under Philip's successors the government returned to contracting with Basque and Cantabrian shipbuilders to produce ships for the Atlantic service. The arguments for "privatization" were the same then as they are today. The government could save money and reduce its own payroll by shifting the expense of finding materials and recruiting workers to contractors. Moreover, as Carla Rahn Phillips showed in *Six Galleons for the King of Spain*, many of the ships may have been built below cost in expectation of royal favors to be received later—tax exemptions, *mayorazgos*, patents of nobility, or favorable terms on other contracts. Every step of construction and outfitting was nevertheless monitored by royal officials and conducted according to strict specifications laid down in the original contracts. The ships seem to have been well built, but a modern student of military contracting would find the disputes, cost overruns, and lawsuits between the crown and its contractors painfully familiar.

Shipbuilding, of course, depended upon the availability of timber and naval stores. Masts and hemp for cordage had to be imported from the Baltic, a region whose trade was dominated through much of this period by the Dutch enemy. Spain's supplies of oak for frames and planking, however, exceeded those of its adversaries. The massive shipbuilding program of Philip II, coupled with demand for charcoal from the Basque iron industry, seriously depleted the great forests of northern Spain. An extensive program of reforestation, remarkable even by modern standards, restored them in time for the shipbuilding programs of Philip IV.

By this time, the recruitment of seamen had become a major problem. The sailing ship was by far the largest and most complex piece of machinery known to the early modern world. It required crews whose skill could only be learned by years at sea, and as the sixteenth century progressed, such men became scarce. Some of the finest sailors in the world came from Spain's northern coast, but mortality on the Atlantic voyage and, above all, in the ports of the Caribbean, was very high. Many who sailed with the fleet died, while some stayed in America to seek their fortune. As the population of the Cantabrian ports dwindled, the crown tried to create a kind of maritime register that foreshadowed the system later devised in France under Louis XIV. It was abandoned in the face of great resistance. As long ago as the thirteenth century, Spain's maritime communities had acquired formidable privileges, including almost universal patents of *hidalguía* for most of the maritime population. Spanish seamen may have been as impoverished as their counterparts in other countries, but they knew how to protect their interests.

Despite these problems, Spain had developed the largest fighting navy in the world by the end of the sixteenth century. The service declined under Philip III and revived under Philip IV. As we shall see, it never fully overcame certain deficiencies in gunnery and training, but it remained sufficient to protect the treasure fleet and a threat to Spain's enemies. Despite increasing pressure from the northern powers, important parts of the fleet were lost on only two occasions: in 1628 to the Dutch under Piet Hein, and in 1657 to the English admiral Blake.

THE CHURCH

In much of the Spanish Empire, the church was a close ally of the monarchy. For centuries, the advancement of Catholic Christianity had provided the ideological basis of the monarchy and the primary justification for its conquests. The relationship between church and state, although not without its tensions, had to be symbiotic if either were to flourish. The church, moreover, was the empire's richest, most powerful corporation. The monarchy needed not only its endorsement but its resources and patronage. For this reason, Ferdinand and Isabella had from the beginning of their reign worked to gain control of ecclesiastical appointments and revenues. The conquest of Granada, and the ability of both Ferdinand and Charles V to use their Italian policies as leverage with a series of popes, provided the basis of their eventual success.

Since 1478, Isabella had demanded the right of presentation to Spanish benefices with only modest results. Sixtus IV reluctantly accepted her nominee to the diocese of Cuenca in 1479, but refused to regard this is as a precedent. A few years later, papal support for the Granada crusade enabled the monarchs to use ecclesiastical funds for this purpose and to establish a new precedent with regard to ecclesiastical appointments. In 1486, Innocent VIII granted the crown full rights of presentation in the conquered lands, at least partially in return for Ferdinand's support in Italy. In 1493, the Aragonese Pope Alexander VI granted the monarchs the right to collect ecclesiastical tithes in the conquered kingdom, and in 1501 extended this privilege to the Indies. Julius II, in another tribute to the usefulness of Ferdinand's Italian policies, granted the right to nominate all American bishops in 1508. The crown now held complete control over church finances and personnel in both Granada and the Americas. Finally, in 1523, Charles V secured the right of nomination to Spanish benefices from his erstwhile tutor, Pope Adrian VI.

In theory the American *Patronato Real*, if not its Spanish counterpart, extended to the lowest levels of the clergy. The king personally nominated bishops and abbots to the pope. Members of a cathedral chapter were selected by either the king or the Council of the Indies from a list of three names submitted by the bishop. The crown normally delegated the appointment of parish priests to the viceroy or governor, who also chose from a list of three provided by the bishop. In some cases, however, the crown granted individual subjects—usually powerful landholders—the right to nominate the curate of a particular parish, a practice common to nearly every European monarchy.

These arrangements and the papal concessions on which they were based did not apply to Italy or the Netherlands. Until 1559 the crown had little direct influence on the church in the Netherlands. Philip II's attempts to change this would become a major cause of the revolt that began in 1566. The church in the Italian kingdoms continued to operate in the canonical way, which is to say that cathedral chapters nominated bishops to the pope. The bishops in turn nominated priests, but, as in other parts of Europe, the crown and its officials had many ways of influencing the selection process. Relations between church and state were almost always based on negotiation and the appointment of clergy unacceptable to the secular government was rare.

This relationship violated the separation of church and state so vehemently supported by the medieval popes, but it benefitted the church in several ways. By placing much of the church's patronage and resources in the hands of the state, it deprived the Spanish monarchy of any incentive to support the Reformation. At the same time, it meant that the clergy, albeit a privileged and not always popular class, was so closely interwoven with the fabric of Spanish and Italian society that anticlericalism of the northern type was difficult to sustain. In Spain, the crown's influence made it possible for Isabella and Cisneros to begin a reform of the clergy that continued under Charles V and Philip II (especially the latter). The suppression of monastic abuses and a gradual improvement in the quality of diocesan clergy removed many of the grievances that troubled laymen in other countries including the Netherlands.

But were the clergy of Spain and Italy superior to their counterparts elsewhere? In Spain the warrior bishops of the fifteenth century gave way to prelates chosen for their learning and piety as well as political skill. Kings and often nobles reformed convents and monasteries with great vigor. The sixteenth and early seventeenth centuries were a golden age in theology and devotional writing as well as in politics, but the degree to which reform penetrated the lower ranks of the secular clergy is questionable. Efforts to improve the education of Spanish priests and catechize the laity in conformity to the decrees of the Council of Trent proved difficult at best. Limited royal influence on the Italian clergy thwarted similar efforts in Naples and Sicily, but in the Netherlands, whose church was dominated by the great nobles until the revolt of the 1560s, the situation was far worse.

Despite these difficulties, the church performed vital services for the crown. In America, the primary goal of pacifying the Indians depended upon the work of conversion. The first missionaries were Franciscan, Dominican, and Augustinian friars from every part of Charles V's empire. They performed mass baptisms, established churches, and hoped to create a native priesthood by educating young Indians in the faith. Christian millennialism and the notion that the Indians lived in a state of innocence inspired the Franciscans in particular to isolate their charges from the corrupting influence of Europeans. To that end they concentrated their efforts on converting the Indian power structure and in some cases gathered the Indians into new communities or *doctrinas* where the converts worked in communal enterprises under the friars' direction. At the same time, the friars did their best to obliterate memory of the ancient gods by tearing down temples and destroying cultural artifacts. When it became evident that many conversions were at best superficial, the friars learned native languages and in the process developed a scholarly interest in native culture. It is to them that we owe the preservation of ancient codices that tell us much of what is known about pre-Columbian society.

This stage of missionary activity did not last. The crown began to suspect that the independence of the friars and the isolation of the missionary communities they had created was a potential threat to royal authority. The missionaries reinforced this view by resisting the authority of newly appointed bishops, forbidding the Indians to pay tithes, and in some cases physically attacking secular priests. The growing conflict led Philip II to appoint a commission whose findings led to the gradual secularization of existing *doctrinas*. The ordinances of 1572–1574 took the position that missions were no longer needed in settled areas and that the friars should instead undertake the work of expanding and pacifying the frontiers. Indian parishes would no longer be supported by royal grants, but by tithes collected from the Indians. Frontier missions, however, would be supported by royal donations, and, wherever possible, by a small number of troops for their protection. To their credit, the friars accepted this challenge. Their missions pressed further into the borderlands until the very end of the colonial period. By bringing the border Indians into settled communities they helped the empire to control strategically important but economically marginal regions

The partnership between church and state proved equally fruitful in the area of education. The universities of Mexico and Peru were founded by royal cédula in 1551. They based their statutes and curricula on those of the University of Salamanca and offered degrees in arts, theology, law, canon law, and medicine. Eight other American universities were eventually created on the same model, and all benefited to one degree or another from the participation of clerics. Ten "minor" universities offered more limited curricula and were generally both run and staffed by members of the Jesuit or Dominican orders. As in Spain and Italy, priests largely controlled elementary education. The basic formation of the empire's elites was, however, undertaken by the Jesuits, who from the 1560s onward established scores of *colegios* in Europe and America alike.

Another ecclesiastical institution with ties to the crown was the Spanish Inquisition. Historically, an inquisition was an ecclesiastical court created by a bishop to look into matters of faith or morals within his jurisdiction. The Spanish Inquisition was unique in that, although staffed at all times by clerics, it was created by a secular monarchy. Isabella, Ferdinand, and their advisors founded it in the late 1470s to deal with what they perceived as false converts from Judaism. Many of these *conversos* had come to occupy high positions in church and state, and represented, at least in the minds of many Castilians, a threat to the purity of the faith. The papacy initially opposed the Inquisition's formation, but eventually relented under diplomatic pressure. Under Isabella and Ferdinand, the Inquisition launched a bloody persecution of conversos and gradually extended its authority to the Aragonese kingdoms where it met with varying degrees of resistance as well as support. The Kingdom of Naples resisted all efforts at its introduction. Sicily embraced it in part because its familiars, as informers were called, enjoyed immunity from criminal prosecution—a privilege that appealed to the island's criminal element and its many supporters.

When a growing lack of potential victims caused the persecution of conversos to decline in the reign of Charles V, the Inquisition proved its resilience as an institution by adopting new missions. It devoted the middle years of the sixteenth century to the pursuit of heretics. Only a few of its Spanish and Italian victims were actual Protestants. Most were suspected of Illuminism or of adherence to the teachings of the Dutch humanist, Erasmus. Neither Illuminism, a kind of mysticism, nor Erasmianism resembled the teachings of Luther, but the Inquisition's grasp of Protestant theology was at best weak. In 1569, Philip II nevertheless established tribunals in Mexico and Lima, ostensibly to protect his American subjects against Protestant teachings introduced by foreign sailors. Philip III established another tribunal at Cartagena de Indias in 1610. The danger of proselytizing from this source must have been small, but the Inquisition provided the crown with another means of deterring interlopers whose presence was in any case illegal.

Like its Spanish and Sicilian counterparts, the American Inquisition continued to prosecute conversos on an occasional basis, but from the 1570s onward, it concerned itself primarily with what would today be called morals charges: bigamy, blasphemy, and homosexuality. It also dealt with what it called "propositions," a wide range of popular notions and superstitions which, although incompatible with Catholic doctrine, did not rise to the formal definition of heresy. Protestants and the writers of the eighteenth-century Enlightenment believed that these activities, and in particular the Inquisition's responsibility for censoring books, retarded the intellectual development of Spanish society. It should be remembered, however, that all early modern states, with the qualified exception of the Dutch Republic, demanded religious uniformity and practiced official censorship. The presence of banned books even in American libraries suggests that the Inquisition may not have been more efficient than its state counterparts in France or England, while the remarkable quality of Spanish political thought and *belles lettres* during the Golden Age of the sixteenth and seventeenth centuries disputes the notion of intellectual backwardness.

INFORMAL STRUCTURES OF POWER

The formal institutions of government provide an idealized framework within which society is supposed to function. In the Spanish empire, as in all other polities, those institutions were modified by informal structures of power whose roots lay deep within the values of the larger culture. Those cultural values, and the relationships they created, influenced and in some cases perverted, the way in which formal institutions work. Spanish kings and their servants understood this. To a great extent, the edicts they devised in dizzying proliferation attempted not only to limit corruption, but to mediate what amounted to a conflict between public and private virtues. Certain deeply held values in Spanish and Italian society made that conflict especially painful.

Everywhere the desire to help one's friends and family influences politics to one degree or another, but in Spain and Italy kinship and clientage appear to have been more important than in the northern countries. The difference was of course relative. The titled nobility of Spain and the Burgundian Netherlands yielded to no one in their effective use of family connections or in their zeal to develop networks of mutual obligation that extended their power. In southern Europe, however, those tendencies extended to all but the least privileged segments of society. Even the most minor municipal offices often remained in the same family for generations. Extended families, although by no means the norm, were relatively common among those who possessed even modest amounts of property. The lack of familial continuity on Dutch or German municipal councils struck both Italians and Spaniards as odd. The common practice by which aging English people with living children paid room and board to live with friends would have seemed to them incomprehensible.

Partible inheritance, the legal principle that insisted on an equal division of property among one's heirs, may have encouraged the formation of extended families. Siblings often remained under the same roof even after marriage in an effort to maintain the integrity of the family's holdings. (Partible inheritance, however, was common in Germany where extended families were rare). Kinship ties may also have been strengthened by the stronger legal position of women. Spanish women, who normally kept their family name after marriage, retained their dowries and their bride price upon the death of their husbands, and were legally entitled to at least half of his property. Widows also retained the right to manage their husband's property in the interest of minor children. Widows with even modest amounts of property were therefore less likely to remarry than their northern sisters. Powerful widows are a commonplace in Spanish and Italian literature as well as in legal documents. Disgruntled step-siblings who went off to seek their fortune are less so, except among the relatively poor. At the same time Spanish and Italian fathers enjoyed far greater legal powers (*patria potestas*) over their unmarried children than did their northern counterparts, and were more likely to acknowledge their illegitimate children and incorporate them into their family networks. In the end, however, a cultural understanding of family that dates back to Roman times or before may have been more important than legal rights. The great twelfth-century Italian scholastic, Peter Lombard, divided the world into *familia* and *inimici* (enemies). Nothing could be more Italian—or Spanish.

Clientage, too, had its roots in ancient Rome. The term refers to a relationship of mutual dependency between a wealthier, more powerful, individual, and a poorer one. The *patrón* (*padrone* in Italian) protects his client and helps him to find employment or other economic opportunities in return for personal and political support when needed. Unlike feudalism (with which it is sometimes confused) or the clientage of ancient Rome, this relationship has no legal standing. It is, however, openly acknowledged by both parties, and is often related to *compadrazgo*, or godfathership. The patron agrees to serve as godfather to one or more of the client's children—a far more onerous obligation than in the Anglo-Saxon world. A violation of the bonds of clientage by either party was taken very seriously and, at the very least, brought dishonor. Personal honor, a concept with little meaning in the modern world, was terribly important in the sixteenth and seventeenth centuries. Contemporaries thought that in Spain and Italy it was an obsession. The political history of the age is replete with bitter vendettas and struggles for precedence that make sense only in the context of what anthropologists call "shame" societies: societies in which reputation is more important than law as a means of social control.

Kinship, clientage, and the demands of honor ensured that most towns were divided into two or more clientage groups that struggled endlessly over economic resources and political privilege. These groups could be diagrammed as pyramids whose base reached into the artisan class and whose apex, a noble or—more rarely—merchant family, might have connections with the court either through the patronage of a great noble dynasty or with one of the secretarial "schools" that were themselves patronage networks with clients in the lower ranks of the bureaucracy. Each of the secretarial schools was in turn affiliated with a faction of courtiers who, like the senior secretaries, enjoyed personal access to the monarch. At the top of the pyramid stood the king, the greatest *patrón* of all.

Ties of clientage and kinship subverted the government's good intentions in two main areas: official appointments and the letting of government contracts. Officials or prominent figures at court nominated candidates for the most important offices. The candidates had to meet certain basic qualifications—old Christian ancestry, a legal degree when appropriate, and so on—but the Council or other appointing body gave its greatest deliberations to balancing the claims of different patrons. Once installed, officials then used their own rights of appointment to reward friends and relatives and build up patronage systems of their own within the lower bureaucracy. Those who had the power to award government contracts inevitably used it to advance their influence in the same way. Everyone, including the king, understood this. In fact, to neglect friends and family and reward one's enemies would have been inconceivable. A major exception involved audiencia appointments in the Indies. There the crown made heroic efforts to appoint only outsiders with no connection to the communities they governed, and passed edicts to isolate them in an effort to control favoritism. Marriage to a local woman was, for example, strictly forbidden. Even this policy broke down in later years when, in the face of economic difficulties, the government resorted to the sale of certain American offices.

In some ways, the structure of Spanish government actually enhanced the importance of kinship and clientage. The king's absolute authority was, as we have seen, mitigated by the subject's absolute right to complain, persuade, and petition. This reciprocity permitted the peaceful resolution of grievances and was therefore essential to the maintenance of stability. In practice, as John Elliott has pointed out, it meant that important matters were almost always decided through private negotiation, rather than through debate in a public forum. The personal nature of the king's government strengthened the power of personal relationships in politics, which in turn tended to subvert legislation designed to limit its influence.

In Spanish America, racial attitudes intensified the problems created by an obsessive concern with kinship and status. Few societies have created more elaborate hierarchies based on race, yet the very complexity of these categories reflects a racialism quite different from that of modern times or from the kind that later developed in the English colonies. Pseudo-scientific theories of racial inferiority, the product of nineteenth-century anthropology, did not yet exist. Neither Spanish law nor Catholic theology denied that the Indians were rational beings who could become good Christians and loyal subjects of the crown. They could not legally be enslaved, and for all the terrible mortality of the conquest, Spanish governors made no effort to exterminate the Indians, then or later. This was, of course, due in part to the need for Indian labor. The contrasting attitudes of at least some English colonists arose from a different pattern of colonization. When it became obvious that the English would find no gold and silver in North America and that the Indians melted into the surrounding wilderness to avoid forced labor, they sought to relieve the perceived overpopulation of England by sending large numbers of colonists who had to expel or kill the Indians to cultivate their lands. The English did not regard the Indians as subhuman in law or theory, but England never developed an imperial policy on Indians or the bureaucracy to enforce it. Each colony dealt with the indigenous population as it saw fit.

Spain's treatment of African slaves was also different. Slavery did not appear as a concept in English law until the seventeenth century. Spain possessed a body of law relating to slavery that dated to the *Siete Partidas* of the thirteenth century. Those laws in turn reflected Roman precedents of great antiquity and offered a measure of protection unknown to the slave codes later developed by the English colonies. Spanish slaves had the right to marry, even against their owner's wishes. They could own property and, if the owner was willing, buy their freedom using money they had earned in their spare time. The owner's right of manumission was in any case unlimited and frequently exercised. This was a mixed blessing because, like the ancient Romans, Spanish slaveholders sometimes freed their slaves to avoid supporting them in old age, but it meant that by 1600, freed blacks outnumbered slaves in several parts of the empire.

Once freed, the ex-slave entered into a strange nether-world that reflected Spain's ambivalence about race. Blacks, like Indians, could not hold public office or, with occasional exceptions, attend university. Unlike Indians, they did not have the option of remaining within a community of their own people, but they could, and did, achieve considerable success in business and the trades. Some had already done so while they were slaves. Landholders often used black slaves as overseers of Indian labor, and in the mining districts of Mexico and New Granada, blacks both slave and free served as managers and engineers. The law, at least, accepted interracial marriage, and by 1600, people of mixed race had become numerous, especially in the larger towns.

Underlying this was the view, supported by the Church, that all people were equal in God's eyes, and the legal premise that all free men were equal as subjects under the king. Race, in the Spanish world, was primarily a matter of status. Status in turn depended heavily upon the medieval concept of blood. It was thought that blood conveyed character traits such as nobility or servility, courage, or refinement. Spain's infamous *limpieza de sangre* statutes, which sought to restrict public employment to old Christians, were based on the theory that (as Philip II himself declared) Jewish blood carried with it a natural tendency toward heresy. Hence, old Christians of pure Spanish ancestry were of higher status than mestizos or people of mixed Spanish and Indian blood. Mulattos were superior to blacks, and lighter mulattos had more status than their darker relatives. The law recognized the inherent foolishness in all this by providing what was known as a *gracias al sacar*, a document stating that the bearer was not in fact black, but white and entitled to all the civil privileges thereof. It could be purchased for a substantial fee, and provided some well-to-do people of African or mixed race with an entrée to public office or the university. Moreover, people of mixed blood often had prominent whites as godfathers, an indication that the ties of clientage could, on occasion, transcend race.

Clientage, kinship, and—in America—race, provided the framework within which the government of the Spanish empire had to operate.

In America, especially, they restricted access to power and opportunity in ways that would eventually weaken the bonds of empire and destabilize the empire's successor states. Spain nevertheless provided an unusually honest and efficient government by the standards of the day, and struggled heroically with problems of distance, corruption, and injustice. It did not always succeed, but as the first modern empire to rule over large and varied populations, Spain developed sophisticated institutions of imperial governance long before France and England. Its system of absolutism tempered by law, openness to criticism, and the kind of commonsense embodied in "*se obedece pero no se cumple*" or the *gracias al sacar* mediated conflicts and for many years found general acceptance in Spain, America, and the Italian kingdoms. Its reception in the Netherlands would be very different.

5

IMPERIAL POLICY

The Spanish Empire of the sixteenth century possessed enviable strengths. Its institutions were well-crafted and deeply rooted in its history and culture. Both Charles V and his son, Philip II, were intelligent, capable rulers whose administrators, soldiers, and diplomats were envied by other states. Above all, Spain's wealth in gold and silver exceeded that of any empire the world had yet seen, but by the time Philip died in 1598, the financial and military resources of his empire had already been stretched to their limits and the domestic economy of Spain itself was in serious disarray. Seventy years later Spain had ceased to be Europe's greatest power, although much of its empire would survive into the nineteenth century. The cause of this decline was an imperial policy which, if defensive in theory, involved the Spanish Habsburgs in two destructive conflicts: the Revolt of the Netherlands, which evolved into a general northern European struggle that lasted for more than 80 years, and the contest with Islam in the Mediterranean.

The goals of imperial policy remained broadly consistent from the time of Charles V until the end of the Habsburg era. Like other vast, multinational empires, the Spanish system faced both external and internal threats. Spanish policy makers knew that the empire was a magnet for the fears and ambitions of other nations, and assumed correctly that it would be the object of frequent attacks on its territories. They believed that failure to repel each and every challenge would encourage further assaults and eventually end in the empire's collapse. This attachment to what a later age would call the domino theory created a near-obsession with maintaining what the Spanish called "*reputación*." Most Spaniards also believed that the empire, based as it was on a specifically Catholic ideology, had to defend itself and its faith against Muslims and Protestants. Their commitment did not, however, imply open-ended support for the papacy, which sometimes opposed Spain's interests in Italy and elsewhere. Within the Spanish empire itself, and especially within the European kingdoms, the government sought to limit dissent by respecting local institutions and cooperating with local elites. This policy, too, remained subject to the constraints of divine and natural law as understood from a Catholic perspective. Spain's neighbors, awed by the wealth and power of the greatest empire the modern world had yet seen, tended to believe that her rulers were bent on world domination. They were not, but even their self-consciously defensive goals caused endless conflict and proved in the end impossible to sustain.

Spain's achievements under Charles V and his son, Philip II, led future generations to call this era the *siglo de oro*, or Golden Century. The phrase implies continuity between the two reigns and hints, rightly, that their glories contained the seed of Spain's eventual decline. Philip and his father shared common values. They differed, however, in style and personality. Charles, within the constraints of his faith, had been pragmatic and cosmopolitan, a warrior prince with extensive combat experience and a gift for delegating authority. Philip was a master bureaucrat, perhaps the first ruler of the modern type. Whereas the father had traveled constantly, rarely spending more than a few weeks in any one place, the son established himself in the center of the Iberian Peninsula near the hitherto unimportant town of Madrid. There he constructed the vast palace/monastery of the Escorial where he remained for the rest of his long life, leaving only rarely except for working vacations at one or another of his nearby hunting lodges.

Philip may have been unlike his father in personality and methods, but their common values and a respect for the virtues of continuity inspired similar policies, and—in the beginning at least—a similar strategy. France, although riven by civil war throughout most of his reign, remained the object of Philip's gravest suspicions. The death of Henry II in 1559 left France under a regency dominated by the Catholic house of Guise. The house of Navarre (which unlike the Guise was of royal blood), contested their dominance and allied themselves with the French Protestants, or Huguenots. The Queen, Catherine de Medici, tried to play each side against the other in an effort to protect the interests of her young sons who would reign in turn as Francis II, Charles IX, and Henry III. This factional conflict continued in one form or another for nearly 40 years, effectively neutralizing France as a major power. From the Spanish point of view, however, the re-establishment of a functioning French monarchy was always a dangerous possibility; the establishment of a monarchy dominated by Huguenots a nightmare. Both posed an immediate threat to the Netherlands and to Spanish power in Italy. For many years Philip attempted (with some success) to manipulate the internal politics of France by providing assistance to the French Catholics.

He also tried, as his father had done, to isolate France diplomatically by maintaining good relations with his Austrian Habsburg cousins and by trying to preserve Spain's historic alliance with England. He managed to avoid an open break with the Austrians, who continued to resent the terms of Charles V's will, but England proved more difficult. The new queen Elizabeth I, a Protestant advised by Protestants more radical than herself, remained deeply suspicious of Philip's motives. She shared his distrust of France but feared his presence in the Netherlands and envied Spain's colonial possessions. In later years, this led to open warfare.

Philip's mastery of Italian affairs was if anything greater than his father's. He continued to honor the nominal independence of the north Italian states while controlling their rulers through patronage backed by the threat of force. Italy remained the strategic center of his European empire. It was also a potential source of conflict not only with France, but with Austria, Venice, and the papacy. Some of the north Italian states were imperial fiefs, while Venice and some of the popes encouraged resistance to Spanish hegemony. In Naples and Sicily the Turks remained a threat to coastal communities as they did to those of Spain. The Ottoman treaty with the Austrian Habsburgs in 1547 did not extend to Spain or Italy, and Ottoman policy in the Mediterranean became more aggressive as the situation in the Danube Valley stabilized. Between 1560 and 1573, an intermittent but very expensive naval war in the Mediterranean carried on the tradition of Charles V—and greatly complicated the European policies of his son.

Domestically, Philip was more determined than Charles to rationalize the government of his empire and its components. In one of his first acts as king he established the Council of Italy and in 1559 he ordered it to suggest reforms for the governments of Naples, Sicily, and Milan. The resulting changes were made within the framework of existing institutions and did not fatally offend local sensibilities. In 1567 he ordered the Council of the Indies to commission a similar review that led to an extensive reform of colonial government according to established principles of Spanish law and administration. Many colonists resented the Council's efforts to protect the Indians, but they could not claim that the government had behaved illegally. In the Netherlands, however, Philip abandoned this moderate approach with disastrous results. From his perspective he had no choice.

THE REVOLT OF THE NETHERLANDS

The Netherlands were an anomaly among Philip's inherited dominions. Not only did they contain a significant minority of non-Catholics, but their tradition of limited religious tolerance and the gritty independence of their municipal and provincial institutions ran counter to Castilian ideas of royal government. Philip, who knew the country well and had lived there during the 1550s, came to believe that failure to reform church and government in the Netherlands would not only undermine the legitimacy of his rule but expose his soul to mortal peril. By attempting drastic reforms with little regard for local sensibilities, he provoked a general revolt that resulted in the loss of seven northern and eastern provinces and the creation of a new nation, the Republic of the Netherlands. The refusal of Philip and his successors to accept that outcome turned the revolt into a generalized European conflict that lasted, for Spain at least, until 1657. By that time, the Spanish empire had gravely weakened itself financially and militarily. Because Spain's policy toward the Netherlands bears an important share of responsibility for the empire's seventeenth-century decline, the conflict must be described in detail.

When Philip became ruler of the Netherlands in 1555, his father's alliance with the old Burgundian nobility remained strong, and a vigorous, if unpopular, persecution had brought the problem of heresy under temporary control. The cost of the emperor's wars and widespread discomfort over his religious policies had nevertheless created serious tensions. In the four years between Philip's succession and his return to Spain in 1559, the government's position began to erode. In the Estates-Generals of 1556 and 1558, leading nobles had protested the presence of Spanish troops in the Netherlands and tried to limit new assessments for the French wars that resulted in the great victory at St. Quentin in 1559. When Philip appointed a government to represent him in his absence, he resolved to limit the nobles' influence. His half-sister, Margaret, Duchess of Parma, became regent. The presidency of the Council of State went to Anton Perrenot de Granvelle, Bishop of Arras, whose arrogant manner coupled with relatively humble origins offended the nobility. Viglius, a distinguished jurist of middle-class origins assumed the presidency of the Privy Council, and Charles, Count of Berlaymont, was given the Council of Finance. It soon became obvious that these three would make most of the major decisions for the region as a whole. All were competent, but the only noble among them was both poor and outside the inner circle of grandees who had long been central to Charles V's system of governance. The nobles, led by William, Prince of Orange and the Count of Egmont, hated Granvelle, looked down on Berlaymont, and regarded Viglius with indifference. Above all, the nobility of the Netherlands feared that their growing exclusion from government would cost them the offices and financial rewards they needed to preserve their status in an age of rising costs and declining rents.

Philip's religious policies aroused even greater hostility. The ecclesiastical structure of the Netherlands had been created in the early middle ages when the region was still rural and relatively under-populated. There were only four bishoprics, three of which fell under the jurisdiction of Reims in France, and one under the Archbishop of Cologne. Few of the great cities had bishops of their own, and many, even in the Netherlands, regarded the clergy as corrupt and ignorant. The emperor had known that such a church could scarcely provide pastoral care much less cope with the rise of heresy, and had been tinkering with the idea of a complete reorganization since 1551–1552. In 1558 Philip brought his father's schemes to fruition by asking the pope to create 16 new bishoprics to be grouped into three provinces along linguistic and regional lines. The king would have the right of nomination to all but one of the new prelates, and only candidates of good moral character with degrees in either theology or canon law would be accepted.

The pope responded with unusual speed on May 12, 1559. The bull *Super Universalis* authorized the proposed changes, and the crown appointed a commission to implement them. The commission resolved the problem of funding 16 new bishops, in part by proposing the transfer of revenues from Spanish dioceses, many of which were poor enough to begin with. The rest of the money would be found by incorporating monastic foundations and their revenues into the new dioceses. The new bishops would displace the abbots and assume their revenues. Bulls of circumscription confirming these arrangements were issued in May and August of 1561. The Bishop of Arras, who guided the process from the start, had already been named Cardinal Granvelle and Archbishop of Mechelen.

The prospect of an effective church organization in the Netherlands terrified both the Protestant minority and those in municipal government who felt that a more effective prosecution of heretics would harm their trade with England and Germany. The nobles were infuriated. Many of them had held the right of nomination to church offices that were an important source of income and patronage as well as a means of providing for younger sons. Few of the latter were noted for their piety or learning and under the new rules would be excluded from church office in any case. The nobles would also lose influence in the powerful Estates of Brabant where three abbots, all from noble families, would be replaced by three bishops appointed by the crown. The reform, in short, was not only an infringement of local autonomy, but struck directly at the wealth and power of the nobility.

In 1564, the leading nobles engineered Granvelle's dismissal with the help of friends at Phillip's court. Flushed with new confidence, they dispatched the Count of Egmont to demand a reorganization of the governing councils. Their goal was to restore their authority and halt the executions for heresy. Egmont's mission, however, reinforced the king's growing belief that heresy in the Netherlands was becoming uncontrollable. To avoid the appearance of open conflict, Philip showered Egmont with favors and sent him home thinking that his mission was a success. Nothing could have been further than the truth. After the king made his true position known in May, 1565, the nobles launched a series of dramatic protests, the most importance of which was the *Compromise des nobles*, a document later regarded in the Netherlands as a declaration of independence. After the loyalist Berlaymont referred to the protesters as beggars, the dissidents adopted the epithet as the name of their party and appeared in public wearing beggar's bowls around their necks. Fearing the worst, Margaret of Parma, issued the so-called *Moderation*, which effectively permitted the exercise of Protestantism in areas where it was already established. When Philip repudiated this measure as well, the Protestants removed or destroyed images in churches throughout the region with the encouragement of the nobles and some of the city governments.

The Iconoclasm of 1566 outraged Philip. Margaret's government, supported by Egmont and the Prince of Orange, soon restored order, but the king decided that this would not solve the underlying problem. In 1567 he dispatched the Duke of Alba with an army of veterans to root out those he regarded as rebels and heretics. When Alba had finished his work, the king would come to the Netherlands, dismiss the duke for exceeding his instructions, and issue a general pardon. The scheme, to which Alba was a party, shows Philip II at his most devious. Alba arrived in Brussels in August, 1567, and arrested Egmont and the relatively innocent count of Hornes. Margaret resigned in protest on September 13, and Alba became Governor-General of the Netherlands with what amounted to proconsular authority over foreign and domestic affairs. Acting on decisions already made in Spain, he executed Egmont and Hornes and established a Council of Troubles to enforce the placards against heresy and condemn the signers of the *Compromise* as traitors. Between 1567 and 1576, the Council of Blood, as it was known in the Netherlands, condemned 8957 individuals, most of whom had long since fled to England or Germany. More than 1000, however, were executed. William of Orange, who had wisely retired

to his estates in Germany before Alba's arrival, raised an army of mercenaries and invaded the southern Netherlands. A second army under his
brother, Louis of Nassau, invaded Friesland. Alba defeated both of them,
and by Christmas, 1568, the entire country was once again reduced to
obedience.

At this point, Philip should have come to the Netherlands as planned, but
he did not do so. His son Don Carlos, whose strange behavior had long been
a problem, died on July 24, 1568, leaving Spain without an heir. Then, on
Christmas Eve of that year, the Moriscos of Granada rose in a bloody revolt
that would require two years to suppress. This reminder that the Reconquest was not yet complete required the monarch's presence, and Alba,
already hated for his repressions, remained in the Netherlands for four
more years. The duke distrusted his new subjects, and governed through
what amounted to a military government of occupation administered by
Spaniards and Italians. He imposed a badly needed uniform code of criminal law and installed the bishops who had been appointed in 1561—in some
cases at gunpoint—but opposition to what most Netherlanders now saw as
an alien regime continued to grow. The breaking point came in 1571–1572
when Philip's troubles converged in an improbable and nearly catastrophic
sequence of events.

Alba's regime depended upon the support of an expensive, multinational
army paid for by Spain. Philip, however, was forced to divert much of his
revenue to quelling the Morisco rebellion. By 1570, pacification was largely
complete, but in January of that year the North African corsairs recaptured
Tunis, and in June, the Turkish fleet attacked Cyprus. Spain, together with
most of the Italian states, formed the Holy League to combat the Muslim
threat, but the League's forces failed to relieve the island. In October, 1571,
a second and far greater Christian fleet defeated the Turks at Lepanto. Hoping for a final victory over Turkish power in the Mediterranean, the League
planned an even more ambitious effort for 1572. Philip's commitment to
war against the Ottomans now came into conflict with his commitment to the
Netherlands. The cost of massive operations on two widely separated fronts
was more than Spain could bear. Philip ordered Alba to impose new taxes
on the Netherlands to, at the very least, pay his own expenses. Spanish contributions to the army in Flanders dropped to almost nothing in 1570–1571
while taxes in the Netherlands rose dramatically. It was not enough. Alba
proposed a version of the Castilian alcabala known as the Tenth Penny. The
new scheme aroused intense opposition, especially among the rich. When
Alba finally imposed it without the approval of the Estates General, popular
outrage approached uncontrollable levels.

As opposition to Spanish rule increased, the diplomatic situation in north-ern Europe began to deteriorate. Elizabeth I of England saw the presence of a large Spanish army in the Netherlands as a potential threat to her rule. In 1568 she seized a Spanish fleet carrying money for Alba's troops and offered shelter to the Sea Beggars, a ferocious group of Netherlandish exiles who, under letters of marque from William of Orange, attacked shipping in the Channel and raided the smaller coastal towns of Holland and Zeeland. Alba responded by embargoing all trade with England. The Netherlands began to sink into an economic depression. France, too, became a prob-lem when the Huguenots, under their leader Coligny, gained ascendancy over the young king Charles IX, and began to contemplate an attack on the Netherlands in support of their fellow Protestants. To forestall them, Alba dispatched a contingent of Spanish troops to France on his own authority.

In these circumstances, Philip's involvement in the Ridolfi Plot ranks as one of the more bizarre misjudgments of his career. The king had for a decade tried to preserve the English alliance. Elizabeth's actions in 1568 made it apparent to him that he had failed, and that England now repre-sented a threat to his interests in the Netherlands. Misled by the Spanish ambassador Roberto Ridolfi and by the English Catholics who had taken refuge at Madrid, he ordered Alba to invade England in 1571 if Ridolfi or the English Catholics made good on their promise to assassinate the queen. Alba, who believed throughout his career that it would be madness to invade England, protested and did nothing. The assassination plot failed, as Alba—and perhaps Philip—knew it would (the king's reasoning in this case has never been adequately explained), but the damage was done. Elizabeth responded by signing a treaty with France which raised the specter of a joint Anglo-French effort against Spain.

The Revolt of the Netherlands began in earnest when Elizabeth expelled the Sea Beggars from English ports. Ironically, this was neither a hostile act nor a consequence of the Ridolfi Plot, but an attempt to defuse the political situation in northwest Europe. The embargo had caused great distress in England as well as in the Netherlands, and Elizabeth now hoped to reach an accommodation with Alba on trade. The Beggars had in any case worn out their welcome by seizing the ships of neutral powers. Driven from Eng-land and with nowhere else to go, the Beggars seized the fishing village of Brill near Rotterdam on April 1 and called for a general revolt in the name of William of Orange. By this time, the harsh winter of 1571–1572 and the refusal of butchers, brewers, and bakers to sell their goods as a protest against the Tenth Penny added greatly to the distress caused by the paralysis of trade. Orange's adherents had become a majority in several town councils, especially in Holland and Zeeland. In others, council members who were themselves loyal came under intolerable public pressure to declare for the rebels. At the same time, a rebel army under Count van den Bergh successfully invaded the northeastern provinces. Within weeks, much of the country was in revolt.

A more serious threat to Spanish rule came in the south. Orange's brother, Louis of Nassau, seized Mons on the main road between Paris and Brussels. There, an army of Huguenots was to join forces with Orange and 20,000 Germans for an attack on Brussels. Alba, however, surrounded Mons long before either army arrived, and on July 17 destroyed an advance force of 6000 Huguenots at St. Ghislain, five miles from his lines. Orange, who crossed the border at about the same time, resolved to await a French declaration of war before going further. It never came. Charles IX, already embarrassed by the fiasco at St. Ghislain, became convinced that the English, treaty or no treaty, would do nothing to support a French invasion of the Netherlands. He began to think that he could use the situation to rid himself of Coligny and the Huguenots, and in an astonishing reversal of policy ordered the St. Bartholomew's day massacre on August 23. Catholic mobs murdered Coligny and several thousand of his followers, abruptly freeing Alba from all fear of a French invasion. When Orange failed to relieve Alba's siege of Mons, the duke took the city and began to move against the other rebel strongholds, beginning with Mechelen.

Mechelen offered no resistance, but Alba allowed his troops to sack the city because it had been one of the few to accept the Prince of Orange without being pressured to do so by a rebel army. He then sacked Zutphen and Naarden, whose offers to surrender came too late. In each case, these actions were accompanied by the wholesale slaughter of civilians. The duke's campaign of deliberate frightfulness succeeded in that by Christmas every city outside Holland and Zeeland had returned to its allegiance; it failed in that it convinced many in Holland and Zeeland that they would be killed even if they surrendered. Orange retreated to Holland to make his last stand, and began to create the core of a rebel government based on Holland and Zeeland. Alba's men besieged Haarlem, a city garrisoned by 4000 professional soldiers but without modern fortifications.

The siege of Haarlem marked a turning point in the revolt. It lasted eight months with both sides committing terrible atrocities. When the city at last surrendered on terms in July, 1573, Alba violated the agreement by executing some 2000 troops and several of the city's magistrates, imposing a fine of 200,000 florins, and imprisoning a number of the leading townspeople. There could be no further hope of compromise. At one point the citizens of Haarlem had planned to burn the town rather than surrender. Now the people of Leiden claimed that if necessary they would cut off their left arms and eat them (keeping their right arms available to fight), while Alba's next target, Alkmaar, prepared to open its dykes and drown the countryside rather than surrender. Alba thought that his actions after Haarlem had been overly generous, and, echoing his enemies, told the king that it would be better to flood both Holland and Zeeland than to let the rebels have them.

The growing intransigence on both sides owed much to the strain of war but more to the fact that the conflict was becoming increasingly religious in character. The conflict between Protestants and Catholics may not have been the primary cause of the conflict, but it made its resolution impossible. In forming his government, Orange had relied heavily upon the Calvinist minority whose fervor overwhelmed the counsels of the uncommitted. By the time he himself converted in 1573, the Calvinists had become the driving force of the revolt. Alba and the king knew this. To them, as to their Calvinist adversaries, the struggle had become one against evil incarnate: no negotiation was possible. Unfortunately for the Spanish, this conclusion came at a time when Spain no longer possessed the resources to continue. The naval campaigns of 1570–1573 against the Turks had drained the treasury, and when the siege of Haarlem ended, Alba's troops had not been paid in 28 months. His refusal to allow them to sack the city, which would have been permitted under contemporary rules of war, provoked the first of a long series of mutinies that would cripple the Spanish army in years to come. On this occasion his own popularity with the troops defused the situation, but when he ordered a second assault against Alkmaar in September, the men refused. Alba lifted the siege on October 8. Three days later, the rebels defeated a royal fleet in battle on the Zuider Zee and captured its commander.

The king had long known that Alba would have to be replaced. He should have done it early in 1569, but waited until 1570 to appoint the duke of Medinaceli as Alba's successor. He did not, however, recall Alba. Medinaceli stood more or less idly in the wings until January, 1573, when Philip revoked his appointment in favor of Don Luis de Requeséns, a Catalan who had most recently served as governor of Lombardy. The king remained committed to a policy of repression by force, and felt that Medinaceli lacked the toughness and military skill to win. Requeséns arrived in November, 1573, and Alba returned to Spain in December.

The new governor-general tried to continue Alba's policy without the necessary resources. In January, 1574 the rebels destroyed another royal fleet in the Scheldt, and took Middelburg in the following month. Their grip on Zeeland was now secure. Requeséns managed to annihilate an invading army under Louis of Nassau at the Mook on April 14. Louis was killed, but the Spanish army, which remained unpaid, mutinied once again and held the city of Antwerp to ransom for 1 million florins. Paid at last, they besieged Leiden, but the citizens forced them to withdraw by flooding the surrounding countryside. Then in November, they mutinied again, and abandoned most of the places they had taken in Holland and Zeeland to the Orangists. Meanwhile, in September while the siege of Leiden was collapsing, the Turks retook Tunis and the Spanish fortress of La Goletta that controlled the access to the city's harbor.

As 1575 began it seemed that all of Philip's policies had failed. In the Mediterranean, the Turks had not only reversed the verdict of Lepanto, but returned matters to where they had been in 1534. The Spanish army in the Netherlands could no longer be controlled by its commanders, and the king was out of money. He had sent more than 19 million florins to Flanders between 1572 and 1575. Because receipts from the Netherlands had, for obvious reasons, dropped to almost nothing during the same period, it was not enough. Desperate, Philip at last agreed to negotiate, but even at this, one of the lowest points of his reign, he could not accept the rebel's demand for freedom of worship. Negotiations broke down on July 13. In September, the crown again declared bankruptcy, and in October, William of Orange renounced all allegiance to Spain and declared independence. When Requeséns died in March, 1576, Orange controlled Holland and Zeeland with the exception of Haarlem and Amsterdam. The southern provinces, still nominally loyal, were left without an effective government. Finally, after several months, a group of southern nobles led by the duke of Aerschot seized the discredited Council of State in Brussels, and illegally convoked the States-General which had met only twice since 1559. While the States-General opened negotiations with William of Orange, Requeséns's replacement, Don Juan de Austria, arrived in Luxemburg.

Don Juan was Philip II's illegitimate half-brother and the victor at Lepanto, but at this point he had neither troops nor money. The tercios of Spain, together with several of the more important German units, remained in a state of mutiny. In what had by this time become a formal tradition, the soldiers organized themselves into an army under an elected leader (*electo*), and on the day after Don Juan's arrival sacked Antwerp, the largest and wealthiest city in the Netherlands. Over 8000 citizens lost their lives in one of the worst atrocities of the sixteenth century. Four days later, while Antwerp still smoldered, the States-General and the Orangists signed the Pacification of Ghent which recognized the unity of "the common father-land" and demanded the expulsion of the Spanish troops. In the "Perpetual Edict" of February 12, 1577, Don Juan reluctantly accepted the Pacification on condition that Catholicism be maintained throughout the provinces. The States-General paid the mutineers, and the Spanish marched off toward Italy.

At this point, Philip's luck began to change. In August, 2 million ducats in bullion arrived from Peru, the largest shipment to date. The king rene-gotiated his loans and convinced his creditors to loan him an additional 10 million florins (about 5 million ducats). Above all, his diplomats con-cluded a truce with the Turks in the Mediterranean, leaving him free to concentrate on the Netherlands. There, by years' end, the Pacification of Ghent was beginning to unravel on religious lines. Calvinists, although everywhere a minority, controlled most of the towns in Holland and Zeeland and were a substantial presence in much of Flanders and Brabant. Unrestrained by Orange, they embarked on a vigorous campaign to over-throw the Catholic governments of towns whose councils remained firmly Catholic. The provinces of Hainault and Artois formed the League of Arras to protect the Catholic faith and other Catholic provinces withheld their financial support. By the time Don Juan de Austria died on October 1, 1578, the States-General was without money and its troops had mutinied in imitation of their Spanish enemy.

This time, the king wasted no time in appointing a new governor-general: his nephew Alessandro Farnese, son of Margaret of Parma. It was an inspired choice. Skilled at both war and diplomacy, Farnese lost no time in exploiting the tension between the States-General and the Orangists. Before he arrived, Walloon Flanders joined Hainaut and Artois in the league of Arras, and in January, 1579, Holland, Zeeland, and Utrecht responded by forming the League of Utrecht which grew to include the northeastern provinces and the major cities of West Flanders, including Antwerp. On May 17, the Treaty of Arras reunited the Walloon provinces with Spain. Farnese, reinforced by the Spanish veterans who had by now returned from Italy, began a series of brilliant campaigns that within six years restored Spanish control over the provinces south of the three great rivers that bisected the Netherlands: the Rhine, the Maas, and the Waal. Confessional lines hard-ened further as southern Protestants sought refuge in Holland and Zeeland, while northern Catholics moved south.

THE ANNEXATION OF PORTUGAL

As Farnese took command of the army of Flanders, Philip II, his finances and confidence restored, began to plan for the annexation of Portugal and its worldwide empire. The opportunity to reunite the Iberian kingdoms arose from the folly of the Portuguese king, Dom Sebastian. Sebastian, unmarried and only 23 years of age, was Philip's nephew, the son of his sister Juana and the Infante John of Portugal who had predeceased his father John III (d.1557). Sebastian decided to launch a crusade against the Moors, and invaded Morocco against Philip's advice in June, 1578. At the Battle of the Three Kings, fought on August 13 near Alcázarquivir, the Moroccans killed Sebastian and destroyed his entire army, including much of the Portuguese nobility. Sebastian's successor was his celibate, 66-year-old great-uncle, Cardinal Henry. As the oldest male grandson of Emmanuel the Fortunate, Philip II believed that he was next in line for the throne and regarded the addition of Portugal to his empire as a legitimate defense of his dynastic rights. The other plausible candidates were Catherine of Braganza, daughter of the deceased infante, Duarte, and Antonio, Prior of Crato, the illegitimate son of Duarte's brother, Luis, who was also deceased.

Philip used the Portuguese-born diplomat Cristóbal de Moura to lay the groundwork for his succession, but when the Prior of Crato, who enjoyed a measure of popular support, seized Lisbon, it became necessary to occupy the country by force. The Duke of Alba, now 72, commanded the king's forces by land. The Duke of Medina Sidonia launched a second front in the Algarve, while a fleet commanded by Alvaro de Bazán, Marquis of Santa Cruz, supported both from the sea. The Spanish forces behaved with discretion, and Alba in particular showed that, when heresy was not an issue, he had retained his skills as a diplomat. The Portuguese, whose army had perished in Africa, could offer only minor resistance, and in April, 1581, the Cortes of Tomar acknowledged Philip II as Philip I of Portugal. It remained only to secure the Azores. To weaken Spain by keeping the revolt alive, Catherine de Medici, Queen Mother of France, financed an expedition to install the Prior of Crato in the islands. Santa Cruz destroyed the French fleet in July, 1582, and in 1583 captured Terceira, the last stronghold of resistance. The Azores, an important mid-Atlantic base and place of refuge for the treasure fleets was now under Spanish control as well.

Philip's policy in Portugal followed the model established in Italy. He promised to uphold existing liberties and privileges, and decreed that the Portuguese would continue to administer the realm and its overseas empire according to their own institutions. When he returned to Spain in

February, 1583, he established a Council of Portugal, and named Archduke Albert of Austria as viceroy. Albert was the brother of Philip's fourth and last queen, Ana of Austria, who died in 1580 after bearing him four children. Philip treated Albert as a son, and would entrust him with even greater responsibilities throughout the reign. Because the Portuguese, like the Italians, were for the most part good Catholics with a functioning church and an inquisition of their own, Philip could afford to be gracious. In 1591–1592 he showed similar restraint in subduing a revolt in Aragon. Social tension and resentment of Castilian dominance forced the king to restore order with a force of 12,000 men, but he held reprisals to a minimum and ordered that most of the traditional Aragonese *fueros* remain intact. Aragon did not rebel again, and Portugal remained within the empire until 1640.

Portugal's overseas possessions included Brazil, the only part of South America that Philip did not yet possess, together with far-flung colonies in Africa, Asia, and the Spice islands. Although the Portuguese Empire was vast, its contribution to Philip's revenues would be minor. Most of the colonies were little more than heavily fortified trading posts, expensive to maintain and dependent upon fleets that often suffered appalling losses at sea. Profits from the trade in spices, silks, and African slaves remained important to the Portuguese economy, but there was no surplus to share with Spain which now had to assume the burden of the Portuguese empire's defense. Portugal's overseas empire would one day become a strategic liability. For the moment, however, its annexation improved Philip's strategic position in the North Atlantic by providing him with Lisbon, a secure, deep water Atlantic port that could accommodate enormous fleets. It also gave him the Azores, and 12 fighting galleons, ten of them operational. This shift in the balance of power occurred just as the revolt of the Netherlands was becoming a generalized European conflict.

WAR WITH ENGLAND AND FRANCE

As Farnese began his re-conquest of the southern Netherlands, Philip outlawed William of Orange. Four years later, on July 10, 1584, Orange was shot to death at his home in Delft by an assassin. Now leaderless, and with Farnese advancing inexorably through Flanders and Brabant, the Netherlanders sent missions asking for help to Henry III of France and Elizabeth of England. Henry III could do nothing for them. Philip had always funneled support to the French Catholics led by the Duke of Guise and his brother, the Cardinal of Lorraine. New supplies of money and an able Spanish ambassador (Bernardino de Mendoza, son of Charles V's master of the galleys) now induced the Guise to form the Catholic League, a movement which took arms against the king in March, 1585. Henry, deeply unpopular with Huguenots and Catholics alike, submitted to the League's demands in June, leaving Paris and much of the northeast in the hands of Philip's friends.

The League's success, although temporary, removed the threat of French intervention in the Netherlands but increased the danger of war with England. Anglo-Spanish relations had been deteriorating for two decades. Elizabeth and her counselors had feared, even before the Ridolfi plot, that Spain planned to depose her in favor of her Catholic cousin Mary Queen of Scots. English support for the Netherlandish rebels, albeit sporadic and not especially helpful, reflected their concern that the Low Countries might serve as the staging point for an invasion. At the same time, pressure from England's maritime community together with the queen's own piratical instincts had resulted in destructive raids on Spain's American colonies. Philip began to think that war with England was inevitable. When Santa Cruz proposed the construction of an invasion fleet in 1583, the king did not immediately agree, but ordered the construction of nine new galleons nevertheless.

England's intelligence service, headed by Sir Francis Walsingham, was well aware of these developments. Elizabeth banned all trade with the Netherlands, and Philip responded by seizing English shipping in Spanish ports. Tensions increased because Elizabeth felt both threatened by Spain and isolated by the success of the Catholic League in France. When Farnese took Antwerp in August, 1585, she decided to send an expedition of 6000 men under the Earl of Leicester to establish garrisons at Flushing, Brill, and Rammekens. This was ostensibly to help the Dutch, but her main purpose was to occupy ports that might be used as bases by a Spanish invasion force. At the same time she sent out a fleet under Sir Francis Drake that sacked the Spanish ports of Vigo and Bayona, ostensibly to release the embargoed English ships. Drake then went on to raid the Cape Verde Islands, and sailed off to the Caribbean to attack Santo Domingo and Cartagena.

These actions exhausted Philip's patience without producing strategic results. His officials began to assemble a massive fleet in the harbor of Lisbon for the invasion of England. Bad luck and bad management dogged the Armada from the beginning. Santa Cruz proved to be better at fighting than at management. Endless problems with victualing and armament, compounded when Drake attacked Cádiz in the spring of 1587, caused delays and delays caused desertions. Early in 1588, an epidemic of typhus carried off many of the men who remained, including Santa Cruz. Philip replaced him with the very reluctant duke of Medina Sidonia, an able manager with no fighting experience at sea. Storms further delayed the fleet's departure, and it was not until July 29, 1588, that the Armada at last reached English waters.

Catastrophe followed. The basic reason for the Armada's failure was the king's faulty strategy. He ordered Medina Sidonia to take the fleet up the Channel to Calais, where he was to cover the crossing of a force assembled on barges in the Flemish ports by Farnese, now duke of Parma. How he could do this without first neutralizing the English fleet and without an effective means of communicating with Parma remained unclear. At least two of the leading Spanish commanders wanted to blockade the English fleet in its narrow anchorage at Plymouth or try to fight it as it came out, but Medina Sidonia felt that he had to follow the king's orders. He sailed directly to Calais, allowing the English fleet to slip out behind him and take a position to windward from which they could attack or withdraw at will. Before Parma could embark his men, the English used fire ships to force the Armada out of its anchorage, and then engaged the Spanish in a long-range gunnery battle off Gravelines. The English ships outgunned the Spanish, but did not come close enough to do real damage. The Spanish, fighting to leeward, could not close and board as they would have preferred. Tactically, the battle revealed that neither power yet understood how to fight a large fleet action in the age of gunpowder, but strategically, Gravelines was an English victory. It prevented the rendezvous with Parma and forced the Armada to return to Spain by sailing north around Scotland and Ireland. Storms on those inhospitable coasts destroyed at least a third of the ships with great loss of life.

Philip, who before the Armada had answered all objections to his plans by insisting that God would support the Spanish cause, now conceded that providence was inscrutable and began to rebuild his fleet, beginning with the construction of 12 new galleons known as the Twelve Apostles. This program marked the true beginning of a modern Spanish navy. He saw no reason to alter his policies, but the failure of the Armada proved more damaging than he may at first have thought. In France, Spain's defeat temporarily discredited the Catholic League, allowing Henry III to regain Paris. There he arranged the murders of the Guise brothers and designated Henry of Navarre, leader of the French Huguenots, as his successor. When Henry III was himself assassinated in 1589, the Catholic League revived only to be defeated by Navarre at the battles of Arques (September 14, 1589) and Ivry (March 14, 1590).

With the Protestant Henry of Navarre now poised to become king of France, Philip intervened to salvage what was left of his French policy and protect the Netherlands from a possible Huguenot invasion. He ordered Parma to invade France. The duke entered Paris on September 30, but the invasion weakened the Spanish cause in the Netherlands. The Armada's enormous cost—perhaps 10 million ducats—plus the cost of invading France meant that little money remained for the garrisons in Flanders. Parma had consolidated his hold on the ten southern provinces and much of the northeast, but made no further gains after 1588. Encouraged by the Armada's defeat and Parma's lack of money, the seven northern provinces reconstituted themselves as a free republic with William's son, Maurice of Nassau, as its stadholder. Parma thought the situation serious enough to suggest peace with the rebels in November, 1589. He still held Groningen, Overijssel, Drenthe, and Gelderland, all nominal parts of the new Republic, and thought that if the Calvinists of Holland and Zeeland were allowed the right to worship privately, they might once again agree to Spanish rule. He was probably wrong, but Philip summarily rejected the proposal on religious grounds. He would make no compromise with heresy.

The diversion of Spain's limited resources to France left the king's army in Flanders unpaid and increasingly mutinous. When Parma died in 1592, Spanish rule in the Netherlands once again descended into temporary anarchy, and the Dutch (as they may now be called) launched a successful campaign to regain their provinces in the northeast. In a moment of weakness, Philip actually reconsidered Parma's peace plan of 1589, but it was too late. The Republic of the Netherlands had assumed much of its modern shape.

The news from France was equally bad. The pragmatic Henry of Navarre converted to Catholicism, and in 1594 became Henry IV of France. His new faith did not prevent him from invading Artois in 1595 and from concluding an alliance with the Dutch and English in 1596. Somehow, the divided and contentious government at Brussels managed to repel the French, and new Anglo-Dutch attacks on Cádiz and the Azores came to nothing. Philip responded to these provocations by launching another armada against England. Stronger than the first, it numbered no more than 120 ships, but included 24 galleons including six of the twelve *Apostles* built after 1589. Impatient, or perhaps inspired once again by faith in Providence, the king sent his fleet out into the storms of autumn. On October 18, a gale in the Bay of Biscay destroyed 30 of the ships, including six galleons, and forced the rest to retire to Corunna and El Ferrol. A month later, the king declared his third state bankruptcy. Incredibly, the surviving vessels of the 1596 armada, refitted and reinforced by an additional 40 ships, set sail again for England in October, 1597. Once again, stormy weather forced it to return to port, this time with far fewer losses and casualties than before.

For more than 40 years Philip II had defended his faith and his patrimony with unwavering pugnacity. His policies had preserved most of the empire he inherited from his father without, however, halting the spread of Protestantism. Even this limited success had been bought at a terrible price. Between 1590 and 1597 the Army of Flanders alone had consumed more than 40 million florins (20 million ducats). Total expenditures, most of them on war, probably averaged 12 million ducats per annum, or about 130 percent of crown revenues. This was actually an improvement over the 1570s when expenditures amounted to more than 140 percent of revenues. The change did not, however, arise from more careful spending but from the introduction of a massive new levy on Castilian taxpayers called the *millones*. It was not enough. For the government, bankruptcy had become a way of life. The periodic repudiation of asientos in favor of juros had reduced the government's overall debt, but by 1598, Castile's obligation in juros alone amounted to 100 million ducats. Spain was destroying itself to save its empire. In an even more terrible irony, the nation whose rulers sought above all else to preserve its *reputación* had become the victim of a "Black Legend" that persists today.

THE BLACK LEGEND

The journalist Julián Juderías coined the term in the early twentieth century to describe what he and many others regarded as a pervasive tendency among foreign writers to describe Spain—and Spaniards—as uniquely cruel, intolerant, and ignorant. His accusation struck a chord among Spanish intellectuals and produced a modest literature that crested, with Anglo-Saxon contributions, during the early 1970s. Most of those who wrote on the subject agreed that Dutch and English propagandists had produced a large body of writings in the late sixteenth and early seventeenth centuries that portrayed Spanish behavior in Europe and America in the worst possible light. Lurid accounts of such genuine atrocities as the sack of Antwerp worked up popular enthusiasm for war against Spain. Translations of Spanish works on the conquest of the New World were mined for crimes against the Indians and illustrated with memorable engravings by

Theodore de Bry and other artists. In what is perhaps the greatest irony of all, the most effective of these pieces were originally written as part of the campaign by Las Casas and his supporters to protect the Indians from further mistreatment. As part of the Elizabethan campaign against Spain and the Catholic Church, the martyrologist John Foxe contributed vivid tales of Protestant suffering at the hands of the Inquisition in his *Actes and Monuments*. Profusely illustrated in many of its editions, it would long be the best-selling book in English after the Bible.

Literally hundreds of anti-Spanish publications appeared in English, Dutch, French, and German in the sixteenth century. New editions, and new works restating old accusations, would appear in the Thirty Years' War and on other occasions when it seemed useful to stir up anti-Spanish sentiment. Given the pervasiveness of such material, it is not surprising that the authors of scholarly histories absorbed anti-hispanism and transmitted it to later generations. Writers of the French Enlightenment seized upon these works when they attacked what they regarded as superstition, and used Spain as their primary example of clerical bigotry and repression. In the spirit of the enlightenment, travel writers throughout the nineteenth century portrayed the country as a primitive, if sometimes charming, backwater. Others were less tolerant. John Lothrop Motley's otherwise great history of the Dutch Revolt (1855) preserves the Black Legend with a vengeance, as does much work by his Dutch and German contemporaries. Some of their bias was inspired by Protestant liberalism, but it also reflected the sources available to nineteenth-century scholars. All of this and more was revived by publicists and entered American popular culture at the time of the Spanish–American war. In Latin America, the nativist movement known as *Indigenismo* developed a Black Legend of its own in the early twentieth century.

The Black Legend has lost some of its force today, in part because much of the literature on which it was based is no longer widely read, but mainstream scholarship has changed as well. A modern willingness on the part of non-Spaniards to look more closely at their own national myths has revealed that other imperial powers behaved as badly as Spain, and that, in terms of good intentions, no other nation exceeded Spain in its efforts to secure a measure of justice for its new subjects. The fact that those efforts often failed casts more doubt on the morality of colonialism as a whole than on the character of the Spanish people. Pockets of anti-Spanish feeling, of course, remain. In the United States, the old stereotypes perpetrated by the Black Legend may be partially responsible for hostile attitudes toward Latin Americans, but in general it has become difficult for most people to relate them to the prosperous, sophisticated Spain of today. This was not the case in the age of the Habsburgs. The hostility generated by the policies of Philip II and by the misdeeds of his troops would bring endless difficulties to his successors and greatly hamper their sporadic attempts to make peace.

THE "*PAX HISPANICA*"

As Philip II approached the end of life, at war with France, England, and the Netherlands and with his finances in tatters, necessity forced him to reconsider his policies. In May, 1598, he concluded the peace of Vervins with France. Then, in his will, he left the southern Netherlands, not to his son Philip, but to his daughter Isabella Clara Eugenia. She in turn was to marry her cousin, the Archduke Albert, who had served as governor-general of the Netherlands since 1596 after his successful tenure as viceroy of Portugal. When Philip died on September 13, 1598, the Netherlands therefore ceased to be ruled by Spain, at least in theory. After their marriage in April, 1599, the Archdukes as they were called, ruled jointly over the ten southern provinces. They were not supposed to make war or peace without Spanish consent and remained dependent on Spain for a large part of their military budget. The traditional system of government inherited from Charles V would be retained.

The death of Philip II therefore left the Netherlands divided in two parts: the Republic of the Netherlands, whose independence would not be recognized by Spain until 1647, and the Spanish Netherlands, the provinces that would one day become Belgium. Under the Archdukes it once again became the center of a vibrant and fundamentally Catholic culture. Philip's 20-year-old son, Philip III, inherited the remainder of the Spanish empire. The new king has often been portrayed as a weakling dominated by his *valido*, the duke of Lerma (the word can be translated as either "favorite" or "prime minister"), but this judgment is not entirely fair. At least in the early years of the reign, Philip tried to control foreign policy while Lerma concerned himself with domestic affairs. The new king's declared policy was that of his father: war with England, recovery of the rebellious Dutch provinces, and above all, no compromise with heretics or Muslims. He failed, however, to achieve any of these goals.

In the last years of his reign, Philip II had narrowed the circle of his advisors until in the end most of his decisions were made in company with the *junta de noche*, an unofficial group of like-minded courtiers who generally met at night. His son consulted as broadly as possible, reviving the Councils of War and State, and seeking advice from the nobility as a whole. He did not, however, set priorities or merge the views of his councils into a coherent strategy. Moreover, Philip III soon found that the interests of the Arch-dukes were not his own. They and most of their subjects wanted peace at almost any price. Without consulting Madrid, they made diplomatic over-tures to the English in 1600, and in 1601 suggested to the Dutch that the king might tolerate Protestantism in return for peace. The response was understandably cautious. Archduke Albert's conduct of the war was equally problematic. The Army of Flanders failed to defeat Maurice of Nassau at the battle of the Dunes in 1600, and Albert's interminable siege of Ostend, although it prevented an invasion of Flanders, allowed Maurice to besiege Reinburg and threaten Brabant.

Despite Philip III's belligerent rhetoric, his conduct of foreign affairs therefore remained, as his father's had been, essentially reactive. In the first five years of his reign he launched unsuccessful attacks on Ireland and Algiers and was forced to intervene on behalf of the duke of Savoy, whose long-ago annexation of Saluzzo provoked an abortive French inva-sion of northern Italy. Saluzzo was one of a chain of territories that protected Milan, the strategic center of Spain's European empire. No Spanish king could ignore such a threat. Fortunately, Henry IV did not really want a confrontation with Spain, and at the Peace of Lyon (1601), he recognized Savoy's claim to Saluzzo in return for Savoyard lands on the west bank of the Rhone. Milan was safe, at least for the moment, but Savoy's loss was in itself a blow to Spain's strategic interests. It reduced the Spanish Road (the overland route that connected Flanders to Italy), to the narrow Val de Chézery which could be closed by France at any time.

By 1606, Spain was again bankrupt and the Army of Flanders had, for the fortieth time since 1588, mutinied for lack of pay. The 1590s had been a time of economic depression in Castile. Meager harvests, apparently caused by climate change that also affected Aragon, Naples, and Sicily, made Spain's European empire ever more dependent on expensive grain imported from the Baltic by way of Amsterdam. Taxes, notably the *millones*, an excise tax on foodstuffs imposed in 1590 and increased in 1596 and 1600 imposed fur-ther hardships, especially for the poor. Episodes of the plague, culminating in the terrible epidemic of 1599–1600, brought an end to the population increases of the sixteenth century, and launched Castile on a century of demographic decline. The only bright spot on the horizon was that after Elizabeth I of England died in 1603, her successor, James I—as impover-ished by war as the Spanish—made peace with Philip in the following year.

To Philip, and to the duke of Lerma, who now took a belated interest in foreign affairs, it seemed that only peace with the Dutch could prevent financial collapse. In 1609, the two sides agreed to a 12-year truce that tacitly, if not formally, recognized Dutch independence. More ominously, it did nothing to restrict Dutch activities in the East or West Indies, nor did it require the Dutch to raise their blockade of Antwerp by opening the Scheldt estuary to Spanish trade. The resulting truce has been called the *pax hispanica*, but peace remained largely an illusion.

Spain needed peace, but to most of the empire's officials at home and abroad, the Twelve Years' Truce seemed both disgraceful and dangerous. They believed not only that it harmed the empire's vital interests, but that by weakening Spain's reputation it would create a domino effect fatal to Habsburg power. Worse yet, the *pax hispanica* saved little if any money. The Army of Flanders required a subsidy of 4 million florins per annum even in peacetime, and although the Dutch generally honored the truce, the years from 1609 to 1618 were far from peaceful, especially in Italy.

Of all Milan's outer defenses, the marquisate of Montferrat was perhaps the most important. Its great citadel of Casale dominated the upper reaches of the Po and presented a formidable obstacle to French invasions. In 1612 the death of Vincent I, Duke of Mantua, Marquis of Montferrat, and a long-time ally of Spain, precipitated a succession crisis that threatened to place Montferrat in the hands of Charles Emmanuel of Savoy. Charles Emmanuel, who had made a career of playing France off against Spain to his own advantage, asked for and received French help in the form of money and 10,000 volunteers to supplement his own army of annexation. If he succeeded, French access to Montferrat would pose a mortal threat to Lombardy. The Spanish governor at Milan held the allied forces at bay until the pope could arrange a truce in 1617, but the effort was long and very costly to Philip III.

Meanwhile, the Uzkoks, a group of Christian refugees from Turkish Hungary, had established themselves in imperial territory at Gradisca (modern Grado at the head of the Adriatic Sea). Assisted by pirates from the kingdom of Naples, they preyed upon Venetian shipping until, in 1615, the Venetians besieged their headquarters with help from England and the Dutch. The ruler of Gradisca, the Habsburg archduke Ferdinand of Styria, reached out to his Spanish cousin, Philip III. The Venetians had never been friendly to the Spanish presence in Italy, and their enlistment of Dutch and English heretics deeply offended the Spanish king. As king of Naples he had reason to support his subjects who already favored the Uzkok cause, but Ferdinand's offer of Alsace and two strategically important imperial fiefs in Italy, Finale (on the Ligurian coast between Genoa and France) and Piombino, proved irresistible. The resulting treaty between Philip and Ferdinand marked the beginning of a new and far closer relationship between Vienna and Madrid. Philip provided a million thalers for the relief of Gradisca and promised to support Ferdinand's candidacy to succeed his uncle Matthias as Holy Roman Emperor. Gradisca was saved, but in 1618, a new agreement between Ferdinand and Venice removed or executed the Uzkok leaders and guaranteed peace by establishing an Austrian fortress at nearby Zengg. Spain had once again spent its money on a questionable cause, and at the same time set the stage for a deeper involvement in the convoluted politics of central Europe.

THE THIRTY YEARS' WAR

As the Twelve Years' Truce approached its end, it became obvious that the Spanish empire needed a new strategy. By 1618, Europe was drifting into the generalized crisis that became the Thirty Years' War. The Dutch truce had proved so harmful to Spain that few observers thought the king would renew it without major concessions. While Antwerp suffered under a de facto commercial blockade, the Dutch had made serious inroads against the Portuguese empire in Asia and had greatly expanded their activities in the Caribbean. The Portuguese asked how Spanish rule could be justified if the king did not protect them against their commercial rivals. The Council of Indies complained of Dutch inroads in America, while the Council of Finance pointed out that the cost of maintaining the Army of Flanders would be little greater if its soldiers actually fought. All three bodies therefore opposed continuation of the truce.

The Duke of Lerma fell from power in the midst of this debate, albeit for reasons that had little to do with foreign policy. He was replaced by Don Baltasar de Zúñiga, an experienced diplomat who agreed that the existing agreement was untenable and thought that the international situation now favored Spain. England had been a de facto ally since 1605, while the assassination of Henry IV in 1610 had left France under a weak regency that seemed incapable of developing a consistent foreign policy. Neither would intervene to help the Dutch as they had done in the past. The Dutch, too, had become more belligerent. In August, 1618, Maurice of Nassau and the more extreme Calvinists triumphed over a moderate faction led by Johan van Oldenbarnevelt. Although more isolated than ever, the new regime was unlikely to concede anything to Spain.

While Spain and the Dutch debated the merits of the truce, tensions in the Holy Roman Empire reached dangerous levels. Confessional differences had been growing since the 1580s, in part because of the emergence of Calvinism as a major force in German politics. After the Imperial Diet of 1608, both Protestant and Catholic princes created formal unions that sought alliances with non-German powers. The Protestant Union in particular had signed treaties with England in 1612 and with the United Provinces in 1613. By 1618, the old and childless emperor Matthias neared death. His nephew, the devoutly catholic Ferdinand of Styria, was expected to succeed him and had already been designated king-elect of Bohemia by the Bohemian Diet, most of whose members were Protestant. Then, on May 28, a long-simmering dispute over the reversion of ecclesiastical properties prompted the Bohemian Protestants to revolt. Their representatives in the Diet threw two of Ferdinand's regents from a third-story window (the Defenestration of Prague) and set up a provisional government. In the course of the summer, three other Habsburg territories, Lusatia, Silesia, and Upper Austria joined the Bohemians and began the search for a new king. The Protestant Union pledged its support, and in May, 1619, its armies besieged Vienna.

To Zúñiga and his allies at the Spanish court, these actions threatened the survival of the Habsburg dynasty. Of the seven imperial electors, three were already Protestant. If the Bohemians elected a Protestant as they promised to do, the Catholics would be in a minority and sooner or later the Holy Roman Empire would fall into Protestant hands. Over the protests of Lerma's remaining supporters, Zúñiga convinced the king to abort an attack on Algiers and divert the money to Austria together with 7000 Spaniards from the army of Flanders. By this time Ferdinand had raised an army of his own. The Protestant siege of Vienna collapsed in June, but Moravia and Lower Austria joined the revolt, and on August 22, the expanded confederation offered the crown of Bohemia to Frederick, Count Palatine of the Rhine. Frederick was a firm Calvinist and already an elector in his own right. He was also the son-in-law of James I of England and Scotland. If he survived, he would have two votes out of seven in the Electoral College. The emperor Matthias had died in March and Ferdinand now moved quickly to secure the imperial office before Frederick could be confirmed as King of Bohemia. The electors, unaware of events in Bohemia, duly pronounced him Emperor Ferdinand II on August 28.

In the fall of 1619, Spanish policy moved decisively toward open war. The prospect of a Holy Roman Empire dominated by Calvinists and allied with the Dutch was intolerable. Oñate, the Spanish ambassador to Vienna, helped Ferdinand reactivate the empire's Catholic League by offering the Upper Palatinate to Maximilian of Bavaria if Frederick were defeated. James of England, influenced in part by Spanish diplomacy, refused to support his son-in-law, and Spanish agents at the Turkish court convinced the sultan to drop his support for Bethlen Gabor, the Calvinist ruler of Transylvania who had conquered Habsburg Hungary in November. By the following spring, Frederick's support in the Protestant Union had dwindled as the Lutheran princes withdrew their support. They were beginning to fear Calvinists more than Catholics. Genoa, Tuscany, and the pope added to the 3.4 million reichsthalers already provided by the Spanish, and the stage was set for a Calvinist disaster.

In July, 1620, an imperial army invaded Upper Austria, while the Saxons marched into Lusatia. Finally on November 8, Frederick and the Bohemians went down to final defeat at the battle of the White Mountain. The immediate crisis ended, but Spain had not been idle. A detachment of 20,000 men from the army of Flanders occupied the Lower Palatinate, depriving Frederick of his homeland and securing Spanish control over the Rhine. A new Spanish Road that connected Italy with the Netherlands through the Rhineland was now secure. Meanwhile, Spanish and Imperial troops resolved the ongoing struggle for the Valtelline, the upper valley of the Adda that connects Lake Como to the valley of the Inn. The Valtelline had long been ruled by the Protestants of the Grisons. Its Catholic inhabitants rebelled in 1572, 1607, and 1618. In 1620, the Spanish and Austrians sealed off both ends of the valley, allowing the Catholics to rise up and kill the Protestants. The Spanish route from Milan to Austria was now secure as well.

When the Twelve Years' Truce expired on April 21, 1621, a new Spanish strategy was firmly in place. Philip III had died in March of the same year, leaving the government in the hands of Philip IV, aged 16, and Zúñiga. Archduke Albert died at Brussels in July. Zúñiga, who was old enough to have fought in the Armada of 1588, died in 1622, but his nephew, the Count (later Count-Duke) of Olivares succeeded him as *valido* and expanded upon his policies for the next 21 years. Gaspar de Guzmán, Count of Olivares, possessed inexhaustible energy. He also understood, perhaps better than most, that Spain's imperial and foreign policy was in the long run unsustainable for economic reasons, but in light of recent experience the one thing Olivares could not do was avoid war.

The strategy he inherited from his predecessors centered on alliance with Austria, control of northern Italy, and war with the Dutch. It would embroil Spain in almost every aspect of the Thirty Years' War and, eventually, in a disastrous confrontation with France. Few now believed that the Dutch provinces could be recovered, but Spanish policy makers still wanted to limit their depredations overseas and their ability to support the Protestant cause in Europe. Between 1621 and 1626 Olivares therefore tried to strike at the heart of the Dutch economy. The Republic had prospered by serving as an entrepot between inland Europe and the Atlantic world. Cloths and manufactured goods from Germany reached the markets of Amsterdam by way of the great rivers. Grain, timber, and naval stores from the Baltic were traded there as well, and transshipped to Spain and the Mediterranean. In what seemed an intolerable irony, Spain's European empire had in the process become largely dependent upon goods imported from its Dutch enemies. Olivares rebuilt the Spanish fleet, which had been sadly neglected under Philip III, and established a squadron of 70 ships at Dunkirk to disrupt the Channel trade. He then worked with imperial forces to secure a Spanish base in the Baltic and set the army of Flanders to secure the inland water routes between Holland and Germany—all without sacrificing the Spanish armies in Italy.

The new strategy achieved early success. In 1625, the best year for Spanish arms in decades, Ambrogio Spínola, the brilliant Genoese commander of the Army of Flanders, took the strategically important Dutch fortress at Breda. Genoa was rescued from a joint attack by France and Savoy, and a Spanish fleet recaptured the Brazilian city of Bahía from a Dutch expedition that had seized it in May of 1624. In England, Charles I succeeded his father, James, and launched a farcical attack on Cádiz in retaliation for his failure to arrange a marriage with Philip IV's sister, Maria, but fortunately for Spain, England's military capabilities had degenerated since the days of Elizabeth I. It looked for a time as though Spain was about to revive its ancient glories, but by 1628 the Count-Duke's strategy was in tatters. The failure arose in part from the fortunes of war, but its primary cause was that the Spanish empire no longer possessed the resources to achieve its strategic ends.

6

IMPERIAL DECLINE

In retrospect it is easy to criticize the empire's leaders for pursuing an expensive foreign policy with inadequate resources. They would have responded that their many enemies left them no choice, and they may have been right. Empires attract rivals even as they generate dissidents within, and as the Romans, Turks, British, and others have discovered, allowing an empire to unravel can create more problems than it solves. Having inherited his empire, Philip II and his successors felt obliged to sustain it. They may also have believed, at least in the beginning, that with crown revenues greater than those of any other European country they could succeed. Such illusions, if they existed, did not long survive.

Even after large-scale imports of American bullion began in the mid-sixteenth century, the kings of Spain depended primarily on tax revenues from Castile. The structure of the empire bequeathed to them by Charles V determined that nearly all of the money generated from their other European realms, including Aragon, Valencia, and Catalonia, would be spent locally. As we have seen, Castile was not naturally a wealthy country; its institutions alone made it relatively easy for its rulers to extract wealth. Economic and demographic growth under Charles V had masked the inherent fragility of the Castilian economy, as did the dramatic increase in bullion from the New World during the reign of Philip II. When Spanish harvests began to decline in the 1560s and 1570s, the danger signals were largely ignored. As the reign progressed, higher taxes, inflation, and decreased returns from agriculture produced a level of distress that, by the 1590s had become a crisis.

Under Charles V, *servicios* granted by the Cortes increased fourfold, in part to compensate for a decline in returns from the alcabala. Philip increased the rate of the alcabala (the *encabezamiento*) in 1561 and 1576, but the overall level of taxation could not be called excessive until the introduction of the millones in 1590. The millones, so called because it was expected to raise 8 million ducats in six years, did not at first specify how the towns should raise the money. When the Cortes of Castile agreed to increase the tax by a further 1.3 million ducats per year in 1596, it decreed that the new monies should come from excise taxes on essential foodstuffs. They expanded this regressive measure in 1600 by combining the levies into a grant of 18 millions to be raised over six years entirely from excises. The millones enabled Philip II to reduce his annual deficits during the 1590s, but did not eliminate them. It did, however, increase the suffering of the poor, and for the first time brought Castilian tax rates into parity with those in Naples or the Netherlands. The burden of these levies fell on the most productive elements of society: peasant cultivators, artisans, and merchants. When added to the ecclesiastical tithe and señorial dues, they could amount to half of a peasant family's total income. This is a rate comparable to that found in modern industrial societies, but for farmers in a semi-subsistence economy with little or no surplus wealth it caused real hardship.

Under Philip II, increased taxes coincided with a decline in grain production. Climate change may have been the primary cause because Naples and even Sicily, long the granary of Italy, experienced similar shortfalls in the same period. For the first time in its history Castile became a net importer of grain. At the height of the Dutch revolt Spain became increasingly dependent on wheat supplied from the Baltic by Dutch merchants.

Meanwhile, inflation raised prices and wages to levels that made Castilian goods uncompetitive in world markets. Monetarist explanations have held that inflation was created by the massive imports of bullion from America, but for Spain at least, this was only partially true. Under Charles V, when bullion imports had been relatively small, the rate of inflation was far higher than in the heyday of Philip II. Most observers at the time attributed this to the massive export of food, textiles, and hardware to America during the age of conquest. Andalusia experienced the most dramatic price increases as the bulk of local production went to provision the fleets, but the impact was nationwide. Inevitably, wages increased, though not at the same rate as inflation.

When bullion imports began to increase in the 1560s and 1570s, their impact was not a massive and straightforward increase in the amount of money in circulation because relatively little bullion remained in Spain. The crown's fifth went directly to pay for the armies and their expenses and to service the crown's debt, most of which was held by Italian, Netherlandish, and German bankers. When the crown periodically confiscated private silver and issued long-term juros to its owners, that bullion too found its way abroad, as did nearly all of the private silver used by merchants and artisans to pay taxes—an amount far greater than the crown's direct share from the treasure fleets. Vast sums paid for merchandise imported for Spanish or American use from northern Europe or to cover debt owed to the foreign bankers who financed much of Spanish trade. In other words, American bullion contributed to worldwide inflation in the sixteenth century, but its direct impact on Spain may have been less than on the economies of Italy or the Netherlands. Indirectly, of course, the flood of bullion raised the prices of the foreign goods on which Castile was becoming increasingly dependent, but Castile's economic decline had other roots as well.

Even before the crisis of the 1590s, high taxes and declining yields forced a growing number of Castilian peasants to abandon their villages and drift into the larger towns, looking for jobs or charity. There the church could still provide a measure of charity for displaced workers, but jobs were hard to find. The cities of both Old and New Castile had always depended largely on trade with the surrounding countryside. When agriculture declined, their fortunes declined as well. Cities like Segovia, Burgos, and Cuenca whose trade in wool and woolen cloths provided Castile's major export, found their northern markets disrupted by the Netherlands war. Italy provided an alternative until the collapse of the Italian wool market in 1584, after which the business declined dramatically. Faced with Castilian taxes, high wages, and unstable markets, wool merchants gave up and invested in real estate or in government juros. Entrepreneurs in other trades followed suit.

The resulting shortage of capital inhibited new investment in either agriculture or manufacturing. Increases in the alcabala and the introduction of the millones played their part, but distortions in the credit market may have been more important. An unforeseen consequence of the crown's fiscal policy was that its debt tended to absorb whatever capital was available. The high interest rates paid on its loans raised the cost of credit for other purposes while at the same time offering investors a better rate of return than they could expect on more speculative private enterprises. Wealthy Spaniards were coming to believe that a dry, harsh landscape and ever-increasing taxes placed Castilian products at a permanent disadvantage, even in local markets. To invest in government juros, which offered a secure rate of return of 5–10 percent seemed only prudent. Castilian manufacturing therefore declined even further, and Castilian bankers, who had at one time participated at least fractionally in large-scale government asientos, could no longer do so. The transfer of the money markets from the fair at Medina del Campo to Madrid at the end of the sixteenth century symbolized this shift in Spanish finance and marked the permanent decline of Old Castile as an economic center. For a time, Seville and Andalusia in general remained cushioned to some extent by the trade with America. Economic refugees from Old and New Castile migrated there in numbers during the 1580s and 1590s, but by 1620 the south's prosperity, too, had become something of an illusion.

By this time the population of Castile as a whole had declined, owing largely to a decrease in the marriage and birth rates. With little hope of a decent living from agriculture or industry, religious vocations increased dramatically, while laypeople postponed marriage and childbearing. Then, between 1596 and 1600, outbreaks of the plague killed perhaps 10 percent of the population. Demographic failure added to Castile's woes—and to the government's expenses—by increasing wages even further and reducing the number of men available for military service. Signs of distress were everywhere. The poor had become vastly more numerous, but even the rich suffered. The incomes of the great noble families had little more than doubled during a century in which the cost of living had risen fourfold. Most of them were now mortgaging their estates to preserve the standards expected of their class.

ATTEMPTS AT REFORM

The coincidence of economic distress with the failure of the armadas and other setbacks gave birth to a crisis of confidence that found expression in the literature of the age. *Desengaño*, or disenchantment with the empire's crusading ideals, coupled with something like despair seems to have been widely shared by all levels of society. Some, however, tried to seek solutions. The economic problems of Castile inspired a group of intellectuals known as *arbitristas* to propose reforms. Many of their ideas tended to confuse cause with effect. They believed, for example, that the number of grammar schools should be reduced because more people would then devote themselves to trade and agriculture rather than seek entry into the church, the professions, and government service. But when it becomes difficult if not impossible to earn a living in productive occupations, people pursue other courses. Some of them also tended to confuse morality with economics, and condemned such luxuries as the ruffed collars favored by courtiers in the age of Philip II without realizing that the demand for luxuries can in itself promote industry. At times they seemed to think that Spain's problems arose from such staples of the Black Legend as indolence and an unhealthy attachment to aristocratic values when in fact the behaviors they condemned came from rational economic choice. With few outlets for productive investment, the wealthy spent more on paintings, tapestry, and literary patronage. Abbots and bishops invested in new churches and monastic buildings, themselves filled in the baroque style with artistic treasures. This outraged the arbitristas, but helped make the seventeenth century the golden age of Spanish art and literature.

Other ideas, while reasonable in theory, proved impossible to implement. Everyone knew that the crown had to reduce its expenses, but no one knew how to do this without surrendering Spanish power and threatening the security of the empire. A better alternative was to strengthen the Castilian economy. New investment in agriculture and industry would, the arbitristas thought, increase revenues and reduce the kingdom's dependence on foreign imports. Investors disagreed. Investors also tended to ignore the arbitristas' demand for infrastructure improvements. The kingdom's roads were appalling, and few of its rivers were navigable. A scheme to open the Tagus between Toledo and Lisbon was actually begun in the 1580s, but ultimately abandoned. Seville never built a much-need bridge over the Guadalquivir, nor did it act to dredge the river when silting began to strangle the city's trade. The technology to complete these projects existed. They failed in part because of regional jealousies and in part because no one, least of all the government, possessed the capital to complete them.

Tax reform, too, was probably impossible, although most thinking Spaniards knew that it was necessary. In 1600, the crown still derived its ordinary revenues almost entirely from Castile. Roughly 2 million ducats per year came from the crown's share of New World bullion. Another 1.6 million came from concessions granted by the pope from Church revenues (the *cruzada*, the *excusado*, and the *subsidio*). The remainder came entirely from the taxpayers of Castile: about 2.8 million from the alcabala, the sales tax that dated from the middle ages, and another 400,000 from the *servicios* voted annually by the Cortes. Another 3 million came from the millones, the excise tax introduced in 1590 and increased in 1596 and 1600 that had effectively doubled the tax burden on Castilians. All of these taxes were regressive, striking squarely at the well-being of the poor and middle class. Taxes on land or other property were regarded as politically impossible. The nobles, including all those who bore a patent of *hidalguía*, remained tax exempt by law and had the political influence to protect themselves from any reform. Taxing them would in any case have accomplished little. Like Don Quixote, many of the *hidalgos* were already penniless while even the grandees had experienced decades of decline in the rents and fees from their estates and were now deeply in debt. A store of wealth remained, but once it had been taxed it would not be replaced.

The most logical scheme of all, to tax other portions of the empire to pay for the common defense, proved equally unrealistic. In 1599, the government of Philip III managed to extract 1.1 million ducats from the Catalan Corts. Five years later, Valencia contributed another 400,000, but Lerma achieved this only by spending so much in bribes that little was left for the crown. Early in his career Olivares suggested a "Union of Arms" in which the other kingdoms of the peninsula would contribute both men and money to the common defense. Years later, when the Count-Duke, out of desperation, attempted to implement such a plan, it led to revolts in Portugal and Catalonia.

Under Philip III, the problems of Castile continued to fester. The Pax Hispanica, to the degree that it existed at all, was an attempt to alleviate Spain's fiscal dilemma by reducing the costs of war, but in fact Lerma and Philip III had no real options available to them. Desperate to pay the crown's debts, they adopted the time-honored practice of devaluing the currency, and by so doing made matters worse. They authorized the minting of copper coins known as *vellón* as a substitute for silver in 1599, and had the same coins returned in 1603 to be stamped with double their original face value. By doing this, they could divert the crown's silver to the payment of troops rather than placing it in circulation. This was self-defeating if for no other reason than that future tax payments would necessarily be made in devalued vellón rather than silver, but the situation was desperate. The Cortes of Castile briefly stopped these machinations in 1607 by refusing their annual servicio unless the issuance of vellón was dropped, but the approach of war in 1617 forced the crown to resume the practice until 1626. Spain was now flooded with bad money.

There is much truth in the traditional picture of Philip III as ineffectual and Lerma as a prime exemplar of *desengaño*. Although a master of the black arts of patronage and factional politics, Lerma suffered from immobilizing bouts of depression and expended his best energies in enriching himself and his friends. The fact that Olivares, Lerma's temperamental opposite, achieved no more in reversing Spain's decline only demonstrates the depth of the empire's problems. In the first year of the new reign, with crown debt at an incredible 116 million ducats, Olivares established the *Junta Grande* to implement the theories of the arbitristas. On February 10, 1623, the committee published a list of 26 recommendations, the most important of which were the abolition of the millones and the establishment of *erarios*, or regional banks. The theory behind the banks was that they would free the crown from its dependence on the asentistas while providing a source of capital for investment in the economy. The scheme failed because Olivares wanted to fund them by having leading citizens subscribe 5 percent of their property. Those citizens, and their representatives in the Cortes, did not believe the banks would be profitable, but their most important objection reveals much about seventeenth century Castile. They wanted to conceal the extent of their wealth, not because it was great, but because they had become so poor. If their poverty were known, they would lose status in the community. The structure of society—they said—would be endangered.

The Count-Duke's attack on the millones failed as well. From the perspective of the Cortes and the urban elites it represented, there were no viable alternatives. More importantly, when the tax had been introduced in 1590, Philip II had secured the support of the Cortes only by granting that body the right to administer its collection. This gave the Cortes an unprecedented lever in negotiating with the crown on all sorts of issues. In addition, the millones secured the juros which had become a chief source of income for the townsmen represented by the Cortes. By attempting to establish the erarios and repeal the tax, Olivares provoked what might have become a constitutional crisis. Fortunately, he backed down in time. Other initiatives sponsored by the Junta Grande fared no better. An order to reduce the number of municipal officers foundered on the opposition of all whose family members depended on this form of disguised unemployment for their livelihood. Harsh sumptuary legislation was ignored during the celebrations that accompanied the visit of Charles, Prince of Wales, in 1623. Only the ruff vanished, replaced by a flaring collar known as the *golilla* which succeeded because it was adopted by Philip IV and therefore became high fashion.

The inability of metropolitan Spain to feed itself or to provide manufactured goods either for itself or its colonies created a vacuum that was quickly filled by the merchants of other countries. A ban on most foreign imports in 1623, following the renewed embargo on trade with the Dutch in 1621, did more harm than good. In theory, the ban would encourage a revival of Spanish manufacturing; in practice it raised prices, harmed the merchants of Seville and Spanish Flanders, and encouraged even more smuggling. The silting of the Guadalquivir River had made it increasingly difficult for large ships to unload their cargos in Seville. Goods were now off-loaded at San Lúcar de Barrameda or Cádiz and transported overland, in theory at least, to the Casa de Contratación for registration. The Consulado of Seville now connived openly with those who off-loaded silver at night and transferred it directly to northbound ships to pay for imported goods. The goods themselves either disappeared somewhere along the road to the Casa de Contratación or found their way into the holds of ships bound for America. According to an official estimate, 85 percent of the goods shipped to America in the flota of 1624 were contraband. Seville was, of course, desperate to protect its declining trade, but smuggling had serious consequences. Between 1610 and 1624 the crown's share of American bullion dropped by half while the overall volume of silver shipments appears to have remained roughly the same.

A conjunction of events in 1627–1628 revealed the failure of Spanish economic policies and almost brought the country to its knees. A poor harvest in 1627 added to the effects of protectionism and the minting of more vellón currency with a face value of more than 20 million ducats in the preceding five years caused runaway inflation. In September, the Council of Castile reacted by fixing prices and repealing the ban on foreign goods. Prices dropped sharply, but merchants who had paid inflated prices for their merchandise now withheld goods from the market rather than sell them at a loss.

The crown, meanwhile, had once again reached the limits of its credit and repudiated its debts. This time, however, Olivares limited the suspension of payments to Genoese bankers who held most of the asientos. He planned to shift the crown's future business to a consortium of Portuguese conversos who were willing to accept lower rates of interest in return for an edict of grace that would protect them from harassment by the Inquisition. At the same time he floated a scheme to "consume" the vellón coinage. The author of the idea was Gerardo Basso, the Milanese banker and copper importer who had been the chief advocate of *vellón* coinage in the time of Philip III. Basso and Olivares now sought to create *diputaciones*, or consortia, in ten major cities that would accept deposits of vellón at 5 percent interest for 4 years, after which they would return 80 percent of the principle to the depositors in silver. A 2 percent tax on income and capital would provide the basic funding. These proposals scandalized both the Cortes and the Council of Castile. To them, the new *diputaciones* were the old erarios writ new, and to place the crown's finances in the hands of men they regarded as Jews and heretics was unthinkable. The *diputaciones* failed. Instead, with understandable trepidation, court and council agreed in 1628 to devalue the vellón coinage by 50 percent. This helped to relieve pressure on the crown but it destroyed the personal fortunes of many who held the old coinage. The Portuguese bankers, however, became the new asentistas.

WAR WITH FRANCE

The failure to reform its economy left the empire ill-equipped for the struggles to come. From 1623 to 1627 imperial strategy had achieved a fair
measure of success despite the endless problems of finance. By 1628, however, the crown was 2 million ducats short of the funds needed for the years'
campaigns. Then, in September, the Dutch admiral Piet Heyn caught the
treasure fleet from New Spain at anchor in Matanzas Bay, Cuba, and seized
its treasure. The captured bullion enabled the Dutch to launch a new offensive against the Army of Flanders. In another military reversal, Spain's hope
of a base in the Baltic died when the imperial general Wallenstein failed to
take Stralsund. More significant in the long run was the development of
a new Mantuan war that drained Spanish resources. Yet another dynastic
crisis gave Mantua and Montferrat to the duke of Nevers, a member of the
French branch of the Gonzaga family. To protect Milan, Olivares ordered a
siege of the almost impregnable fortress of Casale, hoping that the French
would be too preoccupied with their own siege of rebellious Huguenots at
La Rochelle to intervene. La Rochelle, however, surrendered at the end
of 1628, and in 1629, Louis XIII invaded Italy and forced the Spanish to
abandon the siege. The Mantuan War ground on for another two years, but
by then Spain's attention had turned to a new threat in the north. Swedish
intervention on behalf of the German Protestants emboldened the Dutch to
seize a number of towns along the water line, the most important of which
was Maastricht, which fell on August 23, 1632. Spain had to detach troops
from its defense of the Palatinate against the Swedes, but the death of King
Gustavus Adolfus at Lützen in November blunted the Swedish offensive.
A series of imperial successes beginning with the capture of Breisach in 1633
and culminating in the victory over the Swedes at Nördlingen on September
6, 1634, convinced the Lutheran princes to sign the Peace of Prague (May
30, 1635) and to join with the emperor in hunting down those Calvinists
who still refused to abandon the Swedish alliance.

At this point France declared war on Spain. The French government had
emerged from the problems of Louis XIII's regency, and since 1624, had
fallen increasingly under the influence of Louis's chief minister, Cardinal
Richelieu. Richelieu and the king were determined to oppose what they
saw as a Habsburg consortium that surrounded them on two sides. After
the defeat of the Huguenots at La Rochelle, they felt free to adopt a more
aggressive policy. Its first objectives were to secure their eastern borders
by neutralizing Savoy (hence the Mantuan War) and Lorraine, and by
enforcing a French protectorate over Alsace. Spanish distraction during

the Swedish intervention had helped them to achieve these goals. Richelieu had also supported the Swedes with large infusions of cash. Now the Peace of Prague confronted France with the prospect of a united empire allied with Spain and unmolested by northern invaders. Louis and Richelieu had no desire to become involved in the military quagmire of central Europe, but thought that if Spain could be defeated, the Austrian Habsburgs would cease to be a threat. The French army, however, lacked the training and experience built up by Spain over more than a century of warfare. The army of Flanders easily defeated a Franco-Dutch invasion of the Spanish Netherlands, and in 1637 invaded France, advancing to within 80 miles of Paris. Had a planned invasion of Languedoc taken place at the same time, France might have been forced to make peace. But time was running out for Spain.

The next campaign season brought a French counterattack on Fuenterrabía, the great fortress that guarded the western flank of the Pyrennees. The siege failed, but far away in Germany, the French army managed to retake Breisach after a long siege. France already controlled Alsace, Lorraine, and Savoy. With the loss of Breisach, Spain's land route to the Netherlands—long threatened—was now closed. Only by establishing naval superiority in the Channel and North Sea could Spain maintain communications with Brussels and supply the Army of Flanders. In 1639, Olivares decided to mount a new offensive by sea. His government had rebuilt the fleet, and now had 24 ships at Cádiz and 63 at Corunna. Others from Naples and Cantabria brought the total force up to the level of the 1588 Armada, although the new fleet carried more guns. He ordered its commander to clear the Biscayan Coast of French marauders before destroying the Dutch fleet in the Channel. Spanish diplomacy had neutralized the England of Charles I, and for once, the weather cooperated. The Dutch, unfortunately did not. After making contact with a Dutch squadron in September, the Spanish took refuge in the Downs, a broad anchorage off the English coast near Deal. There, on December 21, the Dutch destroyed most of the Spanish fleet.

THE CATALAN AND PORTUGUESE REVOLTS

For nearly two decades, the Count-Duke of Olivares had preserved the physical integrity of the empire by measures that became increasingly desperate with the passage of time. When reform failed, he—like his predecessors—sold offices, confiscated private silver shipments at Seville,

and manipulated the currency. Castile's economy and its population continued to decline. The quality of leadership declined as well. By the 1630s,
Olivares was lamenting what he called *la falta de cabezas* (lack of leaders) and
the indifference of the nobles to public service. It is true that the decade
produced no one to rival the military leaders of the past, but the fault was
at least in part his own. From the beginning of his tenure, he had circum-
vented the councils by governing through juntas composed largely of his
personal retainers and tried to manage everything himself. As the years
passed, the stress of office showed itself in rude and eccentric behavior that
alienated the nobles and drove many of them to refuse commissions and
eventually to abandon the court entirely. His bullying tactics and penchant
for micromanagement had in effect alienated much of Spain's governing
class. Now without money or trustworthy associates, his situation was clearly
desperate. Not knowing where to turn, Olivares tried to revive the Union
of Arms, and by so doing provoked open revolt.

Catalonia had long resented what it saw as Castilian domination. Aragon
and Valencia, although supposedly poorer, had raised modest sums for
imperial defense, but for 30 years the Catalan Corts had contributed nothing whatever. As the campaign season of 1639 loomed, Olivares hit on the
idea of invading France from Catalonia, thinking that this would force the
Catalans to participate in the war. The French anticipated him by besieging
Salses. With French troops on Catalan soil, the viceroy Santa Coloma, himself a Catalan, managed to recruit some Catalan troops, but most of them
deserted as the siege dragged on into winter. An angry Olivares responded
by suspending the *fueros* of Catalonia in all cases involving the war. In the
end, it was a largely Castilian army that forced the French to abandon the
siege on January 6, 1640, but the mood of the Catalans had grown more
poisonous than ever. Olivares made matters worse by quartering his troops
in Catalonia and calling a meeting of the Corts to change the constitution. In
the face of widespread protests, he then arrested one of the Catalan leaders,
the *diputat* Francesc de Tamarit, and launched an investigation of another, a
fiery canon of the cathedral of Urgel named Pau Claris.

By this time, the discontent had developed a social dimension. Peasant
mobs attacked the Spanish soldiers. On May 22, they marched on Barcelona
and freed Tamarit. Two weeks later, an urban mob murdered Santa Coloma,
who was widely hated as a traitor to Catalan interests. Belated attempts to
conciliate the rebels failed, and on January 23, 1641, Pau Claris proclaimed
the formation of the Catalan Republic under French protection. Richelieu
had of course been working with the rebel leadership for many months,
and a French army had by this time organized the defense of Barcelona. On

January 26, the marquis of Los Velez justified Olivares's low opinion of the Spanish nobility by engaging and then retreating from the Franco-Catalan forces at Montjuich. Catalonia would remain independent of Spain, if not of France, for the next 11 years.

The Portuguese revolt began when Olivares demanded that Portuguese troops commanded by Portuguese nobles help to suppress the troubles in Catalonia, but dissent had been brewing for several years. Spanish rule, although benign, had never been popular. Olivares made matters worse by tinkering with the government's structure and making periodic attempts to inveigle the Portuguese in his proposed Union of Arms. Believing that the viceregal system had collapsed under Philip III, he introduced a triumvirate of governors that proved equally unsatisfactory. Neither they nor the viceroys could extract an annual grant from the Portuguese Cortes. After 1631 the real government of the realm was controlled by Diego Suarez, Secretary of State for Portugal and his representative in Lisbon, Miguel de Vasconcelos. Both were Portuguese, but formed the nexus of a "Castilian" faction opposed by a "Portuguese" faction headed by the Duke of Braganza, a potential heir to the throne.

By this time, most Portuguese had come to believe that Spain could not protect their interests. Association with the Spanish empire had not prevented heavy losses in the far east, nor had it given Portuguese merchants as much access to Spanish markets in the Americas as they had hoped. Now it seemed that Spain was helpless in the face of Dutch threats to Brazil. Brazilian sugar, a commodity far more valuable in the seventeenth century than it is today, had become enormously important to the Portuguese economy. The Dutch, always alert to economic opportunity, had seized Bahía in 1624, only to be driven out by a joint Spanish–Portuguese fleet in 1625. In 1630, the Dutch captured Olinda and Recife. This time the Spanish did nothing. Other priorities intervened until 1634 when plans for a relief expedition foundered. Olivares could find no one willing to command the fleet and the disgusted Portuguese refused to help in recovering their own territory. When Spain finally did send an armada to Brazil in 1638, it remained idle for more than a year before being defeated by a much smaller Dutch force on January 12, 1640.

Long before this, Portuguese disgust with the political squabbling at Lisbon, Spain's failure to protect their interests, fear of the proposed Union of Arms, and what they perceived as royal neglect had reached dangerous levels. It is probable that Richelieu did his best to encourage dissent with promises of financial support as he had done in Catalonia. Thinking that a new viceroy of royal blood would neutralize Portuguese complaints of neglect and stabilize the government, Olivares arranged the appointment of the Duchess of Mantua, Princess Margaret of Savoy, a granddaughter of Philip II. He did not, however, abandon his campaign for the Union of Arms. In 1637, a desperate year financially, the Count-Duke tried to ignore the Portuguese Cortes and collect taxes on a regional basis. Riots broke out at Evora and quickly spread to the neighboring provinces of Algarve and Ribatejo. The government suppressed the incipient revolt in March, 1638 largely because Braganza and his followers refused to support it, but it was a portent of things to come. When Olivares ordered the Portuguese to Catalonia, Braganza, who had until now played his hand with great care, allowed his followers to begin plotting revolt. On December 1, they proclaimed him King John IV of Portugal and expelled Princess Margaret from the country. With the Castilian army then marching toward disgrace at Montjuich, Olivares could do nothing to intervene. Portugal, after 60 years as part of the Spanish empire, regained its independence. Its colonies, which Olivares had hoped to retain, soon declared their allegiance to the new king.

Perhaps surprisingly, the loss of Portugal and Catalonia did not lead to further secessions from the empire. In 1641, the government's agents discovered a plot that apparently aimed at creating an independent Andalusia with Portuguese and Dutch help. The details remain murky, perhaps because one of its leaders, the Duke of Medina Sidonia, was a kinsman of Olivares. The Count-Duke managed to curtail the plot while suppressing evidence that might have discredited his family. Six years later, in 1647, popular revolts broke out in Naples and Sicily. The Spanish viceroys suppressed them with the help of the barons, who, after some initial hesitation, decided that they had no desire to be governed by lower- and middle-class revolutionaries. At about the same time, rumors reached Madrid that Aragon and Valencia might cast their lot with Catalonia, but this, too, came to nothing. The conditions that had preserved Spain's European empire for more than a century still prevailed. Its various components remained steadfast in their localism and wholly incapable of supporting the grievances of the other kingdoms. Moreover, their elites continued to support the crown. This was partly class interest. They could rely on Spain to guard their privileges against social revolutionaries, but they also needed the viceroys to mediate their quarrels—no small matter in countries where the terrible rivalries that had encouraged Spanish rule in the first place continued unabated.

By this time, Olivares was gone, but not before he had promoted another catastrophic devaluation of the vellón coinage. The failure of his policies and his own eccentric and overbearing personality had long since alienated every important segment of Spanish society, and on January 17, 1643, the king at last dismissed him. On May 19, the Spanish infantry met defeat at the battle of Rocroi. The battle itself had few strategic consequences, but it demonstrated that after a century of military superiority, Spain no longer possessed a tactical advantage over the French. Olivares died two years later in disgrace.

SPAIN AFTER OLIVARES

The Count-Duke's successors, led by Philip IV who, after 22 years, now resolved to attend more carefully to the business of government, dismantled his system of administration by juntas and returned the councils to their ancient prominence. But the king's resolve to govern in person soon drowned in masses of paperwork. Luis de Haro, a nephew of Olivares emerged as the new *privado*, although he never claimed such a distinction, nor did he emulate his uncle's hectoring and autocratic ways. Affable and conciliatory, he managed the affairs of the empire until his death in 1661. The situation he inherited may have been dire, but developments in France and the Empire offered reasons for hope. Cardinal Richelieu, the guiding genius of the French government, had died a month before the fall of Olivares. Louis XIII died shortly thereafter, leaving his five-year-old son, Louis XIV in the care of an unpopular regency headed by Cardinal Mazarin. In Vienna, the new emperor, Ferdinand III, was taking the first steps toward ending the Thirty Years' War, an effort that came to fruition four years later with the peace of Westphalia.

After 80 years of struggle it began to appear that peace with the Dutch was now possible. With France temporarily neutralized and Charles I of England facing a revolution of his own, the Dutch lacked allies. Meanwhile, the Portuguese revolt had relieved Spain of responsibility for Brazil, long a major issue between the two countries. Spain's ambassador to the Netherlands, the count of Peñaranda, dropped his government's former demands for Catholic toleration and for the opening of the Scheldt, the estuary that provided Antwerp's access to the sea. He then leaked a secret offer from Mazarin that would have restored Catalonia to Philip IV in return for the Spanish Netherlands. This confirmation of the threat posed by France provided a further impetus to the Dutch, who agreed to the Treaty of Münster on October 24, 1648.

The Dutch Revolt was over, but the war with France continued. In 1652, the Catalans, who had found the tyranny of the French worse than that of the Castilians, offered little resistance when a Castilian army under the king's illegitimate brother, Don Juan José recaptured Barcelona. They reaffirmed their loyalty to Philip IV in return for a general pardon and a confirmation of their traditional rights. In 1656, the Fronde, an aristocratic rebellion against Mazarin's regency in France, provided an opportunity for peace, but this time the Spanish overplayed their hand and talks broke down. Three years later they were forced to negotiate at a disadvantage. In 1654, Oliver Cromwell, leader of England's regicide government, launched an attack on Spain's possessions in the Caribbean. The expedition failed in its major objectives, but managed to take Jamaica, then a poor and under-populated island which nevertheless offered England a base from which to threaten the treasure fleets. Spain reluctantly declared in war in February, 1656, but in September, Cromwell's general-at-sea, Robert Blake, seized two treasure ships containing over 2 million ducats in silver. In April, 1657, he destroyed the remainder of the treasure fleet at anchor in Santa Cruz de Teneriffe. No silver reached Spain for two years, and Haro had no choice but to make peace with France. The treaty of the Pyrennees (1659) was a humiliation. Spain gave up Artois as well as Cerdagne and Roussillon. The eldest daughter of Philip IV, Maria Teresa of Austria, married the 21-year-old Louis XIV.

Incredibly, peace with France allowed Philip IV to think again of recovering Portugal. In 1663 and again in 1665, Spanish invasions were ignominiously defeated by the Portuguese with French and English assistance. A new issue of inflated coinage funded the war and led to further economic instability in Castile. When the king at last died on September 17, 1665, his only surviving son, the four-year-old Charles II, succeeded him. Charles was the child of Philip's second wife, his niece, Mariana of Austria, and the sad victim of generations of royal inbreeding. His long list of physical and mental ailments, including seizures so violent that his subjects dubbed him Carlos the Bewitched after a politically inspired exorcism late in the reign, did not prevent him from surviving until 1700. Philip IV was well aware of his son's weakness. On his deathbed, he established a regency council or *Junta de Gobierno*, carefully chosen not only for competence, but—in a major departure from past practice—to provide representatives from Spanish kingdoms other than Castile. The Queen Mother, herself no model of political wisdom, ignored it and ruled with the aid of her Jesuit Confessor, Father Nithard, until 1669. Thereafter she relied upon her favorite, Fernando de Valenzuela, until he, too, was expelled in 1676–1677.

The Spanish government reached its nadir in the early years of Charles II. Neither he nor the Queen Mother could manage its affairs, and business was conducted almost entirely by the councils. Conciliar government had always been cumbersome. Without guidance from the top it achieved something like paralysis until the duke of Medinaceli became chief minister in 1680. Philip IV left behind a legacy of financial chaos and an American empire that, economically at least, had already drifted far from its Spanish moorings. Years elapsed before the first modest signs of recovery appeared in the peninsula. By that time Spain's status as the major world power was a distant memory.

AMERICA: THE DRIFT TO AUTONOMY

The decline in Spanish trade with the New World that began in the 1590s and the eventual decline in the king's share of American bullion reflected fundamental changes in the American economy. Recent scholarship has dispelled the idea of a seventeenth-century depression in the New World. The level of general prosperity and the level of bullion production fluctuated, but the overall trend appears to have been upward. The first reason for Spain's loss of trade with her colonies was the large-scale development of trade and manufacturing within the colonies themselves. The second was the growing importance of foreign merchants in both the American trade and in the economy of the peninsula. Spain's attempt to preserve its monopoly of colonial trade, in other words, had failed. It could not provide America with slaves or manufactured goods, and the sheer size of the empire made it impossible to exclude foreigners completely.

The loss of a great part of America's native population created labor shortages and reduced the value of Indian tribute to the crown, but the Indians had never been major consumers of European goods. Creoles consumed wheat, oil, and wine as well as luxury goods and manufactured items, and had in the early years of settlement purchased all of this from Spain. Andalusia had grown rich not only from provisioning the treasure fleets but from providing settlers with European foods. In time, however, the high cost of imports and Spain's inability to provide its colonies with manufactured goods encouraged creoles to develop European-style crops and industries of their own. They planted wheat and vineyards and sold their surplus locally or to the vast internal trade networks that developed to provide the mining districts with tools, cheap textiles, brandy, and (in Potosí) coca. Most of the mines were located in remote districts. Potosí, whose population at one point reached 120,000 people, was situated in a barren region 14,000 feet above sea level. Indians who worked under the *mita* were supposed to provide their own food, usually dried and frozen potatoes brought from their home villages. All other food had to be brought in from large farms on the coast that produced wheat, wine, and other products. Cheap textiles for the workers came from as far away as Quito on the backs of mules and llamas.

In Mexico, mine operators developed great estates or *haciendas* to provide meat and other foodstuffs for their workers. The shortage of Indian labor favored the establishment of large estates which, like the latifundia of ancient times, were for the most part self-sufficient, but luxuries for the owners and for the well-paid specialists who ran the mines and smelters had to be shipped from as far away as Mexico City. Sugar came from the coastal regions, tobacco from Cuba, and cacao from what is now Venezuela. Chocolate was becoming a universal indulgence with plantations around Guayaquil supplying the Peruvian market. Some of the Chinese silks and porcelains brought by the Manila Galleon were purchased by Americans. The rest was shipped to Spain in the treasure fleets where some was sold to Spanish consumers. Most, however, was transshipped at San Lúcar or Cádiz for sale in northern Europe, often without paying customs duties. Goods from France, Germany, and the Netherlands could be sent to America legally or illegally in the flota, but much was purchased illegally from Dutch or English merchants who defied the crown's regulations by trading clandestinely with Caribbean ports. Spain's chief export to the New World remained mercury from Almadén, but even that had to be supplemented on occasion by imports from Croatia.

The bullion that paid for nearly all of America's internal trade never reached Spain, nor did the massive amounts of silver shipped in the Manila Galleons. Exports of silver to Asia may have amounted to as much as 3 million pesos in some years. As with all trade figures from this period, exact amounts went unrecorded, especially after the Olivares regime, in an ill-advised attempt to cut its losses, tried to limit not only the Acapulco–Manila trade but the trade between Mexico and Peru. Most of the silver went to the Fukienese traders who controlled the trade between China and Manila, but the Viceroyalty of New Spain financed the galleons and subsidized the government of the Philippines out of its own revenues—also with bullion.

American bullion, of course, supported American governments. Metropolitan Spain contributed nothing, but this, too, reduced the volume of silver shipped to Seville. In the seventeenth century, the growing presence of foreign interlopers in American waters brought with it vastly increased government outlays for defense. In the time of Olivares, the European powers had taken advantage of his preoccupation with the

Continent to establish themselves on the American periphery. The English led the way with their colonies in Virginia and Massachusetts and with the settlement of St. Kitts, Barbados, Nevis, Montserrat, and Antigua between 1624 and 1632. The French followed with Martinique (1635), and the Dutch with St. Eustace and Curaçao (1630–1640). Even Denmark harbored its own colonial ambitions and settled St. Thomas in 1670. Only Cromwell's acquisition of Jamaica in 1655–1656 posed a strategic threat to Spanish interests, but all of the Caribbean colonies were intended not only to produce sugar for their home markets, but to serve as entrepots for the theoretically illegal trade with the Spanish empire. They also provided a refuge for pirates. Spanish weakness, chronic warfare, and changing alliances made the period from 1668 to 1688 the golden age of piracy. Pirates, themselves from every conceivable ethnic group, preyed without distinction on the shipping of all nations. A few, like the Welsh captain Henry Morgan, emulated the Elizabethans by sacking Spanish ports including Portobello and Panama. Others sailed around Cape Horn and raided the Pacific coast.

The cost of fortifying and, in some cases rebuilding, the targets of the buccaneers fell to the colonial governments. The *Armada de Barlovento*, or Windward Squadron, was also maintained at colonial expense. Intended for the Caribbean, the crown reassigned it for convoy duty or use in Spanish waters during most of the period from 1598 to 1672. Its attacks on Nevis and St. Kitts (1629), St. Maarten (1633), and Providence (1641) were mounted during the intervals between sailings of the flota. After 1672, it was again dedicated to it original purpose, largely in response to the depredations of Morgan. In the Pacific, the viceroys of Peru largely neglected the *armada de la mar de la sur* until a pirate attack on Guayaquil in 1687 inspired the merchant consulado to construct a small fleet at its own expense. It is a measure of Spain's inability to provide for its colonies that the ships for these squadrons were either purchased from the Dutch or built locally at yards in Havana and Guayaquil.

The massive growth of a quasi-legal trade with northern Europeans soon reduced the number and importance of the pirates. Much of the slave trade had always been lawful. Spain could not provide its colonies with African slaves, and until 1640 relied for its supply on asientos with Portuguese slavers. After Portuguese independence, the asiento was granted in succession to Genoese and Portuguese financiers resident at Seville and for a time to the city's Consulado. Because these people had no direct access to African slave markets, they subcontracted the business to Dutch and English merchants until 1685 when the asiento was openly granted to a Dutch financier. Spanish traders purchased their slaves from the English in Jamaica or the Dutch in Curaçao and sold them to planters in Venezuela, Cuba, and Vera Cruz.

Philip III had granted limited trading privileges at Seville to English and Hanseatic merchants in an effort to maintain supplies of grain, timber, and naval stores without having to rely upon the Dutch. English ships carried Spanish silver to the army of Flanders. They also carried it to London where English bankers provided bills of exchange to purchase goods from Holland, the Baltic, and France for resale at Seville. Textiles in particular were then sent on to America, often without formal registration or payment of customs. Fundamental change came with the great treaties that marked the end of Spain's predominance in Europe. Westphalia (1648) and the peace of the Pyrenees (1659) granted new and expanded privileges to the Dutch and French, and in 1667 these broader provisions were extended to the English as well. Basically, they granted foreigners the right to establish themselves as "nations" on Spanish soil with their own consuls and their own courts for resolving internal disputes. They could also, for the first time, use their own nationals as *corredores* or agents and, most important of all, gained the legal right to export their profits in silver to their home countries.

The result was a system that provided the Spanish colonies with needed goods and Western Europe with a flood of silver that was no longer channeled through the military system of the Spanish empire. The center of that system was Cádiz. The city occupies a rocky peninsula which in turn shelters a large harbor. The harbor provided anchorage for entire fleets, while its landward side, then relatively undeveloped, offered endless opportunities to smugglers. Because Spanish authorities typically allowed three or four days to elapse before an incoming cargo had to be registered, and because the treaties prohibited them from searching the premises of a foreign merchant, evasion of customs was simple. Gangs of *metedores*, headed by young men from prominent families who were therefore immune to prosecution, simply transferred goods and silver by night to other ships in the harbor or to the mainland.

It was of course necessary to provide a façade of legitimacy by registering at least some goods and paying duties upon them. From 1663 to 1713, the customs was farmed out to Francisco Baéz Eminente, a Portuguese of converso descent, and his heirs. To limit evasion and secure at least something for himself and the crown, he entered into private agreements with the various nations to reduce rates and limit inspections. The merchants, in effect, determined their own customs payments, but Spaniards benefitted as well. *Metedores* received handsome fees. Customs guards were bribed, and the Judges Conservator who supervised the entire system received handsome *donativos* from the proceeds of trade. These men tended to come from the highest levels of the Spanish bureaucracy and were nominated by the foreign nations they regulated. The crown, of course, knew of these practices, and periodically imposed *indultos* or general levies amounting to hundreds of thousands of pesos on the entire business community. *Indultos* were occasionally levied on ships as well.

The system of imperial trade that developed in the seventeenth century was in fact a practical adaptation to Spain's circumstances. Without industries or an agricultural surplus of its own, Spain's trade and that of her colonies necessarily fell into the hands of foreigners. The ingenious arrangements described above kept at least some of the profits in Spanish hands, but at considerable cost. Spain became increasingly irrelevant to the economic life of its colonies. By losing control of the bullion supply, the crown lost its ability to pay for war, and with it, its standing in international affairs. The empire survived for another century because its commerce had become essential to the other nations of Europe. The flood of American silver that fueled the unprecedented development of capitalism in England and the Netherlands had to be maintained at all costs, preferably while Spain shouldered the costs and responsibility of empire.

THE LAST YEARS OF THE HABSBURGS

Dynastic and governmental collapse in Spain coincided with the emergence of France as the dominant power in Europe. Louis XIV assumed full responsibility for the government of France when Mazarin died in 1661, and ruled for more than half a century with considerable skill and an infallible instinct for political theater. France became the political and cultural center of Europe with "the Sun King" as its visible symbol. More practically, Louis intended to secure his borders through the annexation of lands he regarded as historically French. These included the Spanish Netherlands which he claimed as the rightful inheritance of his queen. In 1667 he invaded the southern Low Countries, but was driven off by the Dutch with English and Swedish assistance. A second more successful war from 1672 to 1678 gave him parts of Luxemburg, Hainaut, and southern Flanders, together with Lorraine and the Franche-Comté. All except Lorraine had been part of the Burgundian inheritance of Charles V.

Spain may have lost the ability to defend its possessions in northern Europe, but it was not entirely helpless. The wars of Louis XIV enabled Spain and the Dutch Republic to formalize a relationship that had begun to develop even before the Treaty of Münster reopened the Spanish trade to Dutch ships. As the chief economic beneficiaries of the Spanish empire—and its chief creditors—the Dutch had a keen interest in its preservation. Dutch warships began to provide an escort for Spanish vessels in European waters. With the Treaty of the Hague (1673), the commercial alliance became a military pact. Spain's remaining troops in the Army of Flanders found themselves under the command of the Dutch stadholder, William, Prince of Orange. William was the husband of Mary Stuart, daughter of James II of England and a Protestant. When the Glorious Revolution of 1688 deposed James, Parliament recognized Mary as queen of England and her consort as King William III. Louis XIV now faced one of the greatest crises of his reign. In the War of the Grand Alliance, also known as the War of the League of Augsburg or the Nine Years' War (1688–1697), a Dutch, English, Austrian, and Spanish coalition fought the French to a standstill. The Treaty of Rijswick (1697) allowed Louis to retain his earlier conquests with the exception of Luxembourg, but a later agreement placed some of the most important fortresses in the Spanish Netherlands under Dutch control. To console Louis XIV, Spain had to cede the western portion of Hispaniola to the French, who developed it into the rich sugar colony of St. Domingue (modern Haiti).

The southern Netherlands remained at least nominally under Spanish rule for another 17 years, but it had changed greatly since the time of Philip II. The reduction in Spanish subsidies and the lack of direction from Madrid weakened the States-General and left provincial and municipal governments to fill the political void. Its cities, however, retained little of their former greatness. Heavy war taxation, the ongoing closure of the Scheldt, and Anglo-Dutch competition crippled their economies while leaving the countryside relatively prosperous even in the midst of almost constant warfare. The wars of Louis XIV, although bloody for combatants, were less harmful to civilians than those of the preceding age. Improved discipline and the logistical systems designed by Louis's ministers of war (and copied to some extent by the armies of William III), reduced looting and other forms of direct contact between soldiers and the general population. Some rural districts actually prospered by selling supplies to the armies. Others benefited when the breakdown of trade restrictions forced cloth manufacturers to leave the cities in search of cheaper labor. The great days of

Flemish cultural achievement had faded, but the society itself remained largely intact.

Spain's new relationship with the northern powers helps to explain another great paradox of the age. Despite the appearance of governmental paralysis under Charles II, the Spanish empire did not collapse. In fact its economy and that of metropolitan Spain slowly began to revive. The ministers who served Charles in his last years, notably the count of Oropesa and the marquis of Los Velez, demonstrated a tough, quiet competence that had long been needed. By 1675 the premium of silver over vellón had reached 200 percent. In 1680 the government was forced to devalue even the vellón minted since 1660 by half, producing a nationwide flood of bankruptcies and riots in the major cities. Tax receipts from Castile dropped, but the crown's ministers held firm. From 1677 to 1687 they also attacked the juros that consumed so large a proportion of the crown's income. By annulling much of their value, reducing the interest rates, and taxing the remaining proceeds at 15 percent the government added to the prevailing misery, but by the end of the reign inflation was under control, the economy was growing, and the king was solvent for the first time in memory.

Silver shipments from Mexico and Peru continued at a high level, although the government's share still amounted to only a small fraction of the total. There were even a few modest efforts at expansion overseas. Expeditions from Manila established the Marianas (formerly the Ladrones) as a Spanish colony between 1668 and 1685. In a demographic catastrophe that recalls the fate of the Canaries and West Indian islands two centuries earlier, the native Chamorros died or fled in great numbers, and by century's end only Guam and Rota remained populated. The new colony served primarily as a place for the Manila Galleon to take on food and water, supporting itself through the cultivation of tobacco, sugar, and native crops. Another expedition claimed the Carolines in 1686. These islands were placed under the government of the Marianas in 1696, but no effort was made to settle them until late in the nineteenth century. In North America, the French expeditions undertaken by LaSalle between 1682 and 1687 inspired the Spanish authorities to authorize the first circumnavigation of the Gulf of Mexico followed by the establishment of Texas as a province in 1691. The Texas garrisons proved unsustainable, but the permanent settlement of Pensacola in 1698 gave Spain an important base with which to counter French ambitions on the Gulf Coast and Lower Mississippi valley. These developments proceeded from local initiative with only nominal support from the crown.

On a broader scale, Catalans and Basques began to take a larger role in Spanish economic life, and the informal deregulation of trade seems to have benefited even Castile. In the Americas, improved access to European markets strengthened the economy. It certainly increased the wealth and political influence of the landholding and merchant elites, a development that would have important consequences in the century to come. In short, the government's inability to regulate commerce or even to protect parts of its empire without the help of foreigners may have profited its subjects even as it revealed Spain's eclipse as a military power.

7

THE BOURBONS

The death of Charles II on November 1, 1700 marked the end of the Habsburg dynasty in Spain and the beginning of a gradual but revolutionary transformation in imperial government. On his deathbed Charles staunchly resisted the influence of his Austrian queen and chose Duke Philip of Anjou, second son of the French dauphin and grandson of Louis XIV, to succeed him. The choice had been difficult and would lead to a world war of 12 years' duration.

When the War of the Grand Alliance ended with the Peace of Rijswijk in 1697, there were three potential candidates for the Spanish throne: Philip of Anjou, Prince Joseph Ferdinand of Bavaria, and Archduke Charles of Austria, second son of the Holy Roman Emperor. Louis XIV naturally favored the candidacy of his grandson, while Charles II's queen, Mariana of Neuberg and some members of the Spanish elite supported the Austrian claimant. The Dutch and English favored the Bavarian because the acquisition of Spain and its empire by either France or Austria would threaten the balance of power in Europe. Knowing that France was in no condition to fight another war, Louis XIV signed the First Partition Treaty (October, 1698), a compromise agreement with William III of England and his allies that would give Spain, the Spanish Netherlands, and Spain's American colonies to Joseph Ferdinand. Archduke Charles would get Milan. The rest of Spain's Italian possessions plus the Basque Country would go to the French dauphin.

Charles II, however, was determined to avoid the breakup of his monarchy and drew up a will giving the entire inheritance to Joseph Ferdinand. When the seven-year-old Joseph Ferdinand died in 1699, a second partition

149

treaty between Louis and William gave his inheritance to the Archduke Charles. Still unwilling to countenance the breakup of his empire and fully supported by his Council of State, Charles II wrote a second will in the days before his death that named Philip of Anjou as his sole heir. Louis XIV now realized that war was inevitable. Even if he honored the second treaty of partition he would have to fight the emperor and his maritime allies for Spain's Italian possessions. If he did not, he would still have to fight, but he might at least be able to place a Bourbon on the Spanish throne. With nothing to lose, he refused to exclude Philip from the French succession and in December, 1700, Philip of Anjou became Philip V of Spain.

When the 17-year-old king entered Madrid for the first time in April, 1701 he discovered, apparently to his surprise, that he commanded only a vestigial fleet and an army that was in the last stages of decay. Its 10,000 infantry and 5000 cavalry had obsolete equipment or none at all. The kingdom's fortresses were in disrepair, and the available military budget amounted to no more than about 3 million escudos. Spain was for all practical purposes defenseless. Alarmed, Louis XIV tried to support his grandson's succession by garrisoning Spanish fortresses in the Netherlands with French troops and sending an army to protect Milan. These actions convinced the English, Dutch, and Austrians that Louis still harbored aggressive intentions. They renewed the Grand Alliance in September, 1701 and declared war against France and Spain in May, 1702. Portugal and Savoy joined the Alliance in 1703.

When the War of the Spanish Succession ended in 1713, Spain and its American colonies remained intact, but the European empire assembled by Charles V no longer existed. The 1688–1697 war had provoked an economic crisis in France, and by 1705 it was apparent that France could no longer confront the allies on equal terms nor could it fully protect Spanish interests. The English navy now dominated the seas because Louis had allowed his fleet to deteriorate after the treaty of Rijswijk. France could still raise formidable armies, but they were rarely a match for the allied forces in the north under the Duke of Marlborough or for the Austrians in Italy under Prince Eugene of Savoy. In Spain, the Archduke Charles captured Barcelona and Valencia with the help of the English fleet in 1705, and in 1706 the Portuguese army, to its own amazement, captured Madrid. Spain itself might have been lost had not a Franco-Spanish army under the Duke of Berwick defeated the English and Portuguese in the battle of Almansa on 25 April, 1707. Berwick, one of Louis XIV's greatest commanders, was the illegitimate son of the exiled King James II of England. His victory paved the way for the re-conquest of Aragon and Valencia. Outside the peninsula, however, Spain's position continued to deteriorate. Eugene of Savoy, who had grown up at the court of Louis XIV, forced the French out of northern Italy, and in July, 1707 an Austrian army occupied Naples. One year later, Marlborough having already defeated the French at Ramillies in 1706, defeated them again at Oudenarde, thereby securing most of the Spanish Netherlands for the allies. After the failure of peace talks in 1709, Marlborough completed his conquest of the Netherlands.

The treaties that ended the war, Utrecht (April 11, 1713) and Rastatt (September 7, 1714), reflected conditions on the ground with only a few modifications. Philip V retained Spain, including Catalonia which had been under Austrian control since 1705, and the Indies. The British (as they may now be called after the union of England and Scotland in 1707) retained Gibraltar and Minorca which they had captured during the war. Gibraltar's importance was, and is, largely symbolic, although its survival as a British colony on Spanish soil is still deeply resented today. Minorca became an important base for the British navy which could now hope to control the Western Mediterranean by monitoring the French fleet based at Toulon. The Archduke Charles, who had been elected Emperor Charles VI in 1711, gained the most without actually signing the treaties. The allies gave him Naples, Sardinia, Milan, and the Tuscan forts, all of which enabled him to dominate the remaining states of northern Italy as Spain had done since the 1550s. The Spanish Netherlands was gradually transferred to Austrian rule as well after 200 years of Spanish rule, while Sicily went to Victor Amadeus II of Savoy.

Spain preserved its American empire primarily because France and the maritime powers knew that Philip's cause was popular in America and had little stomach for waging war on the other side of the Atlantic. They hoped in any case to maintain the existing arrangement by which they harvested the profits of the Indies trade without the expense and trouble of maintaining a colonial government. Philip had already granted the French the right to trade in the Caribbean as a condition of Louis XIV's support. By the Treaty of Utrecht he ceded the slave trade asiento to Britain as well.

REFORM AND REVIVAL

Spain's performance during the war confirmed what had long been obvious: its government and finances—to say nothing of its armed forces—required major surgery if the nation was ever again to play an important role in international affairs. The first efforts at reform were undertaken by Jean Orry, a French official sent to Spain in 1701 by Louis XIV to report on the country's finances. Orry called for a reorganization of Spanish government on the French model, replacing the laborious system of councils and consultas with a ministerial system based on that created by Richelieu and Louis XIV in France. Ideally, secretaries should become cabinet ministers with specific portfolios whose primary responsibility was to advise the king and carry out his commands. Orry also hoped to simplify the system of tax collection and to appoint *intendants* on the French model as governors of each province, thereby extending royal authority into even the most remote corners of the realm. It was the beginning of a prolonged effort to introduce foreign ideas, most of them French, in an attempt to transform Spanish society.

Philip V, who was now keenly aware of the problems he faced, put Orry in charge of military finance. The king knew, however, that Spaniards would resent the domination of foreign counselors as they had done in the time of Charles V and was in any case inclined to vacillate in matters that did not involve foreign affairs. Court intrigues caused Orry to be dismissed in 1706. When he returned in 1713 he packed the councils with new appointments to dilute their opposition to his ideas. Four new secretaries of state assumed responsibility for many conciliar functions. The king then appointed intendants to govern the 21 provinces. Secretaries and intendants alike reported to Orry who, in his capacity as *veedor general* became the equivalent of prime minister. These reforms extended to the kingdoms of Aragon and Valencia whose *fueros* had been abolished when they were re-conquered in 1707. The viceroys of these kingdoms were replaced by captains-general who presided over the audiencias of Saragossa, Valencia, Barcelona, and Palma de Mallorca. The Cortes of Aragon and the Corts of Valencia had also been abolished in 1709; the Corts of Catalonia followed in 1724.

Orry's successor, Cardinal Giulio Alberoni, continued his policies. A native of Piacenza, Alberoni had come to Spain as the ambassador of Parma and had helped negotiate the marriage of Philip V to his second wife, the formidable Isabella Farnese. In 1715 the new queen engineered the fall of Orry and his replacement by Alberoni, who reformed the tariff system and in 1717 transferred the administrative powers of the various councils to the new secretaries of estate. The Council of the Indies, for example, retained only its influence on patronage and its function as an appellate court. The Casa de Contratación was moved to Cádiz and placed under the authority of Alberoni's most important appointment, José de Patiño, who became *intendente general de marina*, intendant of Cádiz and Seville, and president of the Casa de Contratación. Born in Milan to Spanish parents, Patiño was a master bureaucrat whose most enduring achievement was the re-creation of the Spanish navy. When Alberoni fell from power in 1719, Patiño followed him into exile but resumed the intendancy of Seville in the following year. In 1726 he was named Secretary of State for the Indies and the Navy, and shortly thereafter assumed responsibility for finance and foreign policy as well. He remained, for all practical purposes, Spain's prime minister until his death in 1736.

The policies of these men reflected the thinking of Richelieu and Jean Baptiste Colbert, Louis XIV's minister of finance and maritime affairs. They had no use for, and may not have understood, the role of councils as sources of information and guarantors of consensus. They cared little for parliamentary bodies or public opinion, and designed their administrative reforms primarily to enhance the power of the crown. In economic matters they were, like Colbert, mercantilists. The Habsburgs had allowed the great river of American bullion to flow directly into the hands of foreigners. The new men wanted to break Spain's dependence on imports by investing in domestic agriculture and manufacturing. Above all, they had begun to think of Spain as a single economic and political unit. In 1717 the crown created a number of chartered companies that effectively opened the Indies trade to Basques, Catalans, and others. The Caracas Company, otherwise known as the Guipúzcoa Company, granted Basque traders a monopoly of the trade with Venezuela that included the lucrative and rapidly growing business in cacao. The Catalonia Company was licensed to trade with Hispaniola. There were several other companies, all of them monopolies. Spanish control over the Indies trade would be improved by reforming the flota system and by licensing private vessels as *guardacostas* to seize foreign interlopers. In a bizarre reversal of recent history, entrepreneurial Spaniards and Creoles became pirates in their own waters, causing outrage among the Dutch and English and leading ultimately to the War of Jenkins' Ear (1737–1748).

From the king's perspective, the purpose of these efforts was not so much to improve the well-being of the Spanish people as to restore Spain's ability to make war. Philip V and Isabella, who still claimed Parma and parts of Tuscany, were determined to restore Spain's lost empire in Italy and Africa. By 1717, Patiño's navy was spending more than 4 million escudos per year. Ships and dockyards had been built, and more ships were leased from other powers to mount a massive and successful invasion of Sardinia. On July 1, 1718, an even larger fleet landed at Palermo. Alarmed at this assault on the provisions of the Treaty of Utrecht, Britain, France, the Empire, and Savoy formed the Quadruple Alliance against Spain. On August 11, a British expedition shattered the new Spanish fleet off Cape Passaro, forcing the Spanish to withdraw from Sicily. Observers, including the British ambassador at

Madrid, concluded that although the new Spanish ships were excellent they were poorly commanded. Philip V had founded a naval academy in 1714, but it was too new to have produced results. In the following year, a French army under Berwick invaded the Basque Provinces while the British ravaged Galicia. After much negotiation the combatants reached an agreement at Cambrai in 1724 by which Philip returned Sardinia and agreed not to attempt the re-conquest of Naples and Sicily in return for the recognition of his claims to Parma and Tuscany.

Neither Philip nor his Queen was satisfied. After a bizarre episode in 1724 during which Philip abdicated the throne in favor of his eldest son by his first wife, Luis (who promptly died), the king resumed his office. His behavior became increasingly erratic, but even during the 1730s when he descended into periodic mental illness, the crown's expansionist policies never wavered. In 1720, after the war of the Quadruple Alliance, a Spanish expedition had finally relieved the North African presidio of Ceuta, which had been under siege by the Sultan of Morocco since 1694. Philip's immediate purpose was to secure the continuation of the *cruzada*, the tax on the church that would have been lost if there were no more garrisons in Africa, but in 1732, a far larger expedition re-conquered Oran. Clearly, the Bourbons meant to restore the Spanish empire in Africa as well.

A second chance to reclaim the Italian portion of the empire arose in 1733. Philip allied with his nephew, Louis XV, to prevent an Austrian candidate from succeeding to the throne of Poland. In the War of the Polish Succession the French successfully invaded northern Italy while a Spanish expedition under the nominal command of Charles, eldest son of Philip and Isabella Farnese, reconquered Naples and Sicily. The change was generally applauded by the inhabitants of both kingdoms, most of whom had come to detest the Austrians.

To increase his son's popularity, Philip chose to proclaim him ruler of a new and independent Kingdom of the Two Sicilies rather than placing the region once again under Spanish administration. His decision annoyed patriotic Spaniards by ensuring that Italy would be forever lost to their empire, but the experiment proved temporarily successful. Charles reformed the Neapolitan administration with the help of local advisors and ruled with skill and energy until 1759 when he abdicated to became king of Spain. Later, under his successor Ferdinand IV, the Two Sicilies turned its back on Spain and fell increasingly under the influence of Austria and Britain. The program of domestic reform begun by Charles faltered after a serious famine in 1764, but Naples continued to enjoy a lively intellectual life. A measure of reform came even to conservative Sicily where Domenico

Caracciolo, viceroy from 1781 to 1785, managed to abolish the Inquisition during his term of office.

The War of Jenkins' Ear broke out in 1739 when the commander of a Spanish *guardacosta* in the Caribbean allegedly tied an English captain to a mast and cut off his ear. When Captain Jenkins displayed his ear, pickled in brandy, to Parliament, Britain declared war and sent a massive fleet to the Caribbean under Admiral Vernon. Vernon briefly took Portobello on the Isthmus of Panama, but failed at Havana, Cartagena, and even at remote St. Augustine. Patiño's reform of the Spanish navy had begun to bear fruit. The War of Jenkins' Ear merged into the War of the Austrian Succession which broke out in 1740. France, Spain, Bavaria, and eventually Prussia formed an alliance against Austria and Britain in another effort to put a Bavarian on the Imperial throne. Spain's primary interest in this affair was not only to protect its colonies against the British, but to weaken Austrian influence in northern Italy. The Treaty of Aix-la-Chapelle (1748), although generally favorable to Austria, secured Parma and Piacenza for Philip, the younger brother of King Charles of Naples.

Philip V died in 1746 leaving Spain and its empire far stronger than it had been in 1713. He and his ministers had rationalized the administration and restored the country's finances. They had united Castile with the former Aragonese kingdoms, which now for the first time contributed their share to the common burden, and recovered at least some of the Italian possessions of Charles V for the Bourbon dynasty, if not for Spain itself. In the process, the Spanish army had at last justified its enormous expenditures by doing well in the war against the Austrians in northern Italy. Moreover, after a lapse of almost a century Spain once again possessed the framework of a respectable navy, although it would never fully resolve the problem of recruiting skilled seamen.

These were remarkable achievements, but the government's success owed much to factors beyond its control. Major visitations of the plague ceased in Spain after 1649, while harvests in both Spain and Italy improved, owing largely to better weather that would persist for most of the eighteenth century. The population of peninsular Spain began to increase in the 1680s. By 1746 it had returned to the record levels of the mid-sixteenth century and would continue to rise thereafter. The resulting growth in economic activity was at least as helpful to the crown's finances as the improved system of taxation introduced by Orry and his successors.

The reign of Ferdinand VI (1746–1759) saw an important re-orientation of Spanish policy. Attempts to reform the finances of Castile and strengthen its economy continued, but Philip's preoccupation with Italy gave way to an emphasis on the Atlantic empire. The new policies are associated with the marquis of Ensenada, a protégé of Patiño and of Patiño's successor, José de Campillo. Ensenada, who occupied the ministry of marine and the Indies from 1743 to 1754, was inspired by the ideas of Colbert and wanted the colonies to help support the economy of metropolitan Spain. His views on colonial affairs were further influenced by critical reports from the travelers Jorge Juan and Antonio de Ulloa and by Campillo himself, who had once served in Mexico and Havana.

Ensenada sought above all to regain a measure of government control over the colonial trade and to protect it with an improved and expanded navy. His efforts at trade reform, however, were cautious and incremental, owing largely to determined opposition from the consulado of Cádiz and the British. Naval rearmament was more successful. He expanded the shipbuilding program begun by Campillo at Havana and improved the dockyards at Cádiz, Cartagena, and Ferrol. When the Seven Years' War broke out in 1756, the navy had increased from 12 major ships to 45. Domestically, his ambitious scheme to replace some of Castile's many taxes with a levy on income failed. The most important result of this effort was a massive *catastro* or economic survey of Castile that remains an invaluable source for social and economic historians.

ENLIGHTENMENT AND THE PROGRAM OF CHARLES III

The reforms begun by Philip V and continued by his sons Ferdinand VI and Charles III (1759–1788) reflected an approach to political economy that had been fermenting in France, the Netherlands, and England for nearly a century. The Enlightenment (*las luces* in Spanish) was not a philosophical or scientific system but a broad intellectual program based on the conviction that human reason alone could uncover the basic laws of nature and society. Early in the seventeenth century Sir Francis Bacon and René Descartes divorced thought from the theological first principles that had informed philosophy, science, and politics since the beginnings of the Christian era. The success of political reforms based on reason in both France and England and the great scientific achievements of the age seemed to justify the belief that real progress could be made in human affairs through the application of rational principles.

The liberation of reason from theology, however, unleashed forces that would disturb and ultimately destroy the traditional order. The Enlightenment was not at first overtly anti-religious or anti-monarchical. It soon became obvious, however, that the assumptions behind it did not necessarily buttress the rule of kings. Rationalist thinkers from Hobbes to Locke to Voltaire rejected the idea that monarchies embodied the divine will. Some believed that states were based on a primeval "social contract" between the rulers and the ruled. Those who believed in the social contract tended to think that the ultimate purpose of the state should be to improve the welfare of its subjects. By the mid-eighteenth century, many of these *philosophes* (the term was not a compliment) had also become actively anticlerical. Stung by the predictable hostility of churchmen and inspired by an optimistic faith in the innate goodness and rationality of human beings, they sought a "natural religion" independent of the church. Some, like Baron d'Holbach, questioned the need for God in explaining nature. Jean-Jacques Rousseau, the most original thinker of the age, claimed that the essential goodness of humanity had been corrupted not only by religion but by society itself.

The more radical of these ideas did not appeal to the Bourbons or to their Spanish subjects, most of whom remained deeply attached to Catholicism and suspicious of foreign ideas. Spanish governments of the eighteenth century hoped to encourage public interest in science and economics while banning the works of those who advocated anticlericalism and republicanism. Their chief purpose was at all times to enhance royal power with little concern for popular welfare or such concepts as the Rights of Man. As a result, the Enlightenment came late to Spain and its empire. Many Spaniards, especially in America, learned of its political dimensions only after the French Revolution of 1789. Many more would continue to reject its tenets until well into the twentieth century, but the Enlightenment would have a profound—although not, as we shall see, decisive—influence on the eventual dissolution of the Empire. Its impact on the nations that emerged from the Empire's wreckage at the beginning of the nineteenth century would be far greater than on the revolutionary movements that created them.

Educated Spaniards first learned of the Enlightenment from Benito Gerónimo Feijóo, a Benedictine monk and professor of theology. His *Teatro crítico universal* (9 vols., 1726–1739 and *Cartas eruditas* (5 vols., 1739–1759, republished in 15 editions by 1786), contained essays on a wide variety of subjects and embodied the spirit of critical rationalism without rejecting religious beliefs. Feijóo's emphasis on science and its practical applications appealed to the leaders of eighteenth-century Spain, who hoped to encourage material progress without offending the country's innate conservatism. Gerónimo de Uztáriz popularized the mercantilist theories of Colbert in his *Theórica y práctica de comercio y marina,* published by royal authority in 1742.

Mercantilism, rather than the more modern theories of the physiocrats or Adam Smith, would determine Charles III's policies on trade and manufacturing. Like Uztáriz, he sought to reduce Spain's balance of payments deficit and tie the economies of its colonies more closely to the mother country.

Charles III, who has been described (perhaps unwisely) as an "enlightened despot" on the model of Frederick the Great and Joseph II, also supported the formation of local societies known as *Los Amigos del País* to discuss schemes for improving their regional economies. By the end of the reign there were 54 of them in the peninsula, although no more than half ever became truly active. In some regions the societies' commitment to change aroused the opposition of the church and of local elites who saw nothing wrong with the status quo. Periodicals sanctioned by the crown to further scientific and economic interests rarely found more than a few hundred subscribers. The shortage of "enlightened" minds and the sheer impracticality of some of the reformers' schemes (especially in agriculture) ensured that Enlightenment, even in the diluted form approved by the king and his ministers, would not penetrate deeply into Spanish society.

Religious policy, too, owed far more to the example of Louis XIV than to any rejection of the church's fundamental teachings. The Bourbon kings demonstrated exemplary piety at all times but wanted greater control over ecclesiastical appointments, the universities, and the Inquisition. They also believed that the vast lands held by the church in mortmain (*en manos muertas*) prevented economic development. A powerful faction within the Spanish church, known rather confusingly as Jansenists after the heretical sect in seventeenth-century France, supported the crown's position. They were not heretics, but regalists and, in the case of the Augustinian order of monks, rivals of the Jesuits who generally defended papal rights. The Concordat of 1753, negotiated between the ministers of Ferdinand VI and the papacy, enlarged the crown's control over ecclesiastical appointments and ended certain clerical exemptions from taxation. It greatly strengthened royal authority over the church, but the expulsion of the Jesuits by Charles III in 1767 remains the most dramatic, and perhaps misunderstood, of the Bourbon reforms.

As the most forceful advocates of papal supremacy, the Jesuits had opposed regalist policies in France and Portugal as well as in Spain. Portugal suppressed the Society in 1759 and France followed in 1764. Charles III had additional reasons to dislike the Jesuits. He feared that their control over the *colegios mayores* at the Spanish universities and their colleges in the New World gave them undue influence over the Spanish and Creole elites. In America, his subjects complained of the Order's dominant position in a number of businesses, and resented its defense of the Indians even as it profited from native labor. Of course, Charles, like his Portuguese and French counterparts, hoped to confiscate the Society's wealth, which he appears to have overestimated. Above all, events in Paraguay and Madrid convinced him—or so he claimed—that the Jesuits posed a substantive threat to royal authority.

For more than a century the Jesuit reductions (missions) in Paraguay had anchored Spain's defenses in the Plata region. Most had evolved into prosperous communities whose Guaraní inhabitants became gifted crafts-men, artists, and writers (they established the region's first printing press in 1700). The Guaraní were also formidable soldiers. The area had long been subject to savage raids by *bandeirantes*, rugged frontiersman from the São Paulo region who hoped to claim the land for Portugal and enslave the Indians. The Guaraní had been granted the right to bear arms as early as 1644 and soon developed their own commanders and a rich military tra-dition. In 1750 Ferdinand VI tried to settle the endless boundary disputes by ceding seven Jesuit missions on the east bank of the Uruguay River to the Portuguese in return for their settlement at Côlonia de Sacramento, a smuggler's haven across the Plata estuary from Buenos Aires. When the Portuguese authorities tried to expel the missionaries and distribute the land to their colonists, the Guaraní refused to leave. It required a bloody campaign by a joint Portuguese–Spanish army (the War of the Seven Reduc-tions) to remove them, and Ferdinand blamed the Jesuits for inciting their former charges to revolt.

When he came to the throne Charles III accepted the official version of this story. Then in 1766 when riots convulsed Madrid and much of central Castile he blamed Jesuit agitation for this as well. The true cause was almost certainly a protest against bad economic conditions and the essentially for-eign character of the regime. In a year of discontent triggered by shortages and rising grain prices, the king's unpopular Italian advisor, the marquis of Squillace, unaccountably decided to ban the long cloaks and slouch hats favored by many Spanish men. Jesuit involvement remains a matter of con-troversy, but Charles used the riots as a pretext for taking action against the order and its properties.

The expulsion of the Jesuits from all parts of the empire in April, 1767 was followed within a year by their expulsion from the now independent Kingdom of the Two Sicilies and Parma. By removing the Jesuits, Charles effectively destroyed the most vital part of the empire's educational system and may actually have harmed the broader interests of the crown. Like the king and his ministers, the Jesuits had long been exponents of the new scientific learning. They supported economic reform while at the same time offering, through their advocacy of scholastic philosophy, an effective challenge to revolutionary political theories that would one day threaten the monarchy. In short, by expelling the Jesuits, the crown neutralized what might have been an intellectual ally. Moreover, the Jesuits had long been an important component of the government's frontier strategy. When the Jesuits left, their missions in North and South America reverted to wilderness or were sold by the crown to Creole entrepreneurs, leaving their Indian inhabitants to drift away into the pagan hinterlands. The expulsion therefore had its greatest impact in America where the Jesuits were more closely integrated into society than they were in Spain. Violent protests broke out in parts of New Spain and had to be put down by force, but the crown's sale of Jesuit properties helped to counterbalance the general sense of outrage by giving prominent colonists a stake in the expulsion.

The government's attempts to reform agriculture and landholding in Spain itself may also have done more harm than good, but its efforts to strengthen trade and industry achieved a measure of success. Under Charles III, economic policy was heavily influenced by the Count of Campomanes, an avid mercantilist and admirer of Feijóo who held a number of high offices before becoming a key legal adviser to the Council of Castile in 1762 and its president in 1783. As we have seen, the Bourbons thought of Spain as a single entity rather than as a collection of kingdoms. Building on the policies of Philip V, his successors gradually relaxed trade restrictions until by 1789 every port within the empire had the right to trade with any of the others. The flota system had been abandoned by 1740, but within the empire, Bourbon policy remained decidedly protectionist. In an effort to strengthen Spanish industry and reduce the balance of payments deficit, the crown placed heavy duties on many foreign imports or prohibited them outright. They banned the import of cloth from India as early as 1718, preferring to depend on cotton imported from the West Indian colonies and woven in Catalonia. The ban was lifted in 1760, but restored in 1770–1771. By 1792 the Catalan textile industry employed as many as 80,000 workers. Much of the finished cloth was then exported to the American colonies. To protect this trade, royal officials forced textile manufacturers in Peru and elsewhere to close. A ban on imported iron and copperware in 1775 greatly strengthened the Basque metalworking industry, which soon found markets in Europe as well as in Spain and its colonies, and Basque shipbuilding revived as well. Logging to provide ships' timbers and charcoal for the iron industry caused large-scale deforestation in northern Spain.

None of this would have been possible without restructuring the Spanish labor market. Campomanes, a long-time foe of the *gremios* or guilds, undermined them by permitting manufacturers to hire workers from any part of the country and even from foreign lands if the workers were Catholic. In an effort to promote manufacturing in Castile, which still suffered from higher rates of taxation than the Basques and Catalans, the government also reduced the alcabala and other taxes, but high transportation costs in Castile's rugged interior continued to limit progress.

The value of other crown policies was even more questionable. The government prohibited the export of coarse grades of wool in 1785 on the theory that the price would fall for Spanish manufacturers if they did not have to compete for raw material in the European market. Its policy on Valencian silks—among the finest in the world—remained punitive and inconsistent, supposedly in an effort to encourage silk production in Catalonia and Andalusia. Heavy duties and periodic embargos on Valencian silk created little more than a bonanza for smugglers. Another policy, copied directly from those of Colbert, established royal factories for the production of paper, porcelain, glass, tapestries, and fine woolens. For the most part, their products were superb, but none of the factories made money. The government maintained them primarily to limit the importation of luxury items and to provide employment for thousands of workers.

Despite these anomalies, the government's reforms achieved a fundamental realignment of the imperial economy. In 1700, no more than 10 or 12 percent of the manufactured goods imported by the American colonies came from Spain. By the 1780s that percentage had risen to more than 50 percent. Spain had at last begun to fulfill the role of a mother country as defined by mercantilist theory.

REFORM COMES TO AMERICA

Between 1764 and 1786 Charles extended his governmental and administrative reforms to the colonies. In general they expanded royal power, increased crown revenues, and aroused serious misgivings among the colonists. In the course of the Seven Years' War (1756–1763), the British seized Havana and Manila and held them for a year. The Treaty of Paris returned the cities to Spain, but gave Florida to Britain with the French ceding Louisiana to Charles III by way of compensation. The failure of Spanish arms to protect two strategic centers of the empire inspired the king to dispatch a series of visitas headed by José de Gálvez, an able administrator who eventually became minister of the Indies. His recommendations led to the establishment of a colonial army and a major overhaul of colonial government.

American defense had long been entrusted to the navy and to colonial militias commanded for the most part by Creole officers. The new orders increased the size of the militias but also created a standing army of full-time soldiers officered by professionals from Spain. New Spain eventually supported more than 6000 of these troops. A further 2000 were stationed in Peru while smaller garrisons protected the chokepoints of the American trade: Havana, San Juan, Cartagena, Portobello, and Vera Cruz. The new force proved to be both expensive and relatively ineffective. As was often the case with eighteenth-century armies, only the desperate were drawn to the low wages and harsh discipline offered by the king. Their peninsular commanders, rarely the cream of the Spanish officer corps, were resented by Creoles who wanted the commands for themselves. The expanded militias remained largely under local control, but often lacked training or decent weapons. Although colonial troops could display extraordinary courage and proved effective in suppressing colonial rebellions, they would remain vulnerable to better-trained, better-equipped forces from Europe in the event of a major crisis.

Defense inspired some of the reforms recommended by Gálvez, but most sought to increase the crown's revenue and its administrative control over the colonies. Cuba became a captaincy-general in 1764, immediately after its restoration by the British. What is now Colombia had long been governed by the viceroy of far-distant Peru; Venezuela by the equally inaccessible Viceroy of Santo Domingo. Philip V created the viceregal Kingdom of New Granada with its capital at Bogotá in 1719, dissolved it in 1723, and restored it in 1739, primarily in response to Vernon's attack on Cartagena but also because the viceroyalty of Santo Domingo had been unwilling or unable to control the coast of Venezuela. Caracas and Cumaná had experienced rapid growth in the first half of the century. Their commerce, however, was still dominated by Dutch traders operating out of Aruba and Curaçao. The new vicreroyalty was not at first a success. Its capital, remote, conservative Santa Fe de Bogotá, was far away in time and spirit from bustling Venezuela. In 1777, on the recommendation of Gálvez, Caracas became a captaincy-general within the viceregal jurisdiction of New Granada. When the new arrangement failed to create effective government or even to pay for itself, the crown dispatched a visita to install the intendant system and reform finances.

The *visitador*, Juan Francisco Gutiérrez de Piñeres, instead provoked a rebellion. When he separated two taxes that had always been collected as one, the alcabala and the levy originally meant to support the *armada de barlovento*, the public thought that he had created a new tax. Then, when he levied forced contributions on heads of households and increased the prices charged by crown monopolies on salt, tobacco, and alcohol, Creoles and Mestizos alike rose in what they called the Comunero Rebellion. The term, which had been adopted by a far smaller rebellion in Paraguay during the 1720s, intentionally recalled the Castilian revolt against Charles V in 1520–1521. The New Granada rebels opened their campaign in November, 1780, but their poor communications and lack of a central command enabled the royal army to restore order by April, 1781. No one at the time raised the specter of independence from Spain. The Comunero revolt—like its sixteenth-century predecessor—was in theory a protest against the king's evil advisors, but it showed that the Creole elite was capable of resisting attacks on its prosperity and status. The crown modified the worst of Piñeres's measures, but retained the intendant system and gave Caracas its own audiencia in 1786.

Far to the south on the Rio de la Plata the Portuguese had ignored the treaty of 1750 and retained their settlement at Colônia de Sacramento. A Spanish force at last dislodged them in 1776. To consolidate its position, the crown created a massive new viceroyalty in 1777 by detaching what are now Argentina, Uruguay, Paraguay, Bolivia, and much of Chile from Peru. It had other motives as well. The commerce of the Plata region had been growing for some years at the expense of Lima. After the demise of the flota system, merchants of all nations found it cheaper and faster to trade with the mining districts through Buenos Aires rather than to rely on the traditional route through Panama. By creating the viceroyalty of Río de la Plata and placing Potosí within it, the crown sought to impose a greater measure of control over the new trade. Buenos Aires received an audiencia of its own in 1786. By this time, Lima and coastal Peru were experiencing severe economic decline, masked to some extent by the architectural and social brilliance of the viceregal capital. Crown officials, perhaps deceived by these outward appearances, made increasingly unrealistic demands for new and expanded revenues from a community that was already under stress.

During this shift in the crown's South American policy, a major Indian rebellion under José Gabriel Condorconqui, who called himself Tupac Amaru II, convulsed the Peruvian viceroyalty. Indian protests were nothing new. There had been more than 50 uprisings in Upper Peru since 1740. The Indians wanted an end to the *mita* and to the hated *repartimiento de bienes*, a system developed in the later seventeenth century by officials who were the crown's primary contact with Indian communities. By controlling their contacts with the outside world, a corregidor or alcalde forced the Indians to sell their produce to him below market price. He then resold it at a profit and profited again by forcing them to buy their tools, cloth, and other necessities at above market prices. The revolt of Tupac Amaru in 1780 was therefore the culmination of a long process. Its leader was captured in May, 1781 and executed with unusual savagery, but fighting continued until the viceroy's army restored order in 1783. At least 100,000 people lost their lives in the bloodiest internal struggle since the conquest.

The government's response to the revolt combined utter ruthlessness with a willingness to address rebel grievances. By 1784 it had abolished the repartimiento and introduced the intendant system to Peru. Sub-delegates, who reported to the intendants, replaced the corrupt and often uncontrollable corregidores and *alcaldes mayores*. Cuzco, which had been the center of the revolt, received an audiencia of its own in response to Indian demands. Unfortunately, the sub-delegates could no more survive on their meager salaries than had their predecessors, and a variant of the repartimiento de bienes soon revived. In general, the intendant system, which was introduced to New Spain in 1786 as well, achieved its greatest success in urbanized areas where enhanced supervision produced improvements in infrastructure, public services, and—perhaps—official probity.

This period of imperial reform coincided with Spain's involvement in the American Revolution. Charles and his ministers had no love for the American rebels, but saw the conflict as an opportunity to strike at British interests. Encouraged by Britain's temporary naval weakness (the same weakness that resulted in the debacle at Yorktown), a Spanish naval squadron drove the British from the Bahamas while Bernardo de Gálvez, the nephew and protégé of Minister for the Indies José de Gálvez, conquered West Florida in a series of well-conceived campaigns. In the peace of 1783 Spain returned the Bahamas to Britain in exchange for East Florida and Minorca. From Spain's perspective, the worst feature of the treaty was that Britain allowed her former colonies to claim all North American lands east of the Mississippi. There would now be no barrier between Spanish Louisiana and what promised to become a horde of land-seeking Anglo-American settlers.

The war of the American Revolution and the Bourbon penchant for bureaucratic expansion increased administrative costs throughout the Spanish colonies, but revenues from America grew dramatically during the period of reform. Although tax collection became more efficient, the real causes of the windfall were demographic growth and increased trade between the colonies and Spain. The population of the colonies, like that of Spain and Europe as a whole, increased in the eighteenth century: in the case of New Spain it nearly doubled. The real growth of crown revenues, independent of inflation, doubled as well until the 1790s when the French Revolutionary wars brought inflation and economic decline. Until then, demographic growth increased revenues from domestic taxes and Indian tributes alike, while the expansion of trade produced massive new revenues from commercial taxes. By 1780 the yield from commercial taxes had reached an average of 4.8 million pesos a year, surpassing that of the mines. Revenue from monopolies produced even more. The monopoly on Cuban tobacco alone, established in 1765, yielded 3–3.5 million pesos annually during the last 20 years of the century.

But if the Bourbon reforms advanced the interests of the crown, they did so at a political cost to the Creole elite. The later Habsburgs, in financial desperation, had sold colonial offices on a large scale. Prominent Creoles purchased them and achieved a dominant position on the audiencias and in lesser offices that persisted until well into the eighteenth century. Ferdinand VI and Charles III reversed this policy. They believed, correctly, that many Creole officials were either corrupt or overly tied to local interests, but they could not dismiss them without repurchasing their offices. Instead, they discontinued the sale of offices and after about 1750 favored the appointment of peninsulars to new vacancies as they occurred. By 1780, creoles had become a small minority on the audiencias. Intendants, themselves almost exclusively of peninsular origin, packed the cabildos with citizens who had been born in Spain, and, as we have seen, commissions in the colonial army were reserved for non-natives as well. The Creole elite, after managing it own affairs for almost a century, found itself largely excluded from influence.

REVERSAL OF FORTUNE

When Charles III died in December, 1788, he had every reason to believe that his reign of nearly 30 years was a success. His reforms had strengthened the crown's authority, its revenues, and its prestige while increasing the overall prosperity of his realms. He could not have known that he had weakened the bonds between the crown and its subjects in a variety of ways that no one at the time fully understood.

The Habsburg system at its best had been slow, cumbersome, and often inefficient. Under weak kings or incompetent ministers it could and did descend into something like anarchy. At the same time it offered advantages that the reforming Bourbons did not appreciate. By never wavering from the medieval ideal of the monarchy as an essentially spiritual institution, the Habsburgs preserved legitimacy even in the face of manifest incompetence. As the agent of divine will and natural law, the king's primary functions remained as they had been in the Middle Ages: to provide justice and to lead the country in war. As warlord, he enjoyed broad, and largely unquestioned, discretionary powers. Domestically, the king's influence rested primarily on his judicial function. For this reason, policy moved from the bottom up. Petitioners and counter-petitioners brought all of their influence to bear on controversial issues. The king and his counselors deliberated—often at excruciating length—and reached a decision which they hoped was in accord with law and the society's prevailing values. If circumstances changed, if a better argument was presented, or even if successful petitioners lacked the power to sustain their victory, the crown could revise its decision without compromising its authority or prestige. In theory, the king was committed to justice, not to specific policy initiatives, and the crown's legitimacy conferred upon his decisions the presumption of his goodwill.

In contrast, the Bourbons determined policy from the top down by identifying problems and attempting to solve them through the application of reason. The crown, while still claiming absolute powers, justified them on the basis of their supposed ability to improve the material condition of its kingdoms. The government thereby forfeited, at least to some degree, the presumption that it was the agent of divine will and made itself accountable in ways that had never applied to the Habsburgs. Philip V had inherited a kingdom in disarray. He and his successors were driven by the need for haste in correcting the empire's weakness both foreign and domestic. In the writings of men like Campomanes this imperative took on an almost panicky quality, and it soon became apparent that the reformers would not waste time on convoluted political processes which they saw as irrational and almost wholly counterproductive. Unfortunately, few Spaniards, especially in America, accepted the Enlightenment concept of reason. They saw only a king who sent forth orders without prior consultation, and ministers who enforced those orders while largely ignoring the traditional means by which subjects had always sought to influence policy. As officers whose job was to implement the king's orders within the hierarchical system originally perfected by Louis XIV, they lacked in any case the authority to negotiate, whether on the basis of reasoned argument or personal influence. To a population steeped in traditional political values, this seemed perilously close to tyranny.

The Bourbons were not, of course, wholly obtuse. They could respond to the concerns of their subjects, although it sometimes required violence to get their attention. The problem was that by ignoring political norms that had been established for centuries they lost—not the passive loyalty—but the active goodwill of their subjects. If their policies seemed to ignore the best interests of their subjects or, worse yet, if those policies failed, they could not take refuge in divine authority or even claim forgiveness. As agents of reason who all too often ridiculed those who disagreed with them as backward and ignorant, the Bourbons could be judged by rational standards. If (as enlightened theorists claimed) there was such a thing as a social contract between crown and people, the Bourbon reformers had gone a long way toward breaking it. The decline of the monarchy under Charles III's successors ruptured it almost completely.

Charles IV had to face one of the greatest crises in the history of Western society without his father's energy or acumen. The outbreak of the French Revolution in 1789 convulsed all of Europe, but it presented the Spanish Bourbons with a series of exceptionally painful choices. The count of Floridablanca, the king's chief minister and a leading supporter of the Enlightenment under Charles III, tried to prevent news of the revolution, and revolutionary literature in general, from reaching the Spanish public. The presence of banned books in libraries as far away as Peru indicates that he failed, but with the exception of a handful of sophisticates, most Spaniards remained indifferent to enlightened ideas and were horrified by events in France. The king's primary interest, however, was in saving the life of his cousin Louis XVI. A French mission convinced him that Floridablanca's hostility to the revolution would endanger Louis and his family, and in February, 1792 Charles replaced Floridablanca with the count of Aranda, another of his father's aging ministers who had once helped to organize the *Amigos del País*. Aranda lasted until November when he, too, was replaced as chief minister by Manuel de Godoy, a handsome young guards officer who was a favorite of the queen.

Godoy held modestly enlightened views and was not without political skill, but the source of his power made him the butt of hostility and ridicule. Outwardly, he was Queen Maria Luisa's *cortijo*, the escort who accompanied her to social events that the king did not wish to attend. The custom was widespread in court circles, but offensive to ordinary Spaniards who tended to believe the worst. In their eyes the king was a cuckold under the control of his frivolous, domineering wife and a social upstart who had achieved power by unsavory means. As in the early years of Charles II when the queen mother and father Nithard had dominated policy, many qualified persons abandoned the court or otherwise refused to serve in the government. Godoy and the royal couple were often forced to govern in a kind of political vacuum.

The failure of this odd triumvirate to develop a coherent foreign policy compounded their problems. In their defense, the king and Godoy faced a truly excruciating dilemma: should they succumb to the military threat posed by revolutionary France and its vast conscript armies or to the naval threat posed by Britain which had opposed the revolution from the first. The execution of Louis XVI in January, 1793, freed Charles to follow his instincts and declare war on the revolutionaries. A Spanish army invaded Roussillon but failed to capture the all-important fortress of Perpignan. After some months of stalemate the French launched retaliatory campaigns in 1794–1795 that captured Fuenterrabía and San Sebastián in the west and Rosas and Tolosa in the east. To end this embarrassing occupation of Spanish territory, Godoy negotiated the Treaty of Basel, giving Santo Domingo to the French as the price of their withdrawal. The king then bestowed a priceless gift on Spain's satirists by granting his minister the title "Prince of the Peace."

The treaty, although far short of an alliance, aroused the hostility of Britain. The British navy began to seize Spain's ships on the high seas and attack Spain's colonial outposts. By 1796, British depredations inspired the king to abandon his anti-revolutionary principles and ally openly with the French. But France, which had gutted both its navy's officer corps and its system for recruiting seamen during the Revolution, could do nothing to protect Spain against Britain. In February, 1797, a British force under Admiral Jervis defeated a larger Spanish force off Cape St. Vincent and captured four ships of the line. Jervis then instituted a naval blockade of Cádiz to supplement British action against other Spanish ports. The war at sea continued until 1802, with Britain seizing Trinidad and recapturing Minorca.

After Napoleon's seizure of power in November, 1799, Godoy and the king fell entirely under his influence. In 1800, Godoy gave France Louisiana in return for Napoleon's empty promise to favor the Italian schemes of Charles's son-in-law, Louis of Bourbon-Parma. Godoy had been convinced since 1795 that Spain could not protect Louisiana from waves of frontiersman from the United States, and hoped that France would provide a barrier between the new republic and the Spanish settlements on the Rio

Grande. Napoleon, in the first of many betrayals, sold the entire region to the Americans in 1803. Meanwhile, in 1801 Napoleon convinced Godoy to invade Portugal at the head of a Spanish army. The campaign succeeded and forced the Portuguese to close their ports to British ships. Both sides now wanted a respite. France and Britain signed the Peace of Amiens in March, 1802, which returned Minorca to Spain while leaving Trinidad under British rule, but the peace proved to be little more than a temporary truce. War resumed in May of the following year when Napoleon closed continental Europe to British trade.

Spain once again allied itself with a France that could threaten but not protect it. On October 21, 1805, the British under Admiral Horatio Nelson defeated a combined Franco-Spanish fleet at the battle of Trafalgar. The bloodiest battle of the sailing age was followed by a hurricane-force gale that struck the battered fleets before they could reach shelter. Casualties numbered in the thousands. Once again, Spain's failure at sea did not arise from cowardice or in any technological deficiency. Spanish ships and guns, like those of the French, were at least the equal of the British, and by 1805 the Spanish high command included men of ability and long experience. Spanish crews were another matter. Bourbon Spain had never been able to fully implement its system for registering seamen (introduced after 1737) and therefore lacked an effective system of recruitment for sea duty. British crews, although often taken from merchant ships by impressment, were overwhelmingly composed of professional seaman and their officers had spent years at sea. The Spanish crews at Trafalgar were composed for the most part of conscripted landsmen. The junior officers lacked sea experience, and the gun crews were headed by artillerymen on loan from the army. Ship handling did not approach British standards, while an appalling disparity of casualties between the two sides revealed the superiority of British gunnery. The French, who had yet to remedy their own deficiencies at sea, fared no better than the Spanish.

Trafalgar further demoralized a Spanish public already disgusted with the policies of Godoy. Financially, the wars with revolutionary France and then with Britain had been a disaster. The French invasion forced the government of Charles IV to borrow heavily from foreign sources. When interest rates inevitably rose, the crown issued domestic treasury bills called *vales reales* whose face value eventually equaled all revenues from the colonies plus about 75 percent of peninsular receipts. The massive deficits forced officials to raise more money in taxes and forced loans on top of the levies that had been required at the time of the

American Revolution. By the mid-1790s, increased taxes coupled with wartime inflation had already begun to create serious hardship in many parts of the empire.

The success of Britain's war against Spanish trade made matters worse. Spanish shipping incurred losses on the high seas, but most of the economic damage came from the British blockade. Only six ships from Cádiz reached the colonies in 1797. Desperate officials in Cuba and Venezuela opened their ports to neutral vessels, and, to prevent economic collapse, the crown followed their example and sanctioned neutral trade throughout the empire in November, 1797. To preserve its now almost useless privileges, the Consulado of Cádiz procured a suspension of the decree in April, 1799, but colonial officials continued to trade with foreigners. The crown had no choice but to restore neutral trade at the beginning of 1801. The term neutral trade was to some extent a euphemism. The crown opened the colonial market to all comers because there was no effective way to exclude the British. Ships from the United States, Britain, and the Netherlands became the Creoles' economic lifeline, and after Trafalgar, no more treasure ships reached Cádiz.

The Napoleonic Wars therefore severed Spain's commercial links with the Americas at a time when financial distress and resentment over government discrimination against Creoles had already weakened the colonists' attachment to the crown. The latter complaint, at least, was soon mitigated by necessity. So desperate was the crown's need for money that Charles IV revived the sale of offices. From the 1790s onward, more and more Creoles purchased governmental appointments and by 1808 the number of colonial officials born in the New World was greater than it had been at any time in recent memory.

By this time the crown was teetering on the edge of bankruptcy. Despite its poverty and the near-collapse of the Spanish economy, Napoleon extorted large subsidies from Godoy's government in 1804 and 1805. With the loss of the annual treasure fleet, the crown's immense burden of bonded debt made the situation seem irretrievable. Many Spaniards, dismayed by military and financial failure and disgusted with the antics of the royal household, began to plot actively on behalf of Charles's son, Ferdinand (*El Deseado*, or the Desired One). Matters came to a head after Charles and Godoy signed the Treaty of Fontainebleau in October, 1807. By its terms, Spain agreed to the French conquest of Portugal, but when the conquest was complete and the Portuguese royal family had fled to Brazil, Napoleon claimed several of Spain's northern provinces as well. Lacking either money or popular support, Godoy could see no way to expel the French and decided that the royal family should follow the example of their Portuguese counterparts and flee to America.

The refugees went no further than the royal palace at Aranjuez. There, on March 17, 1808, a mob of *Fernandistas* forced the dismissal of Godoy and the abdication of Charles IV. The conflict between father and son provided Napoleon with an opportunity to complete the conquest of Spain. He ordered his army to take Madrid, and then invited both Charles and Ferdinand to a conference at Bayonne where the two Bourbons were essentially his captives. On May 5, 1808, after forcing both to abdicate, he named his brother, Joseph Bonaparte, King of Spain.

Three days before the abdication, on May 2, the people of Madrid rebelled against the presence of French troops in the capital. The Dos de Mayo, now Spain's national holiday, marked the beginning of a prolonged and bloody struggle that introduced the term guerrilla warfare to the world. The rebels, who agreed on little except their hatred for the French, established regional juntas and a Supreme Junta at Seville to coordinate revolutionary activities. Most of them were deeply conservative landowners and clergy who were supported by an equally conservative peasantry. They had disliked the Bourbon reforms and were almost wholly untouched by the ideas of the Enlightenment.

The minority of Spaniards who had imbibed enlightened ideas were divided. Some, called *afrancesados*, supported the Bonapartist regime because they believed it offered the best chance of reforming Spanish society. Others, out of national feeling or distrust of Napoleonic authoritarianism, supported the juntas. The revolutionary movement was therefore divided, not only by regionalism but by ideology. It remained effective on the local level, but could not govern nationally. The French, confronted by the guerrillas and after 1812 by the armies of the Duke of Wellington, could do little but fight for their lives. The struggle in the Peninsula, as terrible and chaotic as any in history, left the Spanish empire without a functioning central government for six long years. The American colonies were left to their own devices.

8

THE END OF THE EMPIRE

The independence of Spanish America did not arise from ideological conviction or from a widespread desire to be free of Spain. Many Creoles had long resented Bourbon authoritarianism and what they saw as indifference to colonial interests. Some had lost faith in the moral legitimacy of Bourbon rule, but with the exception of a few bold spirits who had imbibed the rhetoric of the French and American revolutions there was little support for independence in the colonies prior to 1808. America, in other words, did not try to break with Spain; the Spanish monarchy deserted America.

The abdications of 1808 left the empire without an effective government. They were at one level a symptom of dynastic failure, but Spain's problems ran far deeper than the personal inadequacies of Charles IV and Ferdinand VII. Spain's wealth and population had increased during the eighteenth century. Its government, while sacrificing a measure of legitimacy in the eyes of some, had become more efficient. Unfortunately, its rivals had grown wealthier and more powerful by comparison. The flow of New World bullion alone could not protect it from Napoleon's mobilization of the far greater wealth and manpower of France or the vast resources unlocked by Britain's industrial revolution. In 1808 Spain remained a relatively poor nation caught between the opposing threats of the French army and the British navy. It saved itself in the end through sheer heroism and bloody-mindedness, but it could not at the same time continue to rule an empire.

The realization that they were essentially on their own provoked a crisis among the Creole elite. They knew, as outsiders sometimes did not, that Spanish American society appeared more stable and unified than it

172

actually was. Cultural imperialism, painstakingly cultivated by generations of churchmen and officials, had ensured the dominance of Spain's language, religion, and even architecture. The monarchy, its laws, and its system of imperial government had provided common institutions and a common—although now much weakened—ideology, but this apparent unity masked deep fissures that had been present since the conquest.

The most important of these fissures were of race and class. Each of the colonies was a multiracial society that included people of European, Indian, and African ancestry in every possible combination. There were no academic theories of racial superiority and the monarchy had never countenanced the harsh racialism of Anglo-American law, but prejudice was widespread and deeply resented by its victims. The almost perfect correlation of wealth and skin color in a society that boasted few rich and many poor made matters worse. The crown had protected the Creole elites against the wrath of Indians, poor people (often of mixed blood), and slaves. A majority of the white and wealthy feared that the end of the monarchy would unleash social instability or even racial warfare of the kind that had recently afflicted the French colony of St. Domingue. In 1791, a violent slave revolt had given birth to the Black Republic of Haiti. The Haitians repelled a French invasion in 1802, but by 1808 the country had split into two halves: a southern Republic under President for Life Alexandre Pétion and a northern kingdom ruled by the terrifying Henri Christophe. By this time, those whites who survived had long since fled, carrying with them tales of horror that revived memories of Indian revolts in the past.

The other great fissure of Spanish American society was geographical. The colonies had always been separate, geographically isolated kingdoms united only by their common allegiance to the king of Spain. Their primary lines of communication had been with Spain rather than with each other. Their economies and economic interests differed, and few of their leading citizens knew their counterparts in other colonies. Internally, the viceroyalties of New Spain, Peru, La Plata, and New Granada were fragmented as well. Transport and communication between regions was often poor, and each region had its own ruling elite. In the event of war or a revolution, there would be little hope of mutual assistance or cooperation.

It is not surprising, then, that at the beginning of 1808 few dreamed of independence, but the events of that year left the American colonies with little choice. Since the advent of neutral trade in the 1790s, their economies had become dependent on countries other than Spain. The abdication of the Bourbons therefore severed the only remaining tie that bound them, and confronted both Creoles and royal officials with choices for which they were wholly unprepared. Few if any wanted to recognize the usurper Joseph Bonaparte. Beyond that, the possible options were, almost without exception, agonizing. If they chose independence, could social stability be maintained? If the colonies were to remain under Spanish rule, whose rule would they accept? Should they continue to support the remaining viceroys and hope for the eventual restoration of Ferdinand "*El Deseado*," or should they accept the rule of the Supreme Junta at Seville which claimed the powers of a regency until the king could be restored?

The latter option became more complicated when Napoleon's army conquered Andalusia in 1810 and the Junta took refuge at Cádiz. Confined to a crowded peninsula at the farthest corner of the Peninsula, the Junta fell under the control of *liberales* (the term, like *guerilla*, appears to have been first used at this time) whose enlightened views did not reflect those of the nation as a whole. Given the French occupation and the anarchic conditions it had created, delegates from many of the regional juntas could not go to Cádiz. The Junta gave their seats to substitutes (*suplentes*) whose geographical origins did not necessarily reflect the districts they were to represent, but who could be expected to support the Junta's program. The nature of that program became clear when the Junta convened a Cortes for the purpose of writing Spain's first constitution. The document itself appeared in 1812 and became a manifesto for the liberal cause that would attract adherents for decades to come. It envisioned a limited constitutional monarchy based on civil equality, personal liberty, and the rights of property. Creoles were to be granted citizenship and representation, but, as might be expected, the Cortes of Cádiz had close ties to the local merchant community and carefully limited the number of Creole representatives under the new constitution. It made no concessions whatever on the subject of free trade, which would have harmed the commercial interests of the city that protected them.

Even if the Cortes and its constitution were to survive, which many doubted, its program held little attraction for many Creoles. For those who admired the French and American revolutions, it did not go far enough. They wanted independence and a republican form of government. For royalists who longed for a church-supported monarchy based on divine right and natural law, the constitution was an abomination. They, together with a majority of peninsular Spaniards, hoped for the restoration of Ferdinand VII. *El Deseado* in fact recovered his throne in 1814 after the allies' defeat of Napoleon, but ended by disappointing even many of his followers. Stubborn and vindictive, he rejected the Constitution of 1812, persecuted its adherents, and restored the Inquisition without making himself beloved, even among the loyalists. He may have rejected the enlightened theories of his immediate predecessors, but like them he tended to rule arbitrarily with little consultation or concern for the interests of his subjects. He also intended to preserve his American empire, but circumstances and his own failings prevented him from doing so.

Ferdinand believed, correctly, that a majority of his subjects remained deeply conservative, but gravely overestimated his personal popularity and underestimated the influence of liberals among Spain's urban elite and in the army. In 1820 a military coup led by Colonel Rafael Riego secured his person and forced him to restore the Constitution of 1812. Significantly, the revolt was triggered by the refusal of several army units to serve against the rebels in the New World. Spanish conservatives did nothing to rescue him, but the liberal triumph was short lived. Ferdinand appealed to his fellow monarchs in France, Austria, and Russia, whose goal since the Congress of Vienna had been to restore the pre-revolutionary order throughout Europe. In April, 1823 a French army conquered Spain in a matter of weeks and released the king from his captors. Ferdinand then abolished the Constitution of 1812 for the second time. The acceptance of a French monarchist invasion by Spaniards who had fought Napoleon to a bloody standstill showed that, if the loyalists were demoralized, the liberals had not yet won the hearts of their countrymen. The Riego Revolt and its aftermath nevertheless halted the crown's efforts to intervene successfully in the problems of America. By 1824, all hope of restoring royal government there had been lost.

THE WARS OF INDEPENDENCE

In each colony, the movement toward independence evolved in response to the unfolding crisis in Spain. The Spanish monarchy's abject failure to govern from the Napoleonic invasion through the restoration of Ferdinand VII and the Riego Revolt eventually left even the most conservative Creoles with no option other than to govern themselves. At the beginning, few Creoles accepted the ideals of republicanism or even of the Enlightenment. Many were no doubt ignorant of either, but where charismatic, dedicated republicans like Bolívar and San Martín offered a credible alternative to the repeated failures of the monarchy their leadership changed the character of the independence movement. Where no such leaders emerged (or survived), the ideal of monarchy died a far more lingering death. The course of each war of independence therefore depended in part on the character of its leaders. The past history and social structure of each colony were more important yet.

The Peruvians, perhaps mindful of the Tupac Amaru revolt a genera-tion before, remained loyal to the crown until independence was forced upon them by outsiders after the Riego Revolt. Events in New Spain may have reinforced their caution. In 1810, Father Miguel Hidalgo, priest of the small town of Dolores, raised an Indian army in support of inde-pendence. His motivation is not entirely clear but, like many members of the lower clergy, he was apparently frustrated by the Bourbon's attitude toward the church and sympathetic to the many grievances of his Indian flock. Nearly three centuries of pent-up Indian frustration erupted in the massacre of Spaniards and heavy destruction of property throughout north-central Mexico. Finally, in 1811 the viceroy's army defeated the insurgents and executed Hidalgo, but the government was too weak to restore order outside the capital. Of the many local warlords who arose to fill the vacuum, one emerged as a potential leader. José Maria Morelos, another priest, estab-lished himself in what is now the state of Guerrero and developed a plan for nationhood that involved popular sovereignty and the breakup of large estates. A more disciplined and thoughtful man than Hidalgo, he attracted supporters even among the elite, and by 1813 his forces controlled much of southern Mexico. In 1814 a congress of delegates from the area met under his guidance at Chilpancingo to draw up the first Mexican constitution, a document that would long serve as an inspiration to Mexican liberals.

The end of this phase of the revolution came when the Cádiz government, in one of its last acts before the restoration of the king, belatedly appointed General Felix Calleja as viceroy. A master of counter-insurgency, Calleja and his army, which was commanded in the field by the Creole Colonel Agustín de Iturbide, gradually recovered the territory lost to the rebels and on December 22, 1815, executed Morelos. Ferdinand VII replaced Calleja with his own appointment in 1816 and Mexico enjoyed relative peace until the revolt of 1820 forced Ferdinand to accept the Constitution of 1812. Iturbide and the Creoles saw themselves abandoned. With the restored monarchy no longer capable of defending itself or them, they decided to support independence.

In concert with the remnants of Morelos's revolutionaries Iturbide devised the Plan of Ayala, a compromise document declaring Mexico an independent monarchy based on the Spanish Constitution of 1812 with either Ferdinand or one of his brothers as emperor. Central America, heretofore the Captaincy-General of Guatemala, followed suit. Ferdinand, still a virtual prisoner of the Spanish military, refused either to accept

Mexican independence or do anything to stop it, and in May, 1822, Iturbide had himself proclaimed Emperor Agustín I. His rule lasted less than a year. Iturbide had always sided with the Creole elite, but was distrusted by them for his Mestizo and merchant origins and for his compromises with the republicans. Vicente Guerrero, the successor of Morelos and co-signer of the Plan of Ayala, soon came to distrust him for his allegiance to the elites, and in March, 1823, a military coup replaced Emperor Iturbide with a republic headed by Colonel Antonio López de Santa Anna. The military coup became a precedent that would be much copied in the years to come.

In the Viceroyalty of Río de la Plata, the road to independence began even before the tumults of 1808. The British had long dominated the trade of Buenos Aires, and in 1806 a force under Admiral Sir Home Popham captured the city, thinking that they would be welcomed by the inhabitants. The viceroy promptly fled, but the Creoles under Santiago Liniers, a French-born officer in the Spanish navy, drove the British out. The British returned in the following year. Once again the viceroy fled and the Creoles expelled the invaders. Neither Spain nor its viceroy did anything to help them on either occasion. Finding themselves essentially on their own, Liniers and his followers called a *cabildo abierto* of all propertied citizens in 1807. Such bodies had been convened since the sixteenth century, usually in frontier areas and usually in response to a major crisis. This one promptly imprisoned the viceroy as soon as he returned to the city, and for the next three years Buenos Aires governed itself. When the Supreme Junta at Seville appointed a new viceroy in 1810, he found it impossible to establish his authority. The *porteños* soon expelled him and established a governing junta "loyal to Ferdinand VII."

Buenos Aires could not, however, impose its authority on the rest of the viceroyalty. The royalists of Upper Peru defeated an army sent against them in 1811, thereby retaining control of the silver mines. Córdoba, Jujuy, and the other intendancies of northwestern Argentina demanded and received representation in the junta as provinces, while Paraguay declared itself independent. The dominant figure at Asunción was Dr. José Rodríguez de Francia, who acquired dictatorial powers in 1814 and ruled Paraguay as "El Supremo" until his death in 1840. After a second attack on Upper Peru failed in 1813, the Buenos Aires junta convened a representative assembly of the provinces, but refused to seat delegates from the Banda Oriental, the region on the east bank of the Rio de la Plata whose capital was Montevideo. The infuriated *orientalistas*, who had demanded a federal republic of the Río de la Plata modeled on that of the United States, seized the provinces of Corrientes and Entre Ríos and threatened to attack Buenos Aires. This triggered a three-way struggle among the *orientalistas*, the Argentines, and the Portuguese at São Paulo that lasted until the Banda Oriental achieved independence as the Republic of Uruguay in 1828.

Undeterred by these struggles, the Argentines continued their efforts to conquer Upper Peru and its silver. The prime mover of these schemes was José de San Martín. Born in northern Argentina, he had gone to Spain at an early age and become a lieutenant colonel in the Spanish army. Like many of his fellow officers he was an ardent liberal. In 1812 he went to Buenos Aires to further the cause of independence. San Martín believed that the independence movement as a whole depended on defeating the Peruvian loyalists, and that this could only be done by freeing Chile and then attacking Lima from the sea. In 1810 a cabildo abierto at Santiago had rejected viceregal authority and created a junta of local leaders that included Bernardo O'Higgins, the son of a former governor of Chile and viceroy of Peru. Of mixed Irish and Chilean parentage, O'Higgins had been educated in England and was, like San Martín, a liberal. When the loyalist army recaptured Santiago in 1814, O'Higgins fled to Buenos Aires and made common cause with San Martín. Together, with an army trained and commanded by the latter, they crossed the Andes, defeated the loyalists, and recaptured Santiago. Remarkably, San Martín was the kind of idealist who did not seek political power on his own. Chile declared independence in 1818 with O'Higgins as supreme director of the new state, and the two collaborators began to assemble a fleet for the invasion of Peru. Assisted by a contingent of British sailors commanded by Sir Thomas Cochrane, formerly of the British navy, the Chileans captured Lima in 1820. The Peruvian declaration of independence in 1821 was nevertheless premature. San Martín's position at Lima became precarious after Cochrane's departure, while the loyalist army retreated to the highlands and continued to fight for three more years.

The situation in New Granada, with its long history of internal conflict, was even more confusing and violent than the struggles to the south. The flight of the Supreme Junta to Cádiz in 1810 provoked the establishments of local juntas throughout the region. All of them originally supported Ferdinand VII until in 1811 the prominent liberal Antonio Nariño established a republican government at Bogotá with himself as president. The other provinces were at this time trying to organize a federated government of New Granada in which each retained its own administration under a national congress that would control foreign and military affairs. In response to the bitter opposition of Nariño and his followers—and to what they perceived as the characteristic arrogance of the *bogoteños*—the rest of the congress left Bogotá and established itself as a kind of alternative government at Ibagué.

In Caracas, which had always seen itself as separate from Colombia, a cabildo abierto expelled the captain-general and established a junta that was joined by all of the other provinces with the exception of three that remained vehemently royalist. In July, 1811, the anti-monarchists declared independence and asked Francisco Miranda to serve as president. Miranda was a remarkable mixture of visionary and charlatan. A Venezuelan native whose career in the Spanish army included convictions for indiscipline and financial peculation, he took refuge in the United States and became an admirer of its institutions. He later fought for the French Revolution and for Napoleon, and in the summer of 1806 made two attempts to invade Venezuela, first with the help of Americans who thought wrongly that he had the support of Thomas Jefferson, and then with the aid of the British. Both attempts failed, but his republican principles and his admiration for the United States were well known. His term of office was, however, brief. A loyalist reaction, supported by the clergy—and aided by an earthquake that providentially destroyed the revolutionary strongholds while sparing those loyal to the king—toppled him in July, 1812.

At this point, the fate of New Granada became intertwined with that of Simón Bolívar, one of the most extraordinary personalities of the age. A native of Caracas, Bolívar was tutored by a follower of Rousseau before continuing his education in France. Steeped in the literature of the Enlightenment, he returned to Caracas in 1808 and played an important role in installing Miranda's government. When it collapsed, he fled to Cartagena where he issued the first of several republican manifestos. Amazingly, the divided government of New Granada granted him a military commission and helped him to raise an army with which he recaptured Caracas in 1813. The campaign was a bloody "war to the death" intended to make any future compromise with the loyalists impossible, and once in Caracas, he had himself proclaimed Liberator of Venezuela with dictatorial powers. Like many republicans of the day, Bolívar believed in the rights of man, but felt that states required the guidance of a strong, if enlightened, executive power. For the moment, a majority of Venezuelans disagreed. The loyalists enlisted the support of the llaneros or cowboys of the Orinoco valley, and in a campaign as filled with atrocities as Bolívar's "war to the death" drove the Liberator and his supporters from the country.

After failing to establish himself at Santa Marta in Colombia, he fled to Jamaica. There he called for the establishment of a federation of Spanish

American republics in his "Letter from Jamaica," and sought help from Britain and the United States. When they refused, he received guns and money from Alexandre Pétion of Haiti. Bolívar returned to New Granada, but could accomplish nothing. In 1815 Ferdinand VII, still buoyed by the enthusiasm surrounding his restoration, sent a powerful army to New Granada under General Pablo Morrillo. It was Spain's most serious attempt to reclaim its American colonies and could have been a model for expeditions to follow. Morrillo restored royal authority in New Granada, Bolívar's military efforts failed, and once again he fled to Haiti.

Finally, in 1817, he decided to establish himself in the wilderness of the Orinoco valley, where the fierce *llaneros* had changed sides and now favored the revolution. Two years later, with an army that included a substantial British contingent, Bolívar crossed the Andes and surprised the royal army at Boyacá in the Colombian highlands near Bogotá. The march itself bordered on the incredible, and the campaign remains among the high points of the wars of independence. He entered Bogotá in August, 1819, and in December proclaimed the Republic of Gran Colombia. The new state was to contain Ecuador and Venezuela, although both as yet remained loyalist and Morrillo's forces were largely intact. Finally, the Riego Revolt in Spain gave Bolívar the triumph he had sought for so long. Utterly demoralized by news of the revolt, Morrillo and his army agreed to a truce. Bolívar took Caracas in June, 1821 and Quito in May, 1822. Only the status of Peru remained uncertain. On July 26, 1822 San Martín met Bolívar at Guayaquil to enlist his support. Bolívar's position was the stronger and he saw no reason to cooperate. San Martín returned to Lima in disgust and resigned his position. Bolívar went on to conquer Lima in December, 1824 with the aid of a brilliant 29-year-old general from Venezuela, Antonio José de Sucre. In the following year, Sucre at last expelled the royalists from Upper Peru and became the first president of Bolivia. Both campaigns were aided by divisions among the royalists, who had split over Ferdinand VII's second abolition of the 1812 Constitution.

The independence of South America, like that of Mexico, had been achieved almost entirely by the efforts of its inhabitants. British intervention played a role in Argentina, Chile, and New Granada, but its importance is difficult to assess. Britain's policy remained tentative and inconsistent throughout the period as Whitehall tried to reconcile its lukewarm support for independence with the need to conciliate the monarchists of the Concert of Europe. From Popham to Cochrane, British efforts remained limited and highly unofficial. The young United States contributed almost nothing.

By 1838 the Spanish Empire in America had splintered into no fewer than 15 independent states. A 16th, the Dominican Republic, which occupies the eastern two-thirds of Hispaniola, had been ceded to France in 1795. The Creoles rebelled in 1808 and restored Spanish rule, but when the monarchy appeared to collapse for the second time in 1821, they tried to join Bolívar's Gran Colombia. Haiti promptly invaded, and it was not until 1844 that the Dominicans at last achieved independence. Only Cuba and Puerto Rico—and in Asia, the Philippines—remained loyal to Spain.

THE LOYAL ISLANDS AND THE SPANISH–AMERICAN WAR

For most of their post-conquest history, Cuba and Puerto Rico had been important primarily as bases for the protection and provisioning of the fleets. Many of those who lived in their heavily fortified capitals, Havana and San Juan, were either royal officials or dependent on government employment. Until late in the eighteenth century, their hinterlands helped to supply the capitals and the fleets, but had little contact with world trade until Cuba became the center of a lucrative government tobacco monopoly. The turning point in the history of both islands was the great slave revolt in St. Domingue that began in 1795 and gave birth to the independent nation of Haiti. St. Domingue had been the largest producer of sugar in the Caribbean. The revolt brought production to a standstill as plantation owners and managers fled the country. Some went to Louisiana, but most brought their skills and what remained of their capital to Cuba and Puerto Rico. Within a decade, Cuba had replaced Haiti as the center of the sugar industry with Puerto Rico in its wake.

The arrival of the emigrés and the wave of prosperity that accompanied them reinforced the conservatism of a population that had not been inclined toward independence in the first place. The crown's many employees hoped to keep their jobs, while the backcountry farmers and ranchers had never suffered from Spain's economic policies. The new plantations brought a massive influx of African slaves, and with it an increased fear of slave insurrection in the event of secession from Spain. The emigrés, who had experienced the horrors of the Haitian revolt, had no desire to repeat the experience. Moreover, they feared that Britain's efforts to ban the slave trade would cut off their source of labor and thought rightly that Spain, unlike its rebellious colonies, would preserve the institution on which they depended. In 1815 the crown wisely reinforced this loyalty by relaxing trade regulations in favor of the islands. The wars of independence passed them by, and Puerto Rico even helped the crown to recover Santo Domingo in 1808.

The Philippines had always been an anomaly among the Spanish possessions. Manila was in most respects a trading station similar in some ways to the colonies founded by Portugal in the Far East. Spain had actually conquered very little of the archipelago, and had made only meager efforts to introduce Spanish language and culture. Spanish-speaking Filipinos numbered no more than about 5000 in 1800, and even the Dominican friars seemed more interested in the large population of overseas Chinese who controlled much of Manila's economy. A brief protest against Spanish rule had been easily suppressed after the British occupation in 1764, in part because the native population was divided ethnically and linguistically and in part because they hated the Chinese more than the Spanish. The age of independence passed with few incidents. Perhaps the most important change was that the Manila Galleon sailed for the last time in 1811. After that, free commerce removed what might have become a source of grievance, while the presence of two Filipino members in the Spanish Cortes provided the illusion of representation.

Throughout the nineteenth century rotating ministries and bitter disputes between liberals and conservatives prevented Spain from developing a rational colonial policy. Ill-advised and often contradictory decisions produced widespread discontent in its remaining colonies, each of which eventually developed a national movement. In Cuba, for example, the crown awarded arbitrary powers to the governor in 1825, and in 1837 ended the island's representation in the Cortes. The government promised to pass "special laws," but subsequent administrations did nothing. Afflicted by what they regarded as an incompetent tyranny, some Cubans—and Puerto Ricans as well—sought to be annexed by the United States. The annexationist movement achieved a measure of support from the southern states who were at this time hoping to preserve slavery by creating new slave states that would help them to increase their representation in Congress. This strategy influenced the granting of statehood to Texas, the Mexican War, and the filibustering expeditions of William Walker in Nicaragua, but came to an abrupt end—together with the annexationist dreams of Cuban and Puerto Rican slaveholders—in the American Civil War of 1861–1865. Other Cubans, many of whom wanted slavery abolished, preferred independence.

The abdication of Queen Isabella II in 1868 triggered revolutionary movements in both islands. With the future of slavery now uncertain, many landowners now sought local autonomy and a relaxation of the tariffs that hampered trade with the United States. Isabella's government ignored

these Reformists, who then put their hopes in the revolutionary government that overthrew her in September, 1868. That government, however,
reacted inconsistently. It offered a measure of autonomy to Puerto Rico,
but did nothing for Cuba. The Spanish Prime Minister, the Catalan General
Prim, would have been willing to grant autonomy, or even to sell Cuba to
the United States, but he could not overcome severe pressure from the powerful Cuban lobby of Spanish-born traders and bureaucrats who opposed
all reform and the Catalan merchants who supported them. Many of the
disappointed Reformists then joined forces with the secessionist movement
that had been brewing in Oriente and Camagüey provinces. The *peninsu-
lares* formed a volunteer militia which expelled the governor-general from
Havana when he tried to broker a truce. In response, Spain sent 100,000
troops to quell the disturbance and the Cuban insurrection expanded into
the Ten Years' War that cost the lives of more than 200,000 people, Cuban
and Spanish.

The struggle ended in 1878 with the promise of reforms and an end
to slavery. By this time Spain itself had passed through the assassination
of General Prim, an abortive monarchy under Amadeo of Savoy, and the
restoration of Isabella's son, Alfonso XII in 1875. Spain was now a constitutional monarchy in which two rather similar political parties took turns
dominating the Cortes. It was in many ways a good arrangement, but the
torno, as it was called did not produce a consistent colonial policy. Cuba once
again gained representation in the Cortes and slavery was finally abolished
in 1886, but the promised reforms never materialized. Moreover, Spain
insisted that Cuba pay reparation for war damages. In 1887 the same government that had banned slavery suppressed the autonomy movement in
Puerto Rico, and by the 1890s secessionism had revived in both islands.

While Spain dithered, business interests from the United States increased
their investments, especially in Cuba. When Cuba rebelled again in 1895
under the leadership of José Martí's Cuban Revolutionary Party, the giant
to the north began taking a more serious interest in the island's problems.
This time, Spain responded by sending an army commanded by an officer who hoped, vainly, for a reconciliation between the secessionists and
the loyalists. He was succeeded in January, 1896, by General Valeriano
Weyler, whose policy of isolating the rebels in concentration camps led him
to be called "the Butcher." Business interests in the United States began to
clamor for intervention while their supporters in the press provided vivid,
if not always accurate, details of Spanish atrocities. Another group, headed
by Secretary of the Navy Theodore Roosevelt and inspired by the writings
of Admiral Alfred Thayer Mahan, favored war for different reasons. They

believed that American interests demanded the construction of a battle fleet and naval control over a strategic arc stretching from Key West to Hawaii. They thought that control depended upon friendly, if not subservient, governments in Cuba and Puerto Rico and the construction of an American canal across the Isthmus of Panama.

President William McKinley was reluctant to intervene even in the face of strong domestic pressure, but when Spain proved incapable of defeating the insurgents he sent the battleship *USS Maine* to Havana to help protect American lives and property. The cause of the explosion that destroyed the ship in Havana harbor on February 15, 1898 has never been determined, but the resulting popular outrage, coupled with a devastating report on conditions in Cuba by Senator Proctor of Vermont, made war inevitable.

Spain was wholly unprepared for the conflict that began in April, 1898. On May 1, Commodore Dewey destroyed the Spanish squadron that lay anchored in Manila Bay. The Spanish had little coal or ammunition and one of the ships lacked engines. Later that month, another Spanish squadron consisting of four cruisers and three destroyers under Admiral Pascual Cervera arrived at Santiago in eastern Cuba. The US Army, itself poorly prepared and equipped, failed to capture the city on July 1, but two days later the captain-general at Havana ordered Cervera to sea where a much larger American fleet that included four new state-of-the-art battleships destroyed the entire Spanish squadron with virtually no damage to itself. Santiago surrendered two weeks later, and on July 18, Spain sued for peace. The US Army immediately occupied Puerto Rico and an American force of 11,000 men arrived in the Philippines where they occupied Manila a day after the armistice on August 12. In the final treaty, signed on December 10, 1898, Spain ceded Cuba, the Philippines, Puerto Rico, and the southern Marianas to the United States and sold the northern Marianas and the Carolines to Germany. The entire Spanish empire now consisted of two presidios in North Africa: Ceuta and Melilla.

AFTER INDEPENDENCE

The republics that emerged from the collapse of Spain's empire in America faced daunting challenges, many of them economic. A few of the new nations were too small, remote, or lacking in resources to be economically viable. Others, such as Mexico and Argentina, showed great promise, but the wars of independence had disrupted established markets and trading relationships. Moreover, by invoking the demons of regional, class, and racial hatred, the wars caused enormous damage to property and infrastructure. Angry mobs burned farms, businesses, and homes. The already inadequate network of roads, bridges, and port facilities, never a high priority under the crown, had been largely destroyed in the name of military necessity. If the new republics were to revive trade and re-establish communications with their own provinces, they would have to undertake massive construction projects, but war and the loss of overseas trade had left them with empty treasuries and an impoverished citizenry. Peninsular Spaniards, a group hated by nearly everyone in the colonies, returned to Spain or fled to Cuba with their wealth and managerial skills. The result was a shortage of investment capital that persisted for many years. Spanish America found it extremely difficult to expand or even to maintain its already modest industrial capacity and became more dependent than ever on manufactured goods from Europe and the United States.

At the same time, a decline in the availability of cheap, forced labor crippled the mining industry and plantation agriculture. Slaves had been manumitted in large numbers during the wars, often in return for military service. Most of the new republican governments abolished slavery in their first constitutions, and by 1830 the institution had largely disappeared from the former Spanish Empire. Without slaves, the sugar and cacao industries could not compete with the plantations of Brazil and Cuba where slavery persisted. Colombian gold output declined as well. When the Andean Republics abolished the *mita*, Indian laborers returned to their homes and silver production dropped by two-thirds. It never fully recovered. These former staples of imperial trade were replaced to some extent by other products including copper, tin, hides, wool, and grain. Venezuelan coffee growers prospered for a time, but the high cost of capital and competition from slave-holding Brazil eventually took their toll.

In the face of these difficulties, the economy of Spanish America became more truly colonial after independence than it had been under the empire. Without capital for investment or new technology, artisan manufacturers could not compete with low-cost tools and textiles mass-produced in Europe. To pay for these imports, each country depended upon a limited number of commodities, all of which were subject to extreme market fluctuations. The trade itself was controlled by outsiders, especially the British, because Latin Americans now lacked ships and the commercial institutions that could provide credit, insurance, and access to markets. Boom and bust cycles had not been unknown in the old empire, but for obvious reasons they intensified after independence, causing increased social tension and making it all but impossible for governments to budget wisely or to maintain fiscal stability.

The political costs of independence proved equally high. The collapse of Spain's American empire did not arise from any deep-seated impulses within colonial society but from the failure of the Spanish monarchy in Europe. As a result, independence did not change the structure of colonial society or the informal networks of kinship and clientage that made it work. It merely removed the monarchy, the one institution that together with the Church gave the system its legitimacy. Even in its periods of greatest weakness, the royal government and its ministers had refereed disputes between different regions and mediated social and factional conflicts within them. For most of its history Spain had also provided a measure of economic, diplomatic, and military protection that no individual republic could achieve on its own. Britain and the United States might offer support against the ambitions of other powers (the Monroe Doctrine of 1824 is an example of such guarantees), but their assistance came at the price of repeated interventions in support of their economic interests.

As Bolívar had foreseen, one way to deal with these problems was to create broader confederations within Spanish America, but without the crown as a center of allegiance such efforts failed. Gran Colombia, the state he created, did not long survive him, and by 1830 had divided into Venezuela, Colombia, and Ecuador. The United Provinces of Central America survived only until 1838. In all of these regions, and many others, the power of the existing Creole elites was regional if not local in scope. They had no desire to dilute their influence by entering a larger arena, and Spanish America remained politically fragmented, sometimes to the point of open warfare between republics and even among their provinces.

Above all, allegiance to the crown had provided the colonies with an ideological basis for cohesion that was now lost. Colonial elites had relied upon the sacral character of the monarchy to ensure stability and preserve their privileged position. That bond had been greatly weakened by the Bourbons and was now wholly shattered. After independence, some influential Creoles sought to preserve as much of the old order as possible, including the Church, which they saw as a bulwark of social order. Others embraced liberalism as a counter-ideology. Liberalism in the nineteenth century had a different meaning than it does today. It had little interest in social services but, in the tradition of the Enlightenment, emphasized the rights of man, attacked the privileges of the Church, and favored (at least in theory) a kind of laissez-faire capitalism. In some cases, these ideological disagreements did little more than mask long-held rivalries between kinship and clientage groups. Neither liberals nor conservatives intended to cede power to Indians or to the poor, and both often relied on undemocratic methods to preserve their influence.

In the chaotic years that followed independence, many of the Spanish American republics fell under the rule of *caudillos*. The term, which dates to the medieval Reconquest, describes a charismatic leader who combines military force with the manipulation of patronage to maintain power. Caudillos could be found at the national level like Juan Manuel Rosas in Argentina or Santa Anna in Mexico; others were little more than local warlords. Some claimed to be conservatives; others were nominally liberal. With no accepted basis for political unity and their economies in tatters, the new nations reverted to a system that had prevailed under the conquistadors before Charles V imposed the beginnings of imperial government. Bolívar himself, the great advocate of republicanism, had banned elections in Gran Colombia before declaring the country ungovernable and dying on his way to exile in 1830.

Men of the caudillo type would re-emerge as dictators from time to time until well into the twentieth century, but by 1850 European demand for agricultural products had created a limited degree of prosperity in many areas. Improved economic conditions and the growing importance of an urban professional class led some of the republics to develop a more stable political system based on constitutional principles. Liberals and conservatives alternated in power, although the transitions were often accompanied by violence. Both parties remained upper-class factions composed of clientage groups that disagreed on several issues. One was the debate over federalism versus centralism. In Mexico, conservatives from the capital tended to favor the centralization of government functions. Liberals, largely from the provinces, favored federalism. In Argentina, liberal merchants dominated the ruling elite of Buenos Aires and favored centralism in the hope of reining in the more conservative provinces. Conservatives generally sought to preserve the Church and its privileges while liberals sought to limit its influence and confiscate its property, but even this principle was not sacrosanct. All of the republics needed money to provide basic services and improve infrastructure. The dire poverty of most citizens and the ability of the rich to protect their assets limited tax yields, and loans could usually be obtained only from foreign sources at high interest rates. In these circumstances the wealth of the church offered a tempting target to politicians of every stripe.

After the middle of the nineteenth century, liberals in several countries including Mexico, Argentina, and the Andean republics succeeded in imposing a degree of reform. Liberal governments found that by selling church property to prominent conservatives they could largely neutralize the advocates of clerical privilege. At the same time, increased profits from the sale of agricultural products and raw materials to foreign consumers appeared to justify free market theories of economic development. The last years of the century produced considerable wealth for the merchant and landowning classes along with a flowering of the arts and literature. Downtown areas of several national capitals were rebuilt to resemble Paris and Madrid.

Encouraged by their apparent success, liberal theorists pursued the goals of progress and scientific knowledge by attacking everything that seemed primitive, traditional, or superstitious to them. Like their counterparts in Europe and North America, many Spanish American liberals embraced a form of social Darwinism that regarded non-whites as inferior. Their hatred of what they saw as primitivism and superstition often led them to attack Indian as well as popular culture. Above all, their hostility to traditional privilege and their belief in free markets led them to dismantle the Indian communes. The destruction of traditional communities left the Indians more than ever at the mercy of rural landholders and forced them to become impoverished wage laborers living under conditions far worse than anything seen since the days of the conquest. It also became obvious that freedom of economic opportunity did not apply to those outside the white elite. The exclusion of Indians, Mestizos, and even poor whites from the benefits of liberal democracy was not primarily the result of theoretical bias but of the underlying structures of a society still based on the ancient principles of kinship, clientage, and personal honor. Even in today's Spanish America, the would-be entrepreneur faces immense obstacles if he or she lacks friends or family connections in high places.

A reaction was not long in coming. The failure of liberal regimes to ameliorate the tensions produced by race and class, while claiming at the same time to support the rights of man, provoked widespread disenchantment even among the liberal elites. The first half of the twentieth century saw the emergence of radical movements in every Spanish American state. Some, like Emiliano Zapata's attempt to reconstitute Indian communities and restore their lands during the Mexican Revolution of 1910, had strong Catholic overtones. Others, fueled by the political and literary theories of *indigenismo*, sought to restore Indian culture as well. The communitarian values of Indian society made it easy for parties like those of Mariátegui and Haya de la Torre in Peru to fuse Marxist ideas with *indigenismo*, a process replicated in the twenty-first century by Evo Morales in Bolivia. Communist parties on the European model appeared in most countries during the 1920s, but did not attract widespread support until after World War II when they were adopted by urban workers. Ironically, the radical and *indigenista* movements were most likely to invoke the ancient ideal of a polity based on some kind of moral order, while the conservatives embraced capitalism and a market economy that all too often has been anything but free.

Nationalist movements, some with fascist underpinnings, began to appear in the cities. Nationalists resented foreign dominance over their nations' economies and what they regarded as the imperialism of the United States. The role of the United States in Latin American affairs has always been problematic. Much of the hemisphere has long regarded the colossus to the north as a major cause of its problems and deeply resents its tendency to intervene in their internal affairs. In fact the policy of the United States has been inconsistent. In the years prior to the Civil War, southerners who sought to expand slavery sponsored an independence movement in Cuba and filibustering expeditions in Central America. Mexico, "so far from God and so close to the United States," suffered the most. Texas independence and The Mexican War of 1845 cost Mexico a significant portion of its historic territory.

From 1865 to 1898 American interest in Latin America was largely commercial, but after 1898, the seizure of Cuba and Puerto Rico and the new American naval strategy associated with President Theodore Roosevelt led to the age of "Big Stick" diplomacy. In 1903, the United States engineered Panama's declaration of independence from Colombia and, after building the Panama Canal, dominated the politics and economy of the new nation until 1979 when President Jimmy Carter ceded the canal to Panama. In 1904, Roosevelt proclaimed his corollary to the Monroe Doctrine: the United States had the right as an "international police power" to intervene whenever it thought that "civilized" norms of political behavior had been violated. Subsequent administrations used this doctrine to intervene repeatedly in the affairs of Nicaragua and several other Caribbean and Central American countries, often in support of the United Fruit Company's control of the banana trade. The "good-neighbor policy" of President Franklin D. Roosevelt reversed these policies in the 1930s and 1940s, but US interventionism resumed during the Cold War in an effort to prevent the establishment of Marxist regimes in several countries.

Trade policy caused further grievances. During the 1920s, US corporations gained control of much of Spanish America's mineral wealth. Standard Oil and its subsidiaries dominated the oil fields of Mexico, Peru, and Bolivia. American companies acquired the copper mines of Chile and Peru and the tin mines of Bolivia. In most cases they were able to extract valuable tax privileges from their host governments. At the same time, American tariffs virtually prohibited the import of agricultural products with the exception of such items as bananas that did not grow in the United States. When Britain, traditionally the chief importer of Latin American grain, sugar, meat, and cotton, succumbed to pressure from its own dominions and granted preference to their products, the Latin American agricultural sector suffered accordingly. In more recent times, the growth of the illegal drug trade has provoked further intervention by the United States in the affairs of Mexico, Colombia, Bolivia, and Panama, often with destabilizing results.

Nationalism, while understandable in these circumstances, provided no long-term stability even when it was combined with state ownership of selected economic resources and government support for trade unions. The failure of nationalistic socialism to promote economic growth and the absence of any real political consensus forced duly elected nationalists such as Lázaro Cárdenas in Mexico or Juan Perón in Argentina to adopt repressive measures with predictable results. Not all authoritarian regimes, of course, were nationalist. Some were liberal, while others represented an intervention by the military to prevent a Marxist takeover, often with covert American support.

In the early twenty-first century, many of the region's problems remain unresolved. Chile and Costa Rica, with their relative prosperity and fairly homogeneous populations, seem to have achieved a measure of stability, although for Chile the road has not been easy. Argentina's economy has suffered alarming fluctuations. In Mexico, free market reforms threaten to dismantle the corporate state created by Lázaro Cárdenas and the victors of the Mexican Revolution of the early twentieth century. The reformers are opposed by his son, Cuahetemoc Cárdenas, with his substantial following of farmers and workers. Communism continues to dominate Cuba, while the "Bolivarian Revolution" of Hugo Chávez in Venezuela and related movements in Ecuador and Bolivia promise further disruptions to come. In the midst of all this, the legacy of Habsburg political theory lurks in the shadows. The monarchy is long vanished. Few if any would restore it, but the idea of a polity based on a moral order is not dead. Ironically, that dream now inspires radicals and *indigenistas* rather than "conservatives" who have long since embraced a market economy that is all too often anything but free. Meanwhile, tens of thousands of Mexicans, accompanied by the desperate peasants of Honduras, Guatemala, and El Salvador, seek economic opportunity in North America, often at risk of their lives. Costa Ricans complain that they are engulfed by economic refugees from Nicaragua. Peru and

Colombia, long the site of bloody struggles between militias of the right and left, have produced emigrants of their own as has the Dominican Republic, while half a million Cuban opponents of the Castro regime have settled in South Florida.

Political and economic difficulties are not, of course, unique to Spanish America. The histories of Europe and the United States, to say nothing of Asia, Africa, and the Middle East, have produced ample conflict during the past 200 years. It is nevertheless safe to say that under the Spanish Empire the region was more stable than it has been since 1808. On a more positive note, the cultural achievements of the national period have far outstripped those of 300 years under colonial rule. The fusion of Spanish, Indian, African, and European immigrant cultures, together with the intense and varied ideological conflicts in nearly every country, has given birth to a rich body of achievement in art, music, and literature that is now widely appreciated in the West as a whole. Its influence on the United States will certainly grow now that immigrants from Spanish America make up a substantial part of that nation's population, especially in those parts of the country that were themselves once part of the Spanish Empire.

POST-IMPERIAL SPAIN

Spain survived the loss of its empire with little apparent damage. It is estimated that economic losses in the first decades after independence amounted to no more than 2 or 3 percent of the Spanish economy. The domestic failures of the monarchy, however, profoundly affected the nation's politics. Like its former colonies—and many of its European neighbors—Spain experienced more than a century of bitter struggles between liberals and conservatives that culminated in the terrible civil war of 1936–1939. The victory of the conservatives revealed the ongoing strength of traditional ideals. Francisco Franco and his *Movimiento Nacional* created a corporate state influenced by fascist principles, but retained a theoretical allegiance to the ideal of monarchy and, above all, to the memory of Ferdinand and Isabella as exemplars of all that was worthy in Spanish life. After Franco's death in 1975, the modern constitutional monarchy was restored. A subsequent attempt by reactionaries to dissolve the Cortes failed, owing in no small part to the moral authority of King Juan Carlos, and Spain has been governed ever since by freely elected governments of the right and the left like any other Western European nation.

The Spanish economy continued to grow during the nineteenth century, albeit at a slower rate than some of its European neighbors. The prosperity of its former possessions in southern Italy grew more slowly, even after the Bourbons were at last removed in 1860 and Naples and Sicily became part of the Italian monarchy of Victor Emmanuel II. The south remains poorer than Italy as a whole, but Spain has emerged since 1975 as one of Europe's fastest growing economies. By the beginning of the twenty-first century, Spanish banks and corporations were establishing a new commercial empire through mergers and acquisitions rather than by conquest. In a reversal of past history, Spanish interests are now active in the United States, Britain, and continental Europe. In the Spanish American republics, where language and culture gives Spanish businessmen an advantage, Spanish businesses are a growing presence unencumbered by past resentments. The Empire, which made Spain the world's greatest power while doing little for the Spanish themselves, is now only a memory—glorious to some and reviled by others.

GLOSSARY

Adelantado. The governor of a frontier province or the leader of an expedition.

Aides. In the Netherlands, one-time grants of funding from a representative body (see also *beden*).

Alcabala. A sales tax nominally levied as a percentage of final sales. In practice, the rate was usually negotiated with local authorities based on population (see *encabezamiento*).

Alcalde. In medieval Spain, the holder of a landed benefice from the king. From the fifteenth century, the chief magistrate of a Castilian town. In America, the *Alcalde mayor* was a district administrator who reported to the provincial governor and the regional audiencia. Lesser *alcaldes* served as magistrates and police officers in rural areas or in the *barrios* of larger cities.

Alguacil. The police chief of a Castilian town.

Almojarifazgo. An export duty.

Amigos del País. Local associations organized in Spain during the eighteenth century to encourage reform.

Arbitristas. Writers who proposed economic and social reforms in seventeenth-century Spain.

Asiento. A contract, usually to loan money to the crown or to supply slaves to the colonies.

Audiencia. An appellate court. In the American colonies, it also served as an advisory body to the regional chief executive. The territorial jurisdiction of such a court.

Avería. The fee collected by the Casa de Contratación to pay for protection of the Indies fleets.

Ayllu. The basic kinship group among Indians in the Andean region.

Ayuntamiento. A municipal council, also known as a *cabildo.*

Barrio. An urban district or neighborhood. Sometimes called a *colación.*

Beden. The Flemish term for *aides.*

Cabecera. A large Indian town with an elected governor and *cabildo.*

Cabildo. A municipal council or *ayuntamiento.*

Cabildo abierto. An extraordinary session of the *cabildo* attended by prominent members of the community, usually convened in times of crisis.

Cacique. An Indian chief.

Calpulli. The basic kinship unit among Indians in Mesoamerica.

Capitulación. A contract between the crown of Castile and a private individual, in this context setting out the terms for the exploration, conquest, and settlement of new territories.

Casa de Contratación. The House of Trade established at Seville in 1503 to regulate trade with the colonies. It moved to Cadíz in 1717 and was abolished in 1790.

Casta. A person of mixed racial background.

Caudillo. In Spanish America, a leader who rules by military force and patronage.

Cédula. A royal edict.

Colegios mayores. University colleges that specialized in training lawyers and senior ministers.

Collateral Council. The five regents who advised the Viceroy of Naples.

Consulado. A guild of merchants, usually in a particular town.

Consulta. A council's report or recommendation to the king.

Compadrazgo. Godparentage.

Comuneros. Urban rebels against Charles V in Castile. The name was later adopted by urban rebels in eighteenth-century Paraguay and New Granada.

Converso. A convert to Christianity, usually a converted Jew.

Corredores. Commercial agents operating in Spanish-controlled ports.

Corregidor. Originally an official representative of the crown who supervised municipal governments. In America, the magistrate and chief administrative officer of a provincial jurisdiction, often responsible for Indian affairs as *Corregidor de Indios.*

Corregimiento. The province or district administered by a *Corregidor.*

Creole. A Spaniard born in the colonies.

Cruzada. A tax nominally levied to support a crusade against infidels with the pope's permission.

Diputaciones. An unsuccessful scheme proposed by Olivares to establish tax-supported consortia in major cities that would borrow *vellón* (q.v.) and repay the loans in silver.

Doctrina. An Indian parish.

Encabezamiento. The practice of assessing sales, excise, or other taxes on a per capita basis.

Encomendero. The holder of an *encomienda* (q.v.).

Encomienda. A grant of authority over a group of Indians who were to be protected and Christianized in return for labor services or tribute.

Erarios. Regional banks in Castile, first proposed in 1623 but never fully implemented.

Escribano. A town secretary.

Fieles. Officials who supervised the lands and departments of a Castilian municipality. The *fiel ejecutor* regulated weights and measures and tried to ensure the continuity of food supplies.

Flota. The fleet that sailed from Spain to Vera Cruz.

Fueros. Special rights or privileges that might apply to a political unit (e.g., the Kingdom of Aragon), or to a corporate group such as the clergy.

Galeones. The fleet that sailed from Spain to Cartagena and Panama. Also called the *tierra firma* fleet.

Galleon. A large Spanish warship, usually with three or four masts and heavy guns.

Galley. An oared vessel, usually with an open deck, used primarily in the Mediterranean or in coastal waters.

Gracias al sacar. A document that freed people of African ancestry from the civil restrictions that ordinarily applied to them.

Hacienda. A large agricultural estate, often devoted to raising livestock.

Hermandades. Municipal militias in medieval Castile.

Indigenismo. A movement in modern Spanish America that seeks to revive Indian culture as the basis for a new political order.

Indultos. Fees periodically imposed on the business community of *Cádiz* to compensate the crown for losses due to smuggling and corruption.

Intendants. Provincial governors installed by the Bourbon monarchy.

Juro. An annuity paid from government income.

Llanero. A cowboy from the plains (*llanos*) of southern Venezuela.

Mayorazgo. An entailed estate.

Mayordomo. The manager of the king's household. In municipal government, the official responsible for maintaining the town's property.

Mestizo. A person of mixed Indian and Spanish parentage.

Metedores. Gangs that illegally transferred goods and silver from the Indies fleet to foreign ships in the harbor of Cádiz.

Millones. A tax first voted by the Cortes of Castile in 1590. In 1596, the Cortes decreed that the money should be raised by an excise on essential foodstuffs.

Mita. A forced labor draft, based on Inca precedent, to provide Indian workers on a rotational basis, usually for work in the mines of Peru.

Patronato Real. The crown's right to nominate candidates for Church offices and supervise certain aspects of Church administration.

Peninsular. A Spaniard resident in the colonies but born in Spain.

Placards. Edicts against heresy published in the Netherlands.

Presidio. A frontier garrison.

Privado. A favorite of the king who served as his first minister (also known as a *valido*. q.v.).

Repartimiento. In medieval Spain, the allocation of lands to settlers in newly conquered territories. In America, a forced labor draft that allocated an Indian chieftain and his people to a Spaniard.

Repartimiento de bienes. The forced sale of Indian merchandise to Spanish officials.

Requirimiento (The Requirement). A statement read to the Indians before battle, urging them to accept Christianity and allegiance to the crown. Refusal to do so justified war.

Residencia. A judicial review of an official's conduct in office.

Seggi. The branches of the city council of Naples.

Servicios. Annual, non-perpetual levies raised for the crown by the Cortes of Castile.

Suplentes. Delegates appointed to the Cortes of Cádiz as substitutes for those who could not attend.

Taifas. Small Muslim states of medieval Spain.

Tercio. An infantry regiment, nominally of about 3000 men. The basic tactical unit of the Spanish army from 1536 to the end of the seventeenth century.

Vales reales. Treasury bills issued by the government of Charles IV to finance war.

Valido. See *Privado*

Veedor. A royal auditor of accounts.

Vellón. Copper coins used as a substitute for silver after 1599.

Visita. An inquiry into the conduct of officials, usually unexpected.

SELECTED BIBLIOGRAPHY

A comprehensive bibliography on the Spanish Empire is beyond the scope of this or any single volume. The sources listed here are not even a bibliography of works consulted; they have been chosen on the basis of their usefulness to the general reader. Preference has therefore been given to books in English. In those cases where no English-language work exists on a major topic or where a book is simply too important to be ignored, works in other languages have been cited. Nearly all of the books listed contain extensive bibliographies of their own. They can guide the reader to subjects not covered by the present book and to a periodical literature too vast to be included here. The literature on Italy, Germany, and the Netherlands poses special problems. The history of Italy from the Renaissance to the Unification movement of the nineteenth century has received little attention from the English-speaking world. Much of what has been written emphasizes cultural and intellectual developments. Studies on political and economic developments are largely in Italian and all too often buried in journals not readily available to the English-speaking reader. The Netherlands has also been the subject of intensive research, but very little has been translated. In contrast, few subjects have been more intensely studied than Germany in the Age of Charles V. The monographic literature is vast, and with the exception of works on the religious question, almost entirely in German. As Germany is largely tangential to the subject of this book, interested readers should consult one of the many excellent histories of the Reformation that have been published in recent years. Most have bibliographies or contain references to bibliographical reference works.

GENERAL WORKS

The progenitor of all surveys on the Spanish Empire is R.B. Merriman, *The Rise of the Spanish Empire in the Old World and in the New*, 4v. (New York,

198

1918, reprinted 1962). It is still useful. J.H. Elliott, *Imperial Spain, 1469–1716* (New York, 1964) and John Lynch, *Spain under the Habsburgs*, 2v. (2nd printing, New York, 1981) are indispensable. Henry Kamen's *Empire: How Spain Became a World Power, 1492–1763* (New York, 2003) emphasizes the contribution of non-Spaniards to the process of empire-building while his *Spain, 1469–1714: A Society of Conflict*, 3rd Ed. (London, 2005) offers a different perspective on peninsular Spain. F. Braudel's *The Mediterranean and the Mediterranean World in the Age of Philip II*, 2v., trans. S. Reynolds (New York, 1976) is European in scope, but has transformed the way in which scholars look at early modern history and the problems of the Spanish empire.

Imperial ideology and the intellectual problems presented by the acquisition of an empire are analyzed in J.A. Fernández-Santamaria, *The State, War, and Peace: Spanish Political Thought in the Renaissance, 1516–1559* (Cambridge, 1977) and Anthony Pagden's *Spanish Imperialism and the Political Imagination* (New Haven, CT, 1990). As its title implies, Pagden's *Lords of All the World: Ideologies of Empire in Spain, Britain and France c.1500–c.1800* (New Haven, CT, 1995) is a valuable comparative study. John Elliott's *Empires of the Atlantic World: Britain and Spain in America, 1492–1830* (New Haven, CT, 2006) offers a comparison of the two empires on several levels, while his essay, *The Old World and the New, 1492–1650* examines the impact of colonization on both sides of the Atlantic.

Mark A. Burkholder and Lyman L. Johnson, *Colonial Latin America*, 6th Ed. (Oxford, 2008) is an outstanding textbook intended primarily for use in North American universities. It therefore deals with Brazil as well as Spanish America and is strong on social history. D.A. Brading's *The First America. The Spanish Monarchy, Creole Patriots and the Liberal State, 1492–1867* (Cambridge, 1991) is an extended and essential essay on the formation of Spanish American politics and society. A good economic survey is John R. Fisher, *The Economic Aspects of Spanish Imperialism in America, 1492–1810* (Liverpool, 1997), while John Thornton, *Africa and Africans in the Making of the Atlantic World, 1400–1800* provides a fine introduction to an important topic. It should be supplemented by Herbert S. Klein, *African Slavery in Latin America and the Caribbean* (Oxford, 1986).

IMPERIAL BEGINNINGS

Outstanding works on medieval Spain include: Joseph F. O'Callaghan, *A History of Medieval Spain* (Ithaca, NY, 1975); Angus MacKay, *Spain in*

the Middle Ages: From Frontier to Empire, 1000–1500 (London, 1977); Derek W.
Lomax, *The Reconquest of Spain* (New York, 1978); James F. Powers,
A Society Organized for War: The Iberian Municipal Militias, 1000–1284
(Berkeley, 1988); J.N. Hillgarth, *The Spanish Kingdoms, 1250–1516*, 2v.
(Oxford, 1976–1978); and William D. Phillips, Jr., *Enrique IV and the Crisis of
Fifteenth-Century Castile, 1425–1480* (Cambridge, MA, 1978).

C.R. Boxer, *The Portuguese Seaborne Empire, 1415–1825* (New York, 1969)
is the standard treatment of Spain's earliest imperial rival. There are many
works available on the age of exploration in general, but J.H. Parry, *The Age
of Reconnaissance* (New York, 1964) and Carl Ortwin Sauer, *The Early Spanish
Main* (Berkeley, 1966) remain standards.

Ferdinand of Aragon awaits a biography worthy of his importance, but
Peggy Liss, *Isabel the Queen: Life and Times*, Rev. edn. (Philadelphia, 2004) is a
readable study of the queen. Accounts of the war for Granada may be found
in the medieval surveys listed above. For its aftermath, we are indebted to
M.A. Ladero Quesada for *Granada después de la conquista* (Granada, 1988).
On the Canary Islands, see John Mercer, *The Canary Islanders: Their Prehis-
tory, Conquest and Survival* (London, 1980) and Felipe Fernández-Armesto,
The Canary Islands After the Conquest (Oxford, 1982). The literature on
Columbus is vast, but two modern studies are especially useful: Miles
H. Davidson, *Columbus Then and Now: A Life Reexamined* (Norman, OK, 1997)
and William D. Phillips, Jr. and Carla Rahn Phillips, *The Worlds of Christopher
Columbus* (Cambridge, 1992). Samuel Eliot Morison, *Admiral of the Ocean Sea:
A Biography of Admiral Christopher Columbus*, 2v. (Boston, 1942) is a classic, but
highly laudatory and now dated. On the Genoese community and its role
in financing the early voyages, see Ruth Pike, *Enterprise and Adventure: The
Genoese in Seville and the Opening of the New World* (Ithaca, NY, 1966).

THE CREATION OF AN EMPIRE IN EUROPE

General studies of Charles V and his reign include William S. Maltby,
The Reign of Charles V (Basingstoke, 2002) and M. Fernández Alvarez,
Charles V: Elected Emperor and Hereditary Ruler (London, 1975). Both devote
more attention to Spain and its possessions than did Karl Brandi's *The
Emperor Charles V*, trans. C.V. Wedgewood (London, 1939). Hugo Soly,
ed., *Charles V, 1500–1558 and His Time* (Antwerp, 2000) is a massive and
beautifully illustrated collection of essays by noted scholars. Some of them,
like Geoffrey Parker's "The Political World of Charles V," pp. 113–226, are
nearly book-length. M. Fernández Alvarez, *La política mundial de Carlos V*

y Felipe II (Madrid, 1966) summarizes the political ideas underlying the monarchy in its first century, while John Headley, *The Emperor and His Chancellor: A Study of the Imperial Chancellery Under Gattinara* (Cambridge, 1983) describes an important stage in the evolution of Charles's government. Many of the emperor's political problems involved relations with his family. Paula S. Fichtner, *Ferdinand I of Austria, 1503–1564* (Boulder, CO, 1982) is a useful study of Charles V's long-suffering brother, while Mia Rodríguez-Salgado provides a revisionist interpretation of the transition between the reigns of Charles and his son in *The Changing Face of Empire: Charles V, Philip II and Habsburg Authority, 1551–1559* (Cambridge, 1988). On the Ottomans and Africa, see Halil Inalcik, *The Ottoman Empire: The Classical Age, 1300–1600* (London, 1973) and Andrew Hess, *The Forgotten Frontier: A History of the Sixteenth-Century Ibero-African Frontier* (Chicago, 1978).

Ramón Carande analyzes the emperor's finances in *Carlos V y sus banqueros*, 3v. (Madrid, 1965–1967), but Richard Ehrenberg's *Capital and Finance in the Age of the Renaissance* (London, 1928) provides a much clearer explanation in English. Unfortunately, the English translation omits a chapter on Genoese finances that is directly applicable to Charles's affairs. James D. Tracy, *Emperor Charles V, Impresario of War: Campaign Strategy, International Finance, and Domestic Politics* (Cambridge, 2002) offers valuable insights on many subjects, while the same author's *Holland Under Habsburg Rule, 1506–1566* (Berkeley, 1990) is indispensable on politics and finance in the Netherlands. Unfortunately, most works on the Netherlands under Charles V are in Dutch and therefore inaccessible to English readers. Exceptions are J. de Vries, *The Dutch Rural Economy in the Golden Age, 1500–1700* (New Haven, 1974) and H. Van der Wee's *The Growth of the Antwerp Market and the European Economy*, 3v. (The Hague, 1963).

The bibliographic problems related to Germany and Italy have been mentioned above. There are nevertheless several works available on the Kingdom of Naples. Benedetto Croce's *History of the Kingdom of Naples* (Chicago, 1970) is dated and by modern standards polemical, but a useful survey by a distinguished philosopher. More modern works include Giuseppe Galasso, *Alla periferia dell'Impero: Il Regno di Napoli nel periodo spagnolo* (Turin, 1994), Antonio Calabria, *The Cost of Empire: The Finances of the Kingdom of Naples in the Time of Spanish Rule* (Cambridge, 1991), and Antonio Calabria and John Marino, eds., *Good Government in Spanish Naples* (New York, 1990), a valuable collection of essays. The most accessible work on Sicily is H. Koenigsberger, *The Government of Sicily Under Philip II of Spain* (London, 1951). It has been reprinted as *The Practice of Empire* (Ithaca, NY,

1969). Federico Chabod, *Lo stato e la vita religiosa a Milano nell' epoca di Carlo V*
(Turin, 1971) is somewhat eccentric in its organization, but one of the few
works available on sixteenth-century Milan. For the papacy, Ludwig von
Pastor, *The History of the Popes*, trans. R. Kerr, vols. 9–13 (London, 1950) is
still indispensable after more than a century. F.L. Taylor, *The Art of War in
Italy, 1494–1529* (London, 1921) is both old and brief, but still essential to
an understanding of the Italian wars under Ferdinand and Charles V.

THE CONQUEST OF AMERICA

The literature on pre-conquest America is vast and somewhat outside the
subject of the present book. A good place to begin is with the *Cambridge
History of the Native Peoples of the Americas*, vols. 1 and 3 (Cambridge, 1999)
which offers articles and references on many of the major Indian cultures.
The issue of pre-conquest populations and their subsequent decline is cen-
tral to many appraisals of Spanish colonialism and highly controversial.
High estimates are found in Sherburne F. Cook and Woodrow Borah, *Essays
in Population History*, 3 vols. (Berkeley, 1971, 1974, 1979). The essays in
W.M. Denevan, ed., *The Native Population of the Americas in 1492* (Madison,
1976) and in David Henige's, *Numbers from Nowhere: The American Indian
Contact Population Debate* (Norman, OK, 1998) provide other perspectives.
Noble David Cook, *Born to Die: Disease and New World Conquest, 1492–1650*
(Cambridge, 1998) deals with the greatest cause of native mortality.

  Hugh Thomas, *Rivers of Gold: The Rise of the Spanish Empire* (London,
2003) looks at the age of conquest as a whole. One of the best ways
to approach the conquest of Mexico is through contemporary accounts.
Bernal Díaz del Castillo, *The True History of the Conquest of New Spain*, trans.
A.P. Maudslay (New York, 1966) is a riveting narrative by a Spanish partic-
ipant. On Cortés we have not only Francisco López de Gómara, *Cortés: The
Life of the Conqueror by His Secretary*, ed. and trans. L.B. Simpson (Berkeley,
1964), but *Hernán Cortés: Letters from Mexico*, ed. and trans. A. Pagden (New
York, 1971). Miguel León-Portillo, ed., *The Broken Spears: The Aztec Account
of the Conquest of Mexico*, trans. L. Kemp (Boston, 1992) and James Lockhart,
We People Here: Nahua Accounts of the Conquest of Mexico (Berkeley, 1993) provide the native perspective. Modern monographs include R.C. Padden, *The
Hummingbird and the Hawk. Conquest and Sovereignty in the Valley of Mexico*
(Columbus, OH, 1967), Hugh Thomas, *Conquest: Montezuma, Cortés, and
the Fall of Old Mexico* (New York, 1993) and Ross Hassig, *Mexico and the*

Spanish Conquest (New York, 1994). Hassig's *Aztec Warfare: Imperial Expansion and Political Control* (Norman, OK, 1988) is a controversial analysis of Aztec warfare and its purposes.

The conquerors of Peru left fewer literary monuments. Good modern studies of the conquest are: John Hemming, *The Conquest of the Incas* (New York, 1970) and James Lockhart, *The Men of Cajamarca: A Social and Biographical Study of the First Conquerors of Peru* (Austin, TX, 1972). Nathan Wachtel, *The Vision of the Vanquished: The Spanish Conquest of Peru Through Indian Eyes* (New York, 1977) examines the native accounts. For other regions, see Grant D. Jones, *The Conquest of the Last Maya Kingdom* (Stanford, CA, 1998) and an older study by Sir Clements Markham, *The Conquest of New Granada* (Port Washington, NY, 1971).

On the condition of native peoples after the conquest in Mexico, see the pioneering study by L.B. Simpson, *The Encomienda in New Spain* (Berkeley, 1950), Charles Gibson, *The Aztecs Under Spanish Rule: A History of the Indians of the Valley of Mexico* (Stanford, 1964), and James Lockhart, *The Nahuas After the Conquest: A Social and Cultural History of the Indians of Central Mexico, Sixteenth Through Eighteenth Centuries* (Stanford, 1992). Kenneth J. Andrien, *Andean Worlds: Indigenous History, Culture, and Consciousness Under Spanish Rule, 1532–1825* (Albuquerque, NM, 2001) deals with the culture of South American Indians after the conquest. For conditions in the mining districts, see Peter John Blackwell, *Miners of the Red Mountain: Indian Labor in Potosí, 1545–1650* (Albuquerque, NM, 1984) and Jeffrey A. Cole, *The Potosí Mita, 1573–1700: Compulsory Indian Labor in the Andes* (Stanford, 1985). Murdo MacLeod, *Spanish Central America: A Socio-Economic History, 1520–1720* (Berkeley, 1984) is an excellent survey. Lewis Hanke's *The Spanish Struggle for Justice in the Conquest of America* (Philadelphia, 1949) remains the best introduction to Bartolomé de Las Casas and the disputes over the treatment of the Indians. For the beginnings of African slavery (which Las Casas did not oppose), see David Eltis, *The Rise of African Slavery in the Americas* (Cambridge, 2000).

The unforeseen biological consequences of the conquest were explored in a ground-breaking study by Alfred W. Crosby, *The Columbian Exchange; Biological and Cultural Consequences of 1492* (Westport, CT, 1972). Since then, a number of works have examined related aspects of this theme, including Elinor G.K. Melville, *A Plague of Sheep: Environmental Consequences of the Conquest of Mexico* (Cambridge, 1994) and John D. Super, Food, Conquest, and Colonization in Sixteenth-Century Spanish America (Albuquerque, NM, 1988).

IMPERIAL ORGANIZATION UNDER THE HABSBURGS

The government of Spain and its dependencies under the Habsburgs is described in several of the general histories listed in the first section of this bibliography including Elliott, Lynch, and for the Americas, Burkholder and Johnson. That of the Netherlands can be understood in part from the works of James Tracy noted above, and from the histories of the Netherlands Revolt mentioned below under "Imperial Policy." These sources include useful references to monographs on various aspects of government and administration but few are in English. For Italy, please refer to the works listed above. Useful summaries of the Spanish system as a whole may also be found in J.H. Parry, *The Spanish Seaborne Empire* (New York, 1966) and C.H. Haring, *The Spanish Empire in America* (New York, 1947). There are, of course, many works in Spanish on various aspects of administration. One of the most useful is J.A. Escudero, *Los secretarios de estado y del despacho, 1474–1724*, 2nd Ed., 4 vols. (Madrid, 1976), a detailed study of these important functionaries.

On communication and trade, the place to begin is with C.H. Haring's venerable *Trade and Navigation between Spain and the Indies* (Cambridge, MA, 1918). Pierre and Huguette Chaunu, *Seville et l'Atlantique, 1504–1650*, 12v. (Paris, 1956–1960) provide almost overwhelming detail. The financial underpinnings of the trade are described in Antonio-Miguel Bernal, *La financiación de la Carrera de Indias* (Sevilla, 1992). The wool trade between Spain and the Netherlands was important not only in itself but because many of its institutions served as a model for that of the Indies. Carla Rahn Phillips and William D. Phillips, Jr., *Spain's Golden Fleece: Wool Production and the Wool Trade from the Middle Ages to the Nineteenth Century* (Baltimore, 1997) provides an excellent analysis. The study of Spain's Asian trade should begin with William L. Schurz, *The Manila Galleon* (New York, 1939).

Trade and communication depended upon the navy. At the end of the nineteenth century, Admiral Cesareo Fernández Duro accumulated a vast store of information on the subject which he presented in *Armada Española desde la Unión de los Reinos de Castilla y Aragón*, 9v. (Madrid, 1894–1903). It remains indispensable if difficult to assimilate. F.-F. Olesa Muñido, *La organización naval de los estados mediterráneos y en especial de España durante los siglos XVI y XVII*, 2v. (Madrid, 1968) is more accessible, at least to readers of Spanish. David C. Goodman, *Spanish Naval Power, 1589–1665* (Cambridge, 1997) is a good brief description of the fleet during a critical period. Two other works provide valuable insights on naval matters: Pablo Emilio Pérez-Mallaína, *Spain's Men of the Sea: Daily Life on the Indies Fleets in the Sixteenth*

Century, trans. Carla Rahn Phillips (Baltimore, 1998) is as entertaining as it is informative, and Carla Rahn Phillips, *Six Galleons for the King of Spain* (Baltimore, 1986) provides a fascinating study of naval contracting in the early seventeenth century. Military administration and finance on both land and sea is covered admirably by I.A.A. Thompson in *War and Government in Habsburg Spain* (London, 1976). Thompson's *War and Society in Habsburg Spain* (Aldershot, 1992) is a collection of his articles on the same subject. René Quatrefages, *Los tercios españoles* (Madrid, 1979) describes the army's tactical organization.

Relations between the church and the monarchy are described in both Elliott and Lynch. For the church in America, see Adriaan van Oss, *Church and Society in Spanish America* (Amsterdam, 2003) and the earlier collection of articles in Richard E. Greenleaf, ed., *The Roman Catholic Church in Colonial Latin America* (New York, *1971*). John Frederick Schwaller, *Church and Clergy in Sixteenth Century Mexico* (Albuquerque, NM, 1987) is a model study. The literature on the Inquisition is vast and ridden with controversy. Henry Kamen's *The Spanish Inquisition: A Historical Revision* (New Haven, CT, 1998) is good, if provocative; but see also Helen Rawlings, *The Spanish Inquisition* (London, 2005). E. William Monter, *Frontiers of Heresy: The Spanish Inquisition from the Basque Lands to Sicily* (Cambridge, 1990) examines the reception of the Inquisition in Italy and Spanish Europe outside Castile, while the old but still useful Henry Charles Lea, *The Inquisition in the Spanish Dependencies* (New York, 1908) deals with the American tribunals. On missions and the borderlands frontier in general, see John Leddy Phelan, *The Millennial Kingdom of the Franciscans in the New World: A Study of the Writings of Gerónimo de Mendieta, 1525–1604* (Berkeley, 1956). John Francis Bannon, *The Spanish Borderlands Frontier, 1513–1821* (New York, 1970) and David J. Weber, *The Spanish Frontier in North America* (New Haven, CT, 1992) provide a broad overview.

Among the studies that show how family, race, and other non-governmental relationships influenced politics and society in the Americas are Susan E. Ramírez, *Provincial Patriarchs: The Economics of Power in Colonial Peru* (Lincoln, NE, 1999), Susan M. Socolow, *The Merchants of Buenos Aires, 1778–1810: Family and Commerce* (Cambridge, 1978), and Leslie B. Rout, *The African Experience in Spanish America, 1502 to the Present Day* (Cambridge, 1971). For more information on social attitudes in the Americas and on women in particular, begin with Susan Socolow, *The Women of Colonial Latin America* (Cambridge, 2000) and Ann Twinam, *Public Lives, Private Secrets: Gender, Honor, Sexuality, and Illegitimacy in Colonial Spanish America* (Stanford, 1999).

IMPERIAL POLICY

An understanding of Imperial policy in the second half of the sixteenth century begins with the life and policies of Philip II, Three good biographies of the king are Peter Pierson, *Philip II of Spain* (London, 1975), Henry Kamen, Henry, *Philip of Spain* (New Haven, CT, 1997), and Geoffrey Parker, *Philip II*, 4th Ed. (Chicago, 2004). Parker has also written *The Grand Strategy of Philip II* (New Haven, CT, 1998), a policy analysis. A.W. Lovett, *Philip II and Mateo Vázquez de Leca: The Government of Spain, 1572–1592* (Geneva, 1977) provides insight into politics after the collapse of the factions that influenced affairs at court in the 1560s.

For the Revolt of the Netherlands begin with Geoffrey Parker's excellent and readable *The Dutch Revolt*, Rev. edn. (Harmondsworth, 1985), his indispensable *The Army of Flanders and the Spanish Road, 1567–1659* (Cambridge, 1972), and *Spain and the Netherlands, 1559–1659 Ten Studies*, Rev. edn. (London, 1990), a collection of his articles. J.L. Motley, *The Rise of the Dutch Republic*, 3v. (New York, 1851) is old and bitterly anti-Spanish, but still well worth reading. Philip's great proconsuls have found biographers of their own: William S. Maltby, *Alba: A Biography of Fernando Alvarez de Toledo, Third Duke of Alba* (Berkeley, 1983) and Léon van der Essen, *Alexandre Farnèse, Prince de Parme*, 5v. (Brussels, 1933).

On French politics and its influence on the Netherlands, see M.N. Sutherland, *The Massacre of St. Bartholomew and the European Conflict, 1559–1572* (London, 1973) and DeLamar Jensen, *Dogmatism and Diplomacy: Bernardino de Mendoza and the French Catholic League* (Cambridge, MA, 1964).

The drift into war with England is best described in R.B. Wernham's magisterial study of Elizabethan policy *Before the Armada* (New York, 1966), but see also Charles Wilson, *Queen Elizabeth and the Revolt of the Netherlands*, 2nd Ed (London, 1962). For the Armada itself, see Garrett Mattingly's classic *The Armada* (Boston, 1959), Colin Martin and Geoffrey Parker, *The Spanish Armada* (New York, 1988), a collaboration between archaeology and history, and the collection of essays in Mia Rodríguez-Salgado and Simon Adams, eds. *England, Spain, and the Gran Armada, 1585–1604* (London and Madrid, 1988). The continuation of the war after 1588 is described by R.B. Wernham in *After the Armada: Elizabethan England and the Struggle for Western Europe, 1588–1595* (Oxford, 1984) and *The Return of the Armadas, 1595–1603* (Oxford, 1994).

For the Black Legend, see Charles Gibson, *The Black Legend: Anti-Spanish Attitudes in the Old World and the New* (New York, 1971) and William S. Maltby, *The Black Legend in England: The Development of Anti-Spanish Sentiment, 1558–1660* (Durham, NC, 1971).

Neither Philip III nor Lerma have received the attention they deserve, but C.H. Carter, *The Secret Diplomacy of the Habsburgs, 1598–1625* (New York, 1964) and Paul C. Allen, *Philip III and the Pax Hispanica, 1598–1621* (New Haven, CT, 2000) provide an introduction to their foreign policy.

IMPERIAL DECLINE

The prominent role of the Count-Duke of Olivares in the first half of the seventeenth century has inspired a considerable literature including the monumental biography by J.H. Elliott, *The Count-Duke of Olivares* (New Haven, CT, 1989). Elliott has also written *The Revolt of the Catalans* (Cambridge, 1963), an equally detailed study of a major imperial failure. Elliott's *Richelieu and Olivares* (Cambridge, 1984) is a provocative essay comparing the two rival ministers of France and Spain. There was, of course, more to the government of Philip IV than Olivares. A. Domínguez Ortiz, *Política y Hacienda de Felipe IV* (Madrid, 1960) in Spanish and R.A. Stradling, *Philip IV and the Government of Spain, 1621–1665* (Cambridge, 1988) provide a broader view.

Foreign affairs, and in particular, the ongoing problem of the Netherlands are addressed by J. Alcalá Zamora y Queipo de Llano's *España, Flandes, y el Mar del Norte, 1618–1639* (Barcelona, 1975) and Jonathan I. Israel's detailed study *The Dutch Republic and the Hispanic World, 1606–1661* (Oxford, 1982). Israel has also written an essay on the broader topic: *Conflict of Empires. Spain, The Low Countries and the Struggle for World Supremacy 1585–1713* (London, 1997). For a study of Spanish naval policy and organization in northern Europe, see R.A. Stradling, *The Armada of Flanders: Spanish Maritime Policy and European War, 1568–1668* (Cambridge, 1992). The best general study of the Thirty Years' War is Geoffrey Parker, ed., *The Thirty Years' War* (London, 1984), a collaborative effort by several authors that reads like a monograph. C.R. Boxer, *The Dutch in Brazil, 1624–1654* (Oxford, 1957) describes another imperial failure that helped fuel the Portuguese revolt of 1640.

The general issue of Spanish decline is addressed in R.A. Stradling, *Europe and the Decline of Spain: A Study of the Spanish System, 1580–1720* (London, 1981), in a collection of outstanding essays on the situation in Castile by I.A.A. Thompson and B. Yun Castilla, eds. *The Castilian Crisis of the Seventeenth Century* (Cambridge, 1994). James C. Boyajian, *Portuguese Bankers at the Court of Spain, 1626–1650* (New Brunswick, NJ, 1983) deals with an unpopular attempt to change the financial system. Perhaps the best studies of financial issues as a whole are Stanley A. Stein and Barbara Stein, *Silver, Trade and War: Spain and America in the Making of Early Modern Europe*

(Baltimore, 2000) and Artur Attman, *American Bullion in the European World Trade 1600–1800* (Göteborg, 1986). Immanuel Wallerstein's broad overview of seventeenth-century economic development, *The Modern World-System: Mercantilism and the Consolidation of the European World Economy, 1600–1700* (New York, 1980), has been both influential and controversial.

The reign of Charles II was often ignored or denigrated by earlier generations of historians. A more positive view may be found in Henry Kamen, *Spain in the Later Seventeenth Century, 1665–1700* (London, 1980) and in Christopher Storrs, *The Resilience of the Spanish Monarchy, 1665–1700* (Oxford, 2006).

THE BOURBONS

There are several excellent surveys of eighteenth-century Spain, including Gonzalo Anes, *El antiguo régimen: Los Borbones* (Madrid, 1975) and John Lynch, *Bourbon Spain, 1700–1808* (Oxford, 1989). Richard Herr, *The Eighteenth Century Revolution in Spain* (Princeton, 1958) is especially good on the intellectual roots of royal policy. For readable surveys of the War of the Spanish Succession and the reign of Philip V, see Henry Kamen's *The War of Succession in Spain, 1700–1715* (London, 1969) and his *Philip V of Spain: The King Who Reigned Twice* (New Haven, CT, 2001).

G.B. Paquette, *Enlightenment, Governance and Reform in Spain and Its Empire, 1759–1808* (Basingstoke, 2008) covers the reforms first begun under Charles III. Arthur P. Whitaker, ed., *Latin America and the Enlightenment*, 2nd Ed. (Ithaca, NY, 1961) is a collection of essays on the Enlightenment in America, most of which place the movement in a positive light. Colin M. MacLachlan takes a somewhat darker view in *Spain's Empire in the New World: The Role of Ideas in Institutional and Social Change* (Berkeley, 1988). Philip Caraman, *The Lost Paradise, An Account of the Jesuits in Paraguay, 1607–1768* (London, 1975) describes the Society's efforts until its expulsion. One of the best studies of the crown's ecclesiastical policy at the local level is D.A. Brading, *Church and State in Colonial Mexico: The Diocese of Michoacán, 1749–1810* (Cambridge, 1994).

There are a number of excellent studies on trade and finance including John R. Fisher, *Commercial Relations Between Spain and Spanish America in the Era of Free Trade, 1778–1796* (Liverpool, 1985), Geoffrey G. Walker, *Spanish Politics and Imperial Trade, 1700–1789* (Bloomington, IN, 1979), and Herbert S. Klein, *The American Finances of the Spanish Empire: Royal Income and Expenditures in Colonial Mexico, Peru, and Bolivia, 1680–1809* (Albuquerque,

NM, 1998). The all-important mining industry is covered by D.A. Brading, *Miners and Merchants in Bourbon Mexico* (Cambridge, 1970) and Enrique Tandeter, *Coercion and Market: Silver Mining in Colonial Peru, 1692–1826* (Albuquerque, NM, 1993). Stanley A. Stein and Barbara Stein, *Apogee of Empire: Spain and New Spain in the Age of Charles III* (Baltimore, 2003) is also strong on economics as is the broader essay by Peggy Liss, *Atlantic Empires: The Network of Trade and Revolution* (Baltimore, 1982).

Given the diversity of Spain's American empire, it is not surprising that most of the best studies of political and economic reform are regional. An alphabetical listing of selected titles would include: Kenneth J. Andrien, *The Kingdom of Quito, 1690–1830: The State and Regional Development* (Cambridge, 1995), Jacques Barbier, *Reform and Politics in Bourbon Chile, 1755–1796* (Ottawa, 1980), John R. Fisher, *Bourbon Peru, 1750–1824* (Liverpool, 2003), Allan J. Kuethe, *Cuba, 1753–1815: Crown, Military, and Society* (Knoxville, TN, 1986), John Lynch, *Spanish Colonial Administration, 1782–1810: The Intendant System in the Viceroyalty of the Rio de la Plata* (London, 1958), Anthony McFarlane, *Colombia Before Independence: Economy, Society, and Politics Under Bourbon Rule* (Cambridge, 1993), and Miles L. Wortman, *Government and Society in Central America, 1680–1840* (New York, 1982).

Violent reactions to Bourbon policy are described by John Leddy Phelan in *The People and the King: The Comunero Revolution in Colombia, 1781* (Madison, 1978), Ward Stavig, *The World of Tupac Amaru: Conflict, Community, and Identity in Colonial Peru* (Lincoln, NE, 1999), and Sergio Serulnikov, *Subverting Colonial Authority: Challenges to Spanish Rule in Eighteenth-Century Southern Andes* (Durham, NC, 2003). The critical issue of Creole appointments to audiencias is examined by Mark A. Burkholder and D.S. Chandler in *From Impotence to Authority: The Spanish Crown and the American Audiencias, 1687–1808* (Columbia, MO, 1977).

THE END OF THE EMPIRE

The standard modern account of the Napoleonic era in Spain is Gabriel H. Lovett, *Napoleon and the Birth of Modern Spain*, 2v. (New York, 1965). The most recent additions to the vast literature on the Peninsular War are Charles J. Esdaile, *The Peninsular War: A New History* (New York, 2003) and the same author's *Fighting Napoleon: Guerrillas, Bandits and Adventurers in Spain, 1808–1814* (New Haven, CT, 2004).

Good general studies of the Spanish American Revolutions are Timothy E. Anna, *Spain and the Loss of Empire* (Lincoln, NE, 1983), Michael P. Costeloe, *Response to Revolution: Imperial Spain and the Spanish American Revolutions, 1810–1840* (Cambridge, 1986), Jorge Domínguez, *Insurrection or Loyalty. The Breakdown of the Spanish American Empire* (Cambridge, Mass., 1980), and John Lynch, *The Latin American Revolutions, 1808–1826*, 2nd Ed. (New York, 1986). William W. Kaufmann, *British Policy and the Independence of Latin America, 1802–1828* (New Haven, CT, 1951) is an old but thorough study based on Foreign Office papers.

Regional studies are of course essential to an understanding of the movements toward independence. For Mexico, see Brian R. Hamnett, *Roots of Insurgency: Mexican Regions, 1750–1824* (Cambridge, 1986), Hugh M. Hamill, Jr., *The Hidalgo Revolt: Prelude to Mexican Independence* (Gainesville, FL, 1966), Eric Van Young, *The Other Rebellion: Popular Violence, Ideology, and the Mexican Struggle for Independence* (Stanford, CA, 2001), and two studies by Timothy E. Anna: *The Fall of the Royal Government in Mexico City* (Lincoln, NE, 1978) and *The Mexican Empire of Iturbide* (Lincoln, NE, 1990). There are many works on South America as well, including Tulio Halperín-Donghi, *Politics, Economics, and Society in Argentina in the Revolutionary Period* (Cambridge, 1975), Timothy E. Anna, *The Fall of the Royal Government in Peru* (Lincoln, NE, 1979), and Donald F. Worcester, *Sea Power and Chilean Independence* (Gainesville, FL, 1962). The colorful and enigmatic Bolívar has been the subject of several biographies, including David Bushnell, *Simón Bolívar: Liberation and Disillusion* (New York, 2004), John Lynch, *Simon Bolivar: A Life* (New Haven, CT, 2005), and Gerhard Masur, *Simón Bolívar*, 2nd Ed. (Albuquerque, NM, 1969). For San Martín, see J.C.J. Metford, *San Martín the Liberator* (London, 1950). Their nemesis, General Morrillo, is covered in Stephen K. Stoan, *Pablo Morillo and Venezuela, 1815–1820* (Columbus, OH, 1974).

In a sense, the "aftermath" of independence encompasses the entire history of modern Spanish America and has its own massive body of literature. A good place to begin would be with Tulio Halperín-Donghi's, *The Aftermath of Revolution in Latin America* (New York, 1973) and two collections of articles: Jeremy Adelman, ed., *Colonial Legacies: The Problem of Persistence in Latin American History* (New York, 1999) and Jaime E. Rodríguez, ed., *The Independence of Mexico and the Creation of the New Nation* (Los Angeles, 1989). The standard history of modern Spain is Raymond Carr, *Spain, 1808–1975*, 2nd Ed. (Oxford, 1982). David R. Ringrose, *Spain, Europe, and the "Spanish Miracle" 1700–1900* (Cambridge, 1996) is an outstanding work on economic history.

INDEX

211

Breinigsville, PA USA
30 September 2009
225030BV00002B/53/P